MAIN PIKE RIVERS IN NORTHERN ENGLAND

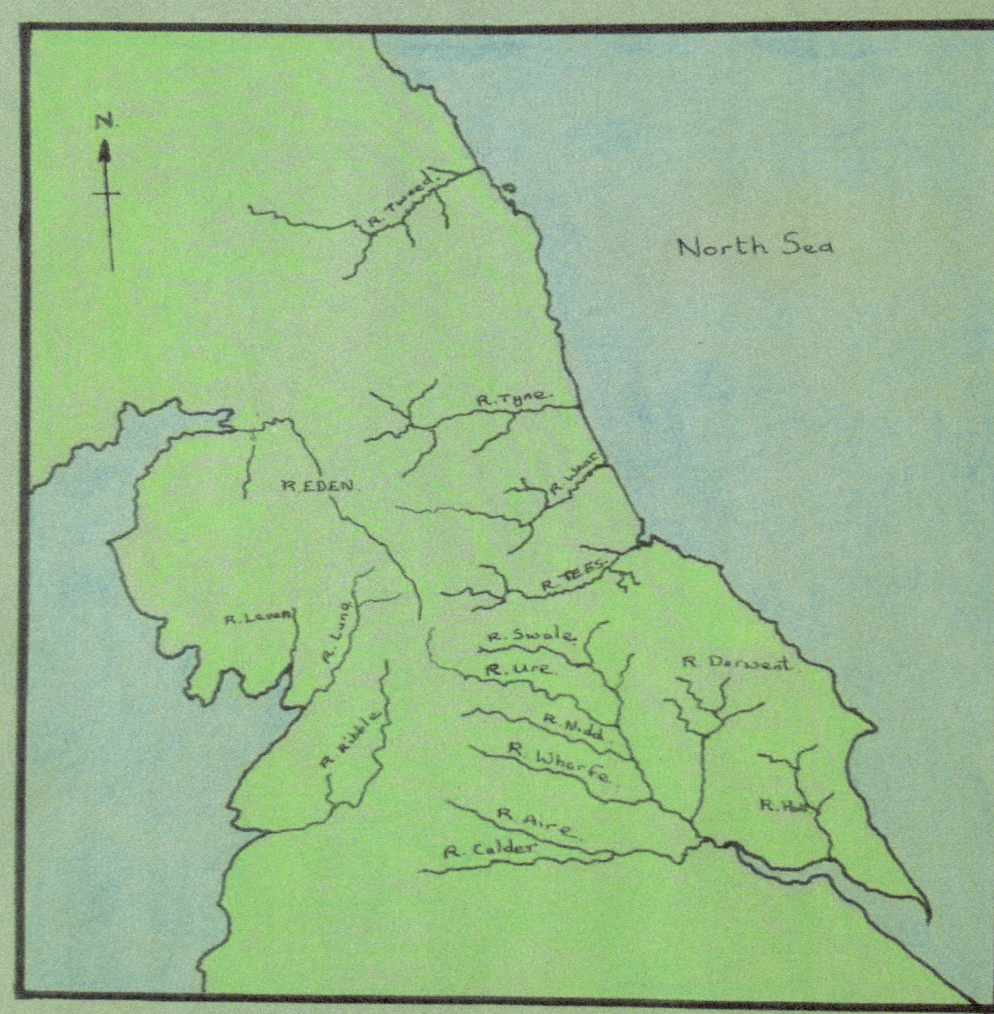

River Pike
in Northern England.

RIVER PIKE
in
Northern England

The Anglers Bible for Catching Big
Northern River Pike

A Lifetime's Testimony Including Memories of
Great Angling Friends.

By

BILL WINSHIP

This book is dedicated to my wife Liz, who has not only welcomed me back from thousands of fishing trips going back over forty-three years but has also edited the chapters for this book. Also, to our offspring Jonathan and Charlotte who put their early angling adventures to such good use in later life.

RIVER PIKE in Northern England

Author: Bill Winship

Copyright © Bill Winship (2022)

The right of Bill Winship to be identified as author of this work has been asserted by the author in accordance with section 77 and 78 of the Copyright, Designs and Patents Act 1988.

First Published in 2022

ISBN 978-1-915164-92-6 (Paperback)
      978-1-915164-74-2 (Hardback)
      978-1-915164-73-5 (Ebook)

Cover Design and Book Layout by:
    White Magic Studios
    www.whitemagicstudios.co.uk

Published by:
    Maple Publishers
    1 Brunel Way,
    Slough,
    SL1 1FQ, UK
    www.maplepublishers.com

A CIP catalogue record for this title is available from the British Library.

All rights reserved. No part of this book may be reproduced or translated by any form or by any means, electronic or mechanical, including photocopying, recording or by any information storage and retrieval system without written permission from the author.

CONTENTS

- Acknowledgements 9
- List of Illustrations 10
- Foreword by David Tipping 14
- Preface 16
- Introduction 18

Angling Heritage and Echoes from the past 23

- Francis Walbran. A Victorian Angling Pioneer on the Northern Rivers 24
- Thomas Sturdy. Pike Fishing in Edwardian Yorkshire 31
- Norris Sturdy. Fishing Mentor and Living link to a rich Angling Culture 42
- John Eastwood. The most important reformer in British Angling History 49
- Barrie Rickards. Sparked a revolution in attitudes towards Pike 54

The Main sixteen Northern Pike Rivers 63

- The main sixteen Northern Pike rivers selected include the rivers Aire, Calder, Eden, Derwent, Hull, Leven, Lune, Nidd, Ouse, Ribble, Swale, Tees, Tweed, Tyne, Ure and Wharfe. 64

Altitude, Atmospherics and the Altostratus 105

- Atmospheric trigger factors. The pike fishing magic starts high up on the roof of England. 106
- Fishing when the river is in flood. 114

Equipment and Methods for Catching Northern River Pike 120

- Landing nets and the importance of safety whilst river fishing 121
- Fishing Reels- Choose your Pleasure 129
- Rods suitable for River Pike Fishing 139
- Handling and Unhooking 146
- Floats and Float Making 153

- Special Hook Rigs and Traces: An early lesson on single hook pike fishing; Deadbait Spinning; Deadbait Spinning as a last resort; Ledger weights for River Piking 165
- Static Deadbaiting and Pike Hotspots 190
- Spoons Spinners and Plugs 199
- Transporting your fishing tackle 215

Red Letter Days - Proof of the Pudding 218

- Two Twenty Pound Pike in One Day 219
- Spinning on the River Ouse 225
- A Brace of Twenty Fours 234
- Fishing with Pike Royalty 241
- Pike Friday and Storm Dennis 247
- A Christmas Cracker 251
- Two from the Lune. A Tribute to Jim. (Guest writer David Holden) 256
- Halcyon Days in a Northern Deer Park. (Guest writer Nigel Winter) 261
- Great Pike Days on River Hull. (Guest writer Adrian Brayshaw) 267
- A Sub Zero Twenty Pounder 279
- A Red-Letter Day on the River Aire (Guest writer Mark Green) 283
- A Giant Pike from the River Wear in county Durham (Guest writer Jonathan Chandler) 290

Appendix 294

- The River Pike Condition Scale 295
- Nurseries for River Pike 302
- Modern Threats to River Pike 307
- Northern River Pike Slide Shows 311
- The trout in spring 323
- Glossary of Pike Fishing Terms 329
- The road to Success 334
- About the Author 338

ACKNOWLEDGEMENTS

This book on Northern River Pike has been something of a lifelong project and has only been made possible thanks to the generous help of the following people. Firstly, I would like to thank my childhood mentor Norris Sturdy for providing the best possible start anyone could have had in River Pike fishing. In the first part of this book I have written a mini biography of both Norris and his father Tom Sturdy to share with the reader an understanding of the old traditions of our early angling culture of the north which without these chapters would mean a whole way of life would be lost forever. Thanks are due to Basil Sturdy, Norris's nephew, for providing photos to illustrate the first part of this book. In the same way thanks are also due to the late Barrie Rickards for his inspiration in all matters concerning the subject of pike. Also, to Dennis, Karl and Paul Winship for support with photography and sense checking various parts of the work. Thanks also to Philip Fowler-Jones and David Harrison for help with photography. Thanks also to Damian McHale for his help on the River Tyne section and to Jonathan Chandler for his local knowledge on Durham Pike. Massive thanks also to my regular fishing partner Nigel Winter who has taken many of the photos in this book and contributed a chapter too. I am also indebted to guest writers Adrian Brayshaw for his chapter on the River Hull and to David Holden for his nostalgic chapter on the River Lune. Thanks also to David's friend Tim Hancock for transferring the slides to digital in David's chapter. We are also indebted to Clive Melhuish for his valuable input and ongoing encouragement and to senior northern angling expert David Tipping for kindly writing the foreword. We are also greatly indebted to the Environment Agency for allowing us to use the fish counter data and for the vast support they provide to the sport of angling generally. Also many thanks to John and his friends at White Magic Studios for their specialist help producing this book. Thanks to Charlotte my daughter for her IT skills and designing the front cover. Last and by no means least I would like to thank Elizabeth my wife for her constant support and especially for her proof-reading abilities making this lifelong work a reality.

A LIST OF ILLUSTRATIONS

- David Tipping displays one of his Northern River Twenties.............................15
- Portrait of Francis Walbran a Victorian Pioneer on the
  Northern Rivers...24
- View of the glorious River Ure looking upstream from
  West Tanfield bridge...27
- The Bruce Arms and stables. Rich in northern angling history. 30
- Portrait of Tom Sturdy. Water Bailif for almost fifty years
  on the West Tanfield beat..31
- Photo of Tom's Father, himself an expert angler and noted
  fly fisherman. 33
- Tom Sturdy after a successful pheasant shoot. 35
- Photo of Church Street where three generations of the
  Sturdy family lived...36
- The Walbran gaff given to Tom Sturdy by Walbran for
  landing big salmon and pike. 37
- Edwardian Pike Fishing photo with Mr Robert Hayton
  and his daughter Mary. 40
- Portrait of Norris Sturdy, a great mentor and living link to
  a rich angling history. 42
- Contemporary sketch of the giant salmon fed Sturdy Pike................................46
- Walbrans angling themed memorial. Funded by his loyal
  fishing friends after tragic accident. 48
- Portrait of the great A.C.A. Founder John Eastwood. A man
  of huge political power and charisma..49
- Badge to mark the 50th anniversary of the A.C.A. Fifty
  years of fighting for clean waterways. 51
- Portrait of Dr Barrie Rickards. Founder of the Pike Anglers
  Club of Great Britain in 1977. 54
- A fishing breakfast with Barrie. The Great Man had a
  penchant for bacon, preferably crispy!..62
- Map of the Northern Rivers. Flowing from the high
  Pennines, the roof of England..64
- Pike scull and vertebrae. Flesh picked clean by the
  ever-present carrion crows. 66
- The mighty river Aire. Now at long last a rich and flourishing
  mixed fishery..69
- Bill at the age of fourteen with his 19lb Pike caught at Castle Howard
  near Malton. 73

River Pike in Northern England

- Bill with his twenty-pound River Derwent pike caught near his childhood home. ... 74
- A very fat River Hull pike caught by Adrian Brayshaw. ... 78
- The glorious River Ribble on a sunny July day. ... 85
- The River Ribble this time on a moody autumn afternoon. ... 87
- James Taylor with his superb twenty-two-pound River Swale pike. ... 89
- The famous river Tees barrage. A salmon run and fish counter is now fully installed. ... 91
- James Taylor with a superb pike taken from the River Tees. ... 92
- Tyne pike in the net. Pike are often caught by salmon anglers along the River Tyne. ... 95
- Hewick Bridge on the River Ure below the market town of Ripon. ... 97
- One of Bills twenty-four-pound pike. ... 99
- Nigel Winter plays a very big pike close to the net but it's not ready! ... 101
- Mark Greens magnificent River Wharfe Twenty-pound Pike. ... 103
- Bill on the 'roof of England'. This is where the weather magic often happens. ... 108
- Sub zero pike in the snow. It was the coldest winter for years. ... 109
- A summer double caught in cooling summer floods. ... 112
- Fishing an angry river in flood. ... 115
- Par digested crows' foot. Proof that pike dine on crow from time to time. ... 116
- Jackdaws and crows have a close symbiotic relationship with the pike. ... 119
- Three different types of landing net, all ideal for landing big pike. ... 124
- An upper twenty-pound pike held safely in a forty-two-inch net. ... 127
- Gently does it. Nigel Winter demonstrates how all pike should be landed. ... 128
- Choose your pleasure, this centrepin is mine. ... 131
- Capturing the excitement of the spinning reel. ... 134
- Another low twenty-pound river pike taken on a favourite centrepin reel. ... 137
- A twenty-pound pike taken on the legendary Allcocks Ariel classic centrepin reel. ... 138
- A collection of the authors favourite pike fishing rods. ... 142
- Open wide please. Gentle pressure on the lower jaw causes pike to open up. ... 147
- A twenty two-pound pike rests safely on a proprietary unhooking mat. ... 149
- Unhooking tools at the ready. ... 151

- Large Pike resting in a carp sack before photographs. 151
- Illustration of a typical snag ridden swim. 154
- Authors range of favourite homemade floats. 155
- The 'Snag Friendly Float' above can be made in a variety of sizes, larger for deep water, smaller for shallows. 158
- It is helpful to keep all your float making equipment in a bag or a box as shown here. 161
- A range of 'Old Favourites' Top layer 'Snag Friendly' versions in varied sizes for fishing deep water. 164
- Single hook rigs. The ideal rig for small baits under six inches long. 167
- Jardine snap tackle above, the authors preferred river rig below. 169
- Adjustable snap tackle, the authors favourite, just so, so good. 172
- River rig set up to fish a seven-inch sardine. 174
- Sliced bait presentation. Ideal for floodwater pike fishing close to bank. 174
- Minnow, small in size but big in its contribution to the food chain. 175
- Good friend Lee Maloney admires a 24lb Northern River Pike. 179
- Bill holds a 22lb River Pike taken on suspended deadbait with single hook. 182
- After a bitterly cold day the mood changes with the capture of this twenty-pound pike. 186
- A range of useful ledger weights for river fishing. With weights, less is always more. 189
- Electronic bite alarm useful, but over sensitive ones of limited use owing to variable water flow. 193
- Bait catapult is essential for positioning ground bait chunks towards far bank. 194
- Jonathan Winship shares the fun of pike fishing on a good day's fishing. 195
- Nigel with his 28lb beauty. This is the largest river pike we have ever seen in 50 years. 197
- The authors favourite spoon baits. 201
- A good selection of spoons and plugs. 203
- Modern Soft baits. Who needs livebaits with realistic lures like this? 210
- Devon minnows. Particularly effective on fast rivers and great fun. 211
- A sparkling shoal of bar spoons. Too good to ignore. 214
- Bill displays his 22lb pike. 221
- James with his first ever big pike. 224
- Evening sunset on the River Ouse 227

- Pike caught just after sunset. 229
- Bills 22lb pike taken in sub zero temperatures on the River Ouse. 233
- A 24lb pike taken on 'lucky 13th' March. 237
- Nigel with his own 24lb pike taken just a few moments after Bills 24lb beauty. 239
- Bill with a Fenland twenty taken on Barrie's rod! 242
- A 22lb pike taken at midnight. 246
- A 25lb pike taken during Storm Dennis! 250
- The 25lb Christmas Cracker. 253
- Brother-in-law Mike and son Jonathan among the pike. 255
- David weighs a very solid 12lb pike from the river Lune. 257
- Another big pike from the River Lune for David. 259
- Big pike engulfs big trout 263
- Nigel displays another big 25lb pike. 266
- The upper River Hull in full flow. 268
- Daren Clark with a tremendous 26lb River Hull pike. 273
- Adrian with a 25lb River Hull beauty. 274
- Sub-zero pike weighing 21lb 281
- An atmospheric view of the River Aire on a pikers dawn. 284
- Deeper Graph 285
- Mark displays his stunning River Aire pike weighing over 22lb. 289
- The River Wear is second to none for its charm and beauty. 293
- The Pike Condition Scale. 299
- This is one of the authors largest Northern River Pike caught or seen in over fifty years of fishing these northern rivers. 300
- A good spawning site, just one of many. 306
- Freshly 'Ottered' pike left to feed the Crows and Rooks. 308
- A moorhen's nest full of beautiful eggs. 309
- Delegates at a Ripon Pike Anglers Club Meeting. 312
- The Aldis projector test run at home. 315
- Bill and Peter enjoy a catch up at the Harrogate P.A.C. National Conference. 317
- Peter receives his well-earned reward. 322
- Trout rising in spring. 323
- A 5lb Brown Trout. 325
- No pressure to catch! 328
- She is not ready for the net yet! 328

FOREWORD

In the thirty-odd years I have known Bill Winship, there have been two overriding passions in his life: his family, and in particular his long-suffering wife Liz, and his love of pike fishing.

To describe him as an out-and-out pike specialist would not be entirely accurate. He has been known to flex a fly rod, and enjoys feeder fishing for the trout, grayling and perch of his beloved River Ure. However, pike are very much his first love. He will talk with enthusiasm about different aspects of the sport, but his eyes light up whenever the conversation switches to pike. If I tried to introduce him to the delights of tench fishing on a misty summer morning or set him up in a seductive barbel swim and told him where to cast, I just know that the minute my back was turned he would have spotted a pike fishing opportunity, and whatever rig I had suggested would have been replaced with a wire trace and a treble hook.

Bill grew up in Wensleydale, and the delightful Yorkshire Dales rivers are in his blood, in particular the River Ure. He is a living link to the history of that river, and to the famous anglers who have walked its banks and waded its waters. As a child, Bill was mentored by Norris Sturdy, the bailiff and fishery manager of the West Tanfield Angling Club, whose grandfather gave his name to the *Sturdy's Fancy*, a fly which finds popularity with grayling anglers to the present day. Nowadays, Bill himself is part of Wensleydale's rich angling heritage. He was also a close friend of one of the most influential pike anglers of modern times, the late and much-lamented Barrie Rickards. In this book, Bill gives a unique insight into the characters behind these (and other) familiar names from the pike fishing world.

However, *Northern River Pike* is far more than just a history of the sport. Bill looks in depth at sixteen different Northern pike rivers and considers the influence of atmospherics – the vagaries of the weather – on feeding patterns. Just how do you adapt to catch pike on a river which might be tap-water clear with cat ice in the margins one day, and a brown, swirling torrent the next?

Tackle and methods are also covered in detail. Bill is not, to use the modern parlance, a 'tackle tart'. He does not use the latest gear just because a cleverly crafted advertising campaign suggests he should or recommend it because a sponsor pays him to do so. Nor is he influenced by changing fads and fashions within the sport, except when he feels a new idea might offer a genuine advantage. He carries his tackle in a Second World War detonator box and some of his rods and reels would not look out of place in an antique shop! However, all his tackle is functional and practical, and his results prove that it is anglers, rather than state-of-the-art equipment, that catch pike.

Finally, if you enjoy a good fishing story – and what angler does not? – Bill delivers in that department too. He covers a selection of days when it all came good...when one of his home-made floats stirred and nodded, or a slowly retrieved plug was met with a rod-juddering swirl. Three guest writers also have stories to tell. If this does not inspire you to head for a Northern spate river with your pike tackle, then nothing will.

For any angler who aspires to catch more and bigger pike from the atmospheric and frequently moody Northern rivers, this book is essential reading.

Dave Tipping, Harrogate, July 2021

David Tipping cradles a truly inspiring pike which weighed just over the magical twenty-pound mark at 20lb 1oz. Without exception all the Northern Rivers highlighted in this book contain specimen pike of this calibre but they are not easy to catch, a fact which makes fish like this especially rewarding on a cold winters day.

PREFACE

Over the last one hundred and fifty years there have been many changes in the angling world. In the mid-nineteenth century almost all pike were classed as vermin and were killed along the full length of our northern rivers. Now all that has been reversed and they are now protected and generally recognised as a worthy quarry with viable sporting and commercial value.

Bill Winship had the good fortune to have been brought up in a friendly rural community where fishing has always been a much-valued part of the local economy. Thanks to Bills invaluable cultural roots and a lot of research it has been possible to track how our angling heritage has developed from the late Victorian period right up to the present day. Special emphasis is given to how pike fit into the angling scene of each period. This has been achieved through a series of case studies of our shared angling forefathers, each of whom give us a developing picture of how angling attitudes have gradually changed through history. Also included in the book is a section on how our northern rivers were in many places "Returned from the Dead" thanks to a relentless and expensive clean-up of our rivers pioneered by John Eastwood and almost wholly funded by anglers. This is an important part of the study because without the seventy-year struggle for clean rivers there would be no fish at all in many of our rivers.

In modern times neither pike nor salmon grow anywhere near as big as they did in the golden age of the 1920s, but we have ourselves caught good numbers of pike up to up to 28lb, about half the maximum size recorded in the 1920s. Interestingly, the newly returning salmon have been recently caught up to the same size of around 28lb, again about half the maximum size recorded one hundred years ago when fantastic salmon and pike over the fifty-pound mark were reported. From these very simple records it is clear our northern rivers are only half recovered from their natural state and there is still a long way to go before we can realise the full potential of our rivers.

My dear old friend Norris Sturdy told me that in the 1920s the River Ure at West Tanfield "Turned black" with thousands of salmon moving upstream. " You really have no idea of how good it was!" I can still remember the excitement in his voice as he told me. Dorris, his sister told me she felt sorry for the youngsters of our generation as we will never really know how rich the rivers once were. Dorris was of course correct, you really do need to experience something that good to fully understand. No matter, we have full faith in the possibility that golden age could return. Even if it never does, it is surely worth trying for. We hope the contents of this book will at least awaken in modern readers some notion of what is possible if we all simply make the right choices…. The Angling Trust have been working very hard to make this a reality so if you are interested in our rivers returning to their full potential you could do nothing better than joining the Angling Trust to support their tremendous push to reconnect our food chain to the North Atlantic Ocean. In the meantime our Northern Rivers still provide great pike fishing and most of this book explains how to get the very best out of it. We have five-chapter contributions by very special guest writers who have given us their inside knowledge of their particular areas. At the heading of each of their chapters they are named. All other chapters unnamed are the work of the author Bill Winship. In the same way photographs donated by contributors are all credited to the originator. Photographs not credited are originated by the author. We see this book as a 'work in progress' we would welcome details of any big pike caught in any of the Northern Rivers as defined on the rivers map. So if you would like to contribute to future editions please don't hesitate to get in touch. My contact details can be found in 'Pikelines' the magazine published by the 'Pike Anglers Club of Great Britain'.

Tight Lines, Bill Winship, January 31st, 2022

P.S. It is my father's birthday today, he is 94. Happy birthday Dad and thanks for your invaluable help on the many historical aspects especially the activities of Norris and his family during the inter war years.

INTRODUCTION

When I first started to compile this book in 2020 one of the first aims was to record some of the local cultural history of pike fishing on our northern rivers based on our contacts with anglers who fished these rivers back in Edwardian England. It was a lifelong ambition which was long overdue and at the age of sixty-six it was a case of now or never if some of this angling heritage stood any chance of being recorded. Interwoven under the same cover we have produced for the first time ever a book on Northern River Pike and share our special approach to river pike fishing which has led to the capture of well over fifty pike upwards of twenty pounds in weight. This figure would be over eighty twenty pounders if you included those landed by my adept partner on the riverbank Nigel Winter.

Having retired from full time work in November 2020 there was finally the opportunity to concentrate on this ambitious project. What an absolute joy it has been to at last, write up so many interesting memories of long-gone friends, and more importantly to log and narrate accounts about local characters reaching back into Victorian times. My friend and mentor Norris Sturdy was fifty-five years older than me; he met and knew Victorian anglers like Walbran and others, thus forming a living link to those far off days. How lucky I was to be introduced by my father to Norris who first fired my lifelong passion for catching river pike. I hope by sharing our combined passion for river pike you the reader will also be inspired to catch these elusive Northern River Pike too.

The first part of the book is based on five important anglers (founding forefathers) with Walbran representing a snapshot of Victorian Yorkshire. Then a mini biography of Tom Sturdy show casing the pike fishing duties of a river keeper in Edwardian Yorkshire, followed by his son Norris from the 1950s era. Then, and in sharp contrast, onto Barrie Rickards who brought about the modern revolution in attitudes towards pike in the late twentieth century. This angling heritage study through the ages reveals the tremendous changes which have occurred in our attitudes to the pike and the reasons for those changes. Last, but by no means least we include the work of John Eastwood, founder of the Anglers Cooperative Association whose work was pivotal in the northern rivers in bringing so many polluted rivers 'Back from the dead'. What we did not plan for or anticipate was the unexpected revelations our research into the past uncovered. Namely, that our northern rivers one hundred years ago were more prolific than we could ever have imagined possible. This discovery, acted as a valuable *realisation* that good as our northern rivers are today, they really do have the potential to be so much better if we continue to get the protection and ecology right as we go forward into the future. This discovery alone has fuelled huge optimism for the future of our sport and inspired a deeper purpose to this book, almost by accident, which alone has made all the work so worthwhile. This is just the start though.

Part two clearly defines the geographical location and scope of our sixteen primary northern spate rivers. These are sizable rivers known to hold big pike, but some are better than others at the time of writing. It is interesting to note that those flowing eastwards to the North Sea are much more prolific pike waters generally than those in the northwest. This alone raises many interesting questions which are discussed in depth. Again, the challenge of writing this section has been an absolute delight to describe the unique qualities of each separate river. Each one with its own completely individual characteristics and all of them holding big pike there for those who understand how to track them down. Just discussing the character of each river and the mouth-watering opportunities to fish them naturally arouses delight in the angler's heart. The kind of feeling which makes one grateful to have been born an angler with the pure lifelong joy it brings. The geographical situation of our northern rivers makes them completely unique in England and a big part of this is to do with the atmospherics of the area. We discuss this specific aspect which has such a huge and unique influence on our pike fishing in northern England.

In the tackle sections we deal with the special equipment and techniques which have brought success and enduring fulfilment over the decades. The northern rivers are not an easy place to catch big pike but by using the specially designed tackles suggested in this section it is possible to do well. To prove it we have dedicated section four to *'Red Letter Days'* so the reader can see what is possible. This is what you could call the *'undeniable proof of the pudding'* section which showcases the awesome pike which now live in our wonderful northern rivers.

On a national scale there has been a wealth of literature contributing steadily to the subject of pike fishing in Great Britain enabling us to track in detail the progress of our sport way back into the nineteenth century. Ireland for example has received huge attention from famous pike authors like Fred Buller who have popularised the sport in this country. Similarly, the Norfolk Broads have enjoyed the same notoriety as a great place to catch pike. The Fenlands of Cambridgeshire too have been written about by various anglers making it another magnet for pike anglers from all over the U.K. All these venues have been so popular that several excellent books have been dedicated to their pursuit in each of these famous areas.

For well over fifty years now these pike books have been a huge source of interest and it has been wonderful to read about these different Pike fishing areas in my ever-expanding private angling library. Yet, in the back of my mind I have always nursed a slight regret that there has never been a pike book based on the northern rivers. It is not as though there is a lack of big pike in the north, indeed, I have caught dozens of pike, over a weight of 20lb in Northern rivers. Furthermore, big fully authenticated 50lb pike, as big if not bigger than anywhere else in the U.K. have been caught in Yorkshire (to be highlighted later in this book). Therefore, there is no obvious reason the northern rivers should have been so shunned, almost as if they did not exist!

A wise man once said, *"It takes a whole lifetime to truly understand a river",* a statement I would completely endorse. At the age of sixty-six, I am still learning about the northern rivers and I discover new things every season. This leads me to suspect the wise man was a master of understatement! Now though, after almost a lifetime of river piking and having endured countless blanks as well as successes I believe I am sufficiently weathered by events to offer a reasoned account of the northern pike scene and justify why it can stand tall alongside the other more well-known pike fishing areas in the south.

Here it is then, the first ever in-depth book on river piking in the North. We would never claim it is easy to catch big pike in the often-fast flowing northern rivers, in fact, the sheer brutal challenge of it is what makes it so rewarding for us in the end. To help the newcomer to northern pike fishing we have revealed our secret tactics and methods which we have found to be useful, where tiny changes in tackle or methods can make all the difference to success. Many of our tackles and techniques are completely novel. In other parts of the book, we strongly defend *well-established* angling practices which have recently been abandoned. There is a wealth of information available at the touch of a button and a generation of virtual angling 'experts' who are undermining established angling practice across social media platforms. For the budding angler, internet-based angling research is a mine field of misinformation. Far too commonly, as I realised whilst recently watching an online video endorsing the practice of not using a landing-net, internet-based research can sow the seeds of bad practice. In this book, we feel duty bound to support best angling practice set up by great masters like Richard Walker, Martin Gay, and other innovators of the mid twentieth century which still hold the highest relevance and bring quality best practice to the sport.

Some of the details of this first section which describe angling customs in the late Victorian period may come as a shock to modern sensibilities. Fishing generally was much different then, but by knowing what went on in the not-so-distant past, enables us to realise how far we have come along the path of conservation. At the same time, I would not want to condemn our Victorian ancestors for killing fish for the cooking pot. Far from it, to this day fishing for food is probably the ultimate justification for angling. However, as the number of anglers has grown over the last century some sort of protection has been necessary to preserve our fish stocks. The progress towards good conservation in our rivers has been achieved within a series of national upheavals which are covered in the first part of this book. It is vital for all anglers to know this national fight to protect our rivers did not come cheap, but it has been bankrolled every inch of the way at a huge cost by we anglers, who to this day continue to fund the fight to preserve the purity of our rivers and lakes. Without knowing all this we are blind to our true status as the ultimate conservers and worst of all completely unaware of the huge efforts and sacrifices made by our predecessors who won for us the privileges, we are in danger of taking for granted today.

Famous academic Professor Barrie Rickards was a great believer in the theory that if we do not learn about the past, we are all doomed to make the same mistakes in the future, repeatedly. In keeping with this wise philosophy, we have started this book way back in the mid nineteenth century by paying full respect to some of the founding fathers of our sport. Some of our champions are nationally famous, others locally famous, others, thousands of others, lost in the mists of time. I am only aware of this last cohort thanks to the silent dedication they invested in building many of our largest angling institutions and in so doing recognising the wide social base upon which our sport has been founded.

When I first began writing this book one of the main aims was to preserve forever an important part of our angling heritage as a kind of nostalgic indulgence. However, as our research progressed, we began to realise just how good the fishing was in the nineteenth century. For example, salmon and pike of over fifty pounds were a distinct reality. Also, rod and line anglers were catching salmon and pike by the hundredweight. All this has made it clear that good as our rivers are now, they are only performing about half as well as they did before the great decline in the 1930s. Therefore, with good husbandry, our northern rivers can be improved much further which is very promising and provides a good target for us to aim for in the future.

To get the most value from this book we recommend the reader to start off by reading the 'Glossary of Terms' featured in the 'appendix' section of the book. Then read the book from start to finish because the middle and later chapters make constant reference to earlier parts.

ANGLING HERITAGE AND ECHOES FROM THE PAST

The Founding Fathers of Angling's Rich Cultural Heritage

We start this book by paying tribute to some of the founding fathers of our sport. The chosen few have been selected because of what they actually contributed to the development of angling. We start off with a short biography of Max Walbran a Victorian angler who travelled widely across Northern England providing guidance to Angling Societies on fish culture and expert angling advice.

Francis Maximilian Walbran 1852-1909

Francis Walbran was born in Ripon in 1852 to a well-respected northern family, his father was a wine merchant and one-time Mayor of Ripon. "Max" as he was known to his friends attended Ripon Grammar School one of the finest in England. After school Max often went fishing in the local river Skell with his cousin, who, because of his infectious enthusiasm, inspired young Max at an early age. As a result of this good company Max became totally engrossed with the sport and declared in his early teens that one of his main missions in life was to become recognised as an accomplished angler.

Several years later as a young man Max became a business executive for a trading firm in Hull. Then later he married and lived at Ivy Cottage in the riverside village of Pool in Wharfedale. His home was only a three-minute walk from his beloved River Wharfe and even as a proud father of two young daughters, Max still had time to indulge in his lifelong love of Angling. Due to starting his angling career at an early age Max was already proficient at both fly fishing and worm fishing. Indeed, he often caught fifteen or twenty fish each session and these catches were fully witnessed. Thanks to his expert grasp of the sport Max began to write with authority for both local and national angling publications like the 'Fishing Gazette' and this further enhanced his reputation as an expert northern fisherman.

At a time long before the motor car was invented, Max relied on the train network to reach quite remote rivers in upper Wensleydale and other more distant destinations. This meant Max had to stay overnight in different coaching houses where he became quite well known and was a much-valued visitor. In Victorian England it was quite normal to kill all you caught whether it was trout, grayling or coarse fish. One can imagine the reception he got at his lodgings turning up with a pannier full of trout, and there was no doubt what would feature on the menu that night. There are several reports about how in the bar after a day's fishing Max enjoyed being the centre of attention with guests and would spend hours telling them all about his fishing exploits. All this helped to build his confidence as an angling orator and his general reputation as an authority about angling.

In addition to his regular fishing trips Max also set up his 'Angling lecture tour' giving local fishing clubs in the West Riding slide shows using the modern and revolutionary oxy-hydrogen lantern. This was state of the art technology at the time and further built up his well-earned reputation. Indeed, Max was particularly good at fly fishing and even wrote his first book on the subject in 1883. Despite these talents his favourite form of fishing was 'swimming the worm' for grayling in autumn and winter. In his books, Max time and time again, extols the virtues of autumn/winter fishing and cannot understand why most anglers fold away their fishing tackle between September and April, missing what he considers the best months of the year. Max must have been a very hardy angler to fish in the depths of winter, he even said once that the weather "Can't be too cold for grayling fishing" and he often caught huge bags of fish when the air temperature was well below freezing. At the age of forty-three, our now nationally famous angling hero opened his own fishing tackle shop in Leeds, called the 'Northern Anglers Depot'. At last with his own fishing tackle business Walbran could give the angling public his expert advice on all matters piscatorial. Furthermore, he had truly realised his childhood ambition of being a recognised fishing expert. Better still and entirely due to his well-earned knowledge he also did good business thanks to his expert understanding of the trade.

In the mid nineteenth century cities like Leeds, Bradford and Manchester were the economic powerhouses of Britain. Massive woollen and cotton mills employed thousands of workers who, on their Sundays off work, loved to escape to the countryside to go fishing. Each mill had its own angling club so by working together they could collectively afford to cover their travel costs. It is interesting to note that the draw of angling for many came from the need to escape those often-terrible working conditions of the Victorian period. These men worked together, fished together and escaped hellish working conditions on chartered trains and later busses, to experience the joy of fishing and the health-giving benefits of fresh country air.

In the 'Northern Anglers Depot' Walbran catered well to the needs of these hard-working men, with good advice and affordable tackle. He also catered for the wealthy classes too. One such wealthy gentleman from West Tanfield was called Mr Tom Ayton and he consulted Max about his six mile stretch of river based in the Tanfield area. By drawing on his influential clients in the West Yorkshire area Max was further instrumental in setting up the Tanfield Fly-fishing club to cater for the high-end game fishing market, drawing further support from some well-heeled northern industrialists. Following a successful meeting at the 'Queens Hotel' in Leeds, the new club was first established with a limited membership of just twenty members paying an annual subscription of four guineas per member. To protect the trout, a full-time water bailiff would be employed at a rate of one guinea per week. As chief advisor and founder Walbran was made secretary and under the guidance of Mr Ayton, he established one of the finest trout fishing clubs in the U.K. which still runs perfectly well right up to this day, some 120 years later.

On reflection one must admit that our Victorian forefathers did not do things by halves. Just like the railways they constructed; their grand designs have so often lasted until this day.

A view of the River Ure looking upstream from West Tanfield road bridge. The fishing here is controlled by Tanfield Angling Club established by Francis Walbran in 1892.

In Walbran's classic book 'Grayling and How to Catch Them' the author openly and honestly admits that in thirty years fishing the Rivers Ure and Wharfe the largest grayling caught was a modest 1lb 6oz. In southern England, his contemporaries had caught grayling almost twice that size by accident, whilst fishing for trout on the southern chalk streams. Perhaps what marked out Walbran as a brilliant angler was on just a short three-day trip to the River Test near Winchester, he not only caught a personal best grayling of 3lb 9 oz, but also broke the local river record for that section of the River Test. Huge praise should be given to his good friends Senior and Halford for obviously inviting Max to a very productive part of the river! Max returned the favour but when Senior came up to Yorkshire, he was not so impressed with what he found as he sat alongside his friend Walbran who just fished on. The fact was that the northern spate rivers of Yorkshire could not compete with the warmer southern chalk stream rivers like the test, the fish though plentiful were only about half the size as those from the more productive southern rivers. Part of the reason may also be that all the bigger fish in the Ure were continually killed for the pot, so perhaps the poor river Ure grayling, like the pike of the same period, rarely got the chance to grow to their full-size potential.

At this point the reader may well ask what has all this got to do with a book on River Pike? Well rather a lot actually.... let me explain. Probably one of the greatest legacies Max left us was the very successful fishing club he had established and in so doing he created a template of success for others to replicate all over England. He did this in 1892 and so was at least one hundred and twenty years ahead of his time. Not only did they enhance the trout fishing out of all recognition due to their well laid out trout hatchery and general protective measures, but the grayling fishing improved too and by the way, the pike got bigger..... much bigger! All thanks to the protection afforded by Maxes management. If you want to know how and why, just read on. The rest of this book will cover the gradual development of pike fishing from the Victorian age when all pike were killed to now when almost all pike are returned. During all that time, a period covering one hundred and fifty years, there have been dozens of books written to extol the virtues of the trout and grayling, good books too, full of fascinating details of fly fishing and worm fishing. Interestingly though, in all that time no one has written a book on the biggest and most dramatic freshwater fish of all which lives in the northern rivers, namely the pike!

In fact, having read Walbrans book on grayling several times the word pike does not enter the book even once and yet his favourite stretches at West Tanfield certainly contained a healthy and thriving number of fish which were at least twenty times bigger than his much-loved grayling. Max stayed overnight at the Bruce inn at West Tanfield for over twenty-five years on a regular basis, he even referred to it as his "second home". In all that time he must have at least seen pike basking in the sun below the road bridge over the river Ure and yet no mention at all, not even to curse them for eating his trout and grayling.

Victorian society was very class conscious. Everyone had their own place in that society where it was vital for everyone to know their place too, provided you knew this simple fact everything ran well. It was not just people who had to fit into the appropriate class, but even fish had their own class too. The "Lordly Salmon" was of course at the pinnacle of the fish class structure. Next down was the "fine game fish the Trout", then, well below the trout came the humble grayling. Walbrans book on grayling fishing was at the time a very controversial plea to get grayling to be recognised with almost equal status to the trout. It did work, and gradually thanks to Walbran and others the grayling became a much more worthy and widely valued quarry almost as respectable as the trout. Well beneath the grayling came the coarse fish, including the pike which were mostly to do with ordinary working people and eccentric anglers like Alfred Jardine. Jardine was very unusual for the Victorian period; he was financially independent and had a strong enough character to put his love of the pike above his social image. Like a lot of modern pike anglers, all he wanted to do was catch pike and cared little about social norms, during that period his attitudes and approach were over a hundred years ahead of his time.

For better or worse our class system is not quite so well defined now, so perhaps it is now safe to write a book about pike fishing in the northern rivers without too much alarm. A lot of northern England is still 'Tweed and Hackle' country, so this book is still a bit edgy. However, as Walbran did with his book on grayling fishing, I will make a similar avant-garde plea for the place of pike fishing within the northern rivers of England, it is the first book ever to do this. This book had to be written though because in my lifetime the northern rivers have given me a continuous sense of joy and purpose in pursuit of big pike and if the reader of this book just gets a fraction of the joy I have had in their pursuit then it will have been all worthwhile. This then is the start of a lifelong testament to be laid down forever within the pages of this book. Like Walbran, all my advice come from real life experiences on the riverbank.

The Bruce Arms was Walbrans 'Second home' for over twenty-five years. Note the Stables where Norris Sturdy weighed his 56lb Pike.

Thomas Sturdy

THOMAS STURDY-WATER BAILIFF FOR ALMOST 50 YEARS.

On March 1st, 1899, Mr Thomas Sturdy was appointed the position of Water Bailiff by Mr Thomas Ayton the owner of the West Tanfield Estate. It was the start of a career which would last almost fifty years, but Tom could not know that at the outset of his career, it was all very uncertain, especially as the job had changed hands several times over the last few years. The task involved maintaining the six-mile beat of the West Tanfield Angling Club and was both physically and mentally demanding. Just patrolling the six mile stretch on foot was a challenge, but that was the easy part. More difficult was raising fickle brown trout fry in the hatchery which required patience and skill of a high order.

To avoid overfishing the club membership was restricted to just twenty anglers. Club membership cost four Guineas per season, about three months wages for the average worker at the time. Membership was therefore restricted, but the subscriptions were only in line with the running costs needed to pay for the upkeep. Along the whole six-mile beat there were no spawning streams for the brown trout, so it was decided to boost natural fish numbers by raising young trout in a purpose-built fish hatchery right next to the River Ure in Tanfield. During this time in the 1890s this was cutting edge husbandry and quite a risky undertaking. Fertilized trout Eggs were purchased from the central Hatchery near Grantham in Lincolnshire and delivered in shallow trays by steam train from the main line Grantham station to Tanfield station on the Masham branch line. A purpose-built hatchery was built and secured by a padlock to provide a protected rearing enclosure fed by local spring water; the Springwater temperature remained almost constant through the whole year so was ideal for rearing stock fish. The tiny fish were brought on by feeding ground liver from the village butchers. In the early stages the fingerlings had to be checked twenty-four hours per day until they grew into a more robust size. By April or May the trout fry had grown to eight inches and at this stage some were stocked into the river. These valuable stock trout were obviously vulnerable to predators like the heron, otters, poachers and pike. Tom the Bailiff therefore bore a lot of responsibility, he was still only a very young man, but he had lots of support from Mr Ayton and the Club secretary Mr Max Walbran who at this time was forty-seven years old and was able to offer professional guidance based on his unrivalled knowledge of fishery matters.

    Tom, now the new water bailiff had a young wife and two twin children Norris and Dorris, so he was very motivated to succeed in his new career. He was a strict Methodist and took his wife Charlotte to Chapel every Sunday making him a well-known and popular member of the community. At the end of the day though his work was funded by the paying customers and his career would live or die on his ability to provide clients with good sport. Yorkshire businessmen at the time would be unlikely to pay four guineas per season if the service or sport were poor. Beautiful surroundings would only go so far, what they really expected was good service and rod bending sport to make it all worthwhile.

    Some members were highly experienced anglers like Walbran who just sought solace and to be left alone amongst the trout and grayling. Others wanted more though. Some of the wealthy businessmen from

Bradford would need setting up in lodgings at the Bruce Arms. They would need help during the day carrying their tackle as well as local guidance to the best fishing swims and even need entertaining during the evening.

This excellent Victorian Photo shows Toms Father who invented the famous grayling fly 'Sturdy's Fancy' and taught Tom all he needed to know about fishing on the northern rivers. (Photo courtesy of Mr Basil Sturdy).

Fortunately, Tom could meet these exacting requirements with ease. His Father was an expert fly fisherman and was the inventor of the famous northern grayling fly called 'Sturdy's Fancy' and Tom had inherited not only the Sturdy name, but also the skill to fly fish and tutored to do so from an early age. He also knew every good trout grayling and pike swim on the whole six-mile beat.

Tom also wanted nothing more than to please his clients, although quiet by nature, his nickname was "Silent Tom" he had the perfect can-do attitude which went down well with fee paying clients and created an easy amicable atmosphere for a good day's fishing. Also, being young and fit Tom could help clients carry their tackle and refreshments on extended days out on expeditions which often required a lot of walking. From the very start Tom proved his worth, and subscription renewals were promptly booked year after year, so much so the club had to form a waiting list. I understand from current club members that now over 120 years later you still must wait for someone to die to get a place!

Let us take a close look at Toms daily activities back in Edwardian England. What we record here is a factual record of the details passed on to Tom's son Norris when we fished together back in the 1960s. Norris is in effect our living link back to the angling scene in Edwardian Yorkshire. This is all part of our valuable local angling heritage and recording the details at last is one of several reasons why we just had to write this book.

The months of April to September were naturally the most demanding months for Tom, having to look after both the fish hatchery and the demanding needs of the clients. From October onwards though Tom's duties changed. This was the start of the shooting season and Tom helped on the estate with organising regular shooting arrangements and employing a dozen or so bush beaters from the village to flush out the pheasants. As a bush beater myself at the age of eight back in 1962 I can remember them as great days out in the woods, very well paid and free lunch at the Bruce arms in West Tanfield. The warm pork pies and Ale, (or for me Shandy as I was too young for strong ale) are all great memories. We were transported from one woodland shoot to another, often sat next to soggy nosed Labradors in large soft top land rovers. There was an atmosphere of military precision in how it was conducted. Indeed, many of the 'Guns' were retired World War two officers and knew how to organise troops. Major Bourne Arton was himself a veteran of the second world war (Royal Artillery) and played a big part in pushing the Germans all the way from Normandy to Berlin. Knowing what a tough character the Major was, I can fully understand why the Germans fell short of winning the war! To this day, sixty years later, the taste of pork pies transports me back to those happy busy days on the 1960s winter pheasant shoot.

A rare photograph of Tom Sturdy after a successful shoot. In addition to his water bailiff duties Tom also helped to organise regular shooting events within the local community. (Photo courtesy of Basil Sturdy).

The Water Bailiffs fishery duties in winter also included squaring up to the enemies of the trout, namely, poachers, otters, heron and pike. On winter patrols along the six-mile beat Tom carried a twelve-bore shotgun, a pike rod, a gaff and a shoulder bag containing food, drink, shotgun cartridges, fold up raincoat and some homemade wagtails and spoons for pike fishing.

Tom knew from his inherent local knowledge that Pike spawned in the weedy sheltered channel below Mickley Weir. If Tom could see the pike spawning in the shallows the first option was to discharge one shotgun cartridge and instantly dispatch them 'Winston Churchill Style'. Failing visual sighting, the spinning tackle was set up, complete with wire trace and a home-made wagtail bait painted to look like a trout. If a pike grabbed the bait, it would be carefully brought to the waiting gaff. After being unhooked it would be humanely dispatched to pay for its trout eating habits!

All this may seem harsh by modern catch and release standards, but things were done differently one hundred years ago. Between the war years and beyond, just about every fish of reasonable size was taken home for the table. Certainly, in West Tanfield, and for as long as Tom was water Bailiff pike were a regular feature in the local diet, often in good quantities too, along with grayling, rabbit, pheasant or hare, all shared out in kind amongst the constantly appreciative villagers.

This image captures the atmosphere of Church Street in West Tanfield where three generations of the Sturdy family lived. Apart from the wheelie bins and cars, nothing much has changed on Church street in the last 120 years.

Otters were another predator which needed to be constantly controlled. These cute little creatures (before they were popularised by Henry Williamson in his book Tarka the Otter) were reviled for killing dozens of trout for fun and blatantly leaving their carcasses rotting on the riverbank. Fortunately, their presence was only intermittent and were a quite easy and slow-moving target and of course were shot on sight. Again, this may seem cruel by modern standards, but trout were very expensive to rear. No one would pay to fish an empty river.

Now we come to dealing with the two-legged trout thieves, namely poachers. Now Toms nickname was silent Tom and was partly earned by his uncanny ability to quietly appear from nowhere and scare the living daylights out of those with a guilty conscience. It is rumoured that Tom could appear from nowhere day or night and once he uncovered the wrong doers they never returned -not ever! We are still no sure how he achieved this but whatever it was it worked and there were never any complaints. It was just one of Toms trade secrets!

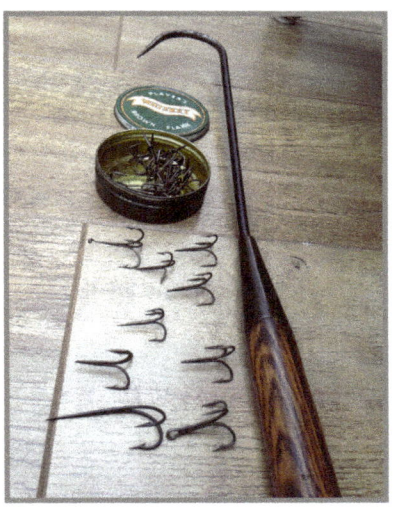

The Salmon/Pike gaff given to Tom by the club secretary Max Walbran This was used to land big salmon and pike. The rare vintage treble hooks were purchased from Walbrans 'Northern Angling Depot' in Leeds. These date back to the late Victorian period of the 1890s. Note there are no eyes on some of the treble hooks so they had to be whipped onto a gimp trace. The photo also shows Toms favourite pipe tobacco!

Now let us return to Tom's summer activities. After feeding the trout in the rearing hut in the Early dawn Tom would attend to the needs of his clients even members who just wanted to be left alone with the trout needed watching – often for their own safety. The loose gravels of the Ure and the slippery smooth glass like limestone slabs on the riverbeds were all quite treacherous for waders, even on a lovely sunny day. On many occasions Tom was there at hand, unbeknown to the fishermen and in perfectly good weather when a loose foothold sent his members sailing down into deep water at the blink of an eye. Tom was at hand several times in this way. Soaked to the skin Tom helped his customers back to the Bruce Arms to dry out in front of the log fire to recharge with a cup of strong tea. This happened numerous times over the years making Tom very highly regarded in the village and in the club too. Alas though, Tom could not always be there on hand as a lifeguard as will be shown in the following chapter.

In his pest control activities Toms main aim was to keep on top of pike numbers so trout fishing members would not even see any pike, let alone get bitten off by them. Over the years Tom became very proficient at catching pike. He discovered where they lived at different times of the year and found lots of different ways of catching them. Any dead trout found in the rearing hut were put to good use as dead bait and they worked very well indeed as a pike bait. Some modern pike anglers claim dead baiting for pike was invented in the 1950s. Not true, Mr Sturdy was doing quite well with them in Edwardian England, about half a century before their later "discovery"!

On a good day he would catch more pike than he could carry home. When this happened, he hid the surplus in a safe place and sent his young son Norris back to collect them after work. Norris was only a teenager then. I met Norris many years later when I was eleven. Norris was sixty-five, but I was captivated by his endless stories of big pike catches. I never had the opportunity to meet Tom as he died ten years before I was born. However, the animated endless recollections Norris gave me about his dad made me feel I knew him very well indeed. I was so inspired I decided I would also like to be a Water Bailiff when I left school at fifteen. That did not happen though as I could find no such job opportunities in Harold Wilsons world of the 1960s. The working world was changing, and it was all about the "White Heat of Technology" As a result of this I decided to take up fishing as a hobby instead and have had no regrets at all.

After reading this section on the duties of Tom the Water Bailiff it is likely that young readers will get the impression that he was a brutal man for killing so many pike and other enemies of the trout. The important thing is that in Victorian England and right up to the 1950s almost all fish were killed for the table. Most villagers at that time, well over half were constantly hungry and very poor. The mortality rate of the average person during Edwardian England was only forty-five, so if you lived to be fifty you were doing very well. Even Tom, with a good house and wage still had to be very careful with his limited resources. For example, on his daily patrols up and down the river Tom collected firewood and stored it outside his house ready for winter. There was a strict rule in the Sturdy household. "No open fire in the house until the first of November." In this way heating was only used when it became very cold in the depths of winter. This was a practice common to many households in the past before the days of electricity, central heating and free government fuel allowances!

Tom was essentially employed in a service industry, and as such one way of seriously improving his income was to secure 'Tips' for attentive service throughout the season. Norris told me his dad could almost double his income in this way by providing good service. This was of course a delicate subject and only known to immediate family. Some of the most generous tippers were the wealthy salmon anglers who relied on Toms expert knowledge to provide guidance as to local conditions. In the early 1900s there were still good numbers of salmon running up the Yorkshire rivers, big ones too up to over fifty pounds in weight. Then as now though their runs were unpredictable and only those who were on the river every day knew when they were present. At certain times, usually in Spring or Autumn, Tom checked the river by standing on Tanfield bridge each morning before going to work. If there was a full run the river below the bridge became black with salmon. Tom knew the run may only last a few days so this is when he contacted the salmon anglers so they could fish whilst the game fish were in. If the river level was on the low side, the salmon progress upstream may be delayed for a few days giving more opportunity to catch them. Thanks to his constant vigilance Tom could keep a track of events and gain huge popularity with his clients making him the most important person in the village. This is partly how Tom made his extra income by being so indispensable. Expressions of appreciation were often presented in the form of a bottle of Whiskey at Christmas, or in Walbrans case free fishing tackle from The Northern Anglers Depot in Leeds. On one occasion Walbran gave Tom a gaff which he used to land big salmon and pike too. On some occasions though, after a very good day Tom would receive a 'Fiver' in appreciation. This was a massive amount of money in the early twentieth century and just shows how wealthy and indeed generous some of the club members were.

It was not just about salmon though, most members were primarily trout anglers and preferred to catch smaller, though more dependable trout and grayling for the table. One member, a Mr Robert Hayton, a great uncle of mine, enjoyed pike fishing on boxing day. Tom could cater for pike lovers too and the photo of Mr Hayton and his daughter Mary shows clearly, if rather faded, a nice leach of pike taken on boxing day 1919. Grayling can also be seen on the photo meaning it was almost certainly a day out on the River Ure. The carefully posed shot was taken in my Great Uncles back garden, all the fish were eaten as was the custom at that time. This photo was given to my mother Mildred by Mary before she died in her eighties. Mary was of course the little girl with her dad in the photo taken in 1919 just after the Great War.

Tom Sturdy died one sunny evening in his chair just outside his back door. The warm pavement and cobbled walls along Church Street in Tanfield still to this day form the perfect sun trap. Tom, like the pike he knew so well, loved to bask in the warm sunlight, and so it was in this way Tom died peacefully facing the evening sunset, a dignified way to go, just before the evening rise. The final closing act for a great angling master; 'Silent Tom'.

This fast-fading photograph captures the results of a good day's fishing on boxing day 1919. The photo shows my great uncle Robert Hayton with a good catch of pike, trout and grayling taken from the river Ure. Note Mary is holding a livebait kettle suggesting that live baiting was the killing method on this day. (Photo courtesy of Mary Hayton and Mildred Winship).

After a lifetime's dedication as River Keeper and all-round expert countryman, Tom's reputation extended beyond his local community. As such he was invited to appear on the BBC National radio commenting on the duties of a Northern River Keeper. This he did with ease and flair. Everyone in West Tanfield was given prior notice of the event so the whole village took time out to 'Tune in on the wireless'. All this was before the advent of modern Television so being invited onto the radio was a big event and was appreciated by all. If only Tom had written an autobiography of his time as River Keeper for Tanfield Angling Club it would today have been a cultural gem. No matter, at least thanks to his son Norris we have been able to record some of the details of his fascinating life and in the next chapter there are more details about both Tom and Norris's activities thanks to Norris and his sister Dorris too who provide a rich testament to their interesting lives.

Norris Sturdy – 1905-1987

There are times in one's life when you meet someone who inspires an interest which can last a lifetime. I will always be grateful to my father for introducing me to his old friend and gifted angler, Norris Sturdy from West Tanfield. Norris was brought up in the centre of a rich angling culture second to none. When his father Tom had died, Norris had taken over his father's reins as Water Bailiff and had become fully conversant in the various demands of the job.

I will always remember my first meeting with Norris. It was one cold dark November evening back in 1965. My father and I had no invite, and yet as old friends we received a very warm welcome despite arriving with no warning. Dorris (Norris' sister) invited us in, plumped up the cushions, made us comfortable next to the log fire and then went out to the kitchen to make tea. Dick, my dad, began updating Norris on his new job as farm manager at Arbour Hill near Bedale. Ten minutes later Dorris returned from the kitchen with a large tray and a big tea pot in the centre covered with a thick tea cosy. She carefully placed her impressive China cups and plates on to a side table and proudly offered us some lovely cakes, "My you have grown Billy, would you like a cake"?

I instinctively knew it would be very bad manners to refuse and they did look delicious. "Are you enjoying School"? she asked, I replied, "Very much thanks, especially the football and Cricket". Dorris poured out the tea, a weak one for me as I had requested. It was the most refreshing tea I had ever tasted, and the home-made cakes were delicious too. These are such vivid childhood memories and the precursor to my first ever pike meeting.

After about an hour's catch up and social formalities my dad skilfully turned the conversation towards the subject of pike fishing and my newfound interest in the sport. "You know a thing or two about pike don't you Norris"? Dad was a real master of understatement! At the very mention of the subject, Norris seemed to somehow shift up a gear, and his voice instantly became more strident. For the next two and a half hours Norris launched into great detail about the methods of catching pike and even rushed out to his shed in the black of night to get us his pike gear to give us a practical demonstration of how it all worked. Dorris quickly moved the tea tray from the table to make way for the tackle, but only after covering the table with a cloth to prevent scratching the surface!

I had never seen proper pike fishing tackle before and there it was laid out before us. Massive spoons, wagtail baits, treble hooks, snap tackles, homemade pike bungs and a special gaff given to Norris's Dad by Walbran. Also, Allcocks Ariel spinning reels of the finest quality. Wow, this was just amazing fishing tackle. Norris showed us how a pike takes a trout sideways on, using an empty cigar case taken from his mantlepiece to illustrate the stage-by-stage process. This was just the start; Norris then went on to describe the capture of his largest ever pike. At this point, Dorris returned to the kitchen to make a fresh round of refreshments. Ten minutes later she returned with even more sweet treats. Her hospitality was amazing and really set the tone and maintained the energy level of the evening.

Norris explained that during the fly-fishing season on the River Ure some club members would complain that they had been "bitten off" by pike when playing trout to the net. Usually the unwanted pike were only five or ten pounds in weight, though occasionally much bigger. On one such occasion Norris' Father came home after a long day and found a handwritten message telling him the exact location of the latest "bite off". Tom was exhausted after a long day so sent Norris to catch the culprit, located just below Tanfield bridge. Equipped with the best tackle money could buy, young Norris set forth on his special mission to catch this troublesome pike.

After about half an hour of searching out the deep pools and undercut banks with his red and silver bait, Norris suddenly had a ferocious take. The rod was wrenched down so hard it was almost bent double. After gaining control the rod was held high to keep the line out of the snag ridden riverbed. It was too late though, the line parted with a crack and all was lost, including the very expensive red and silver Colorado spoon. Norris returned home with the bad news and his dad was not impressed at all. Norris told us that his dad was able to give you a full telling off without even saying a word. His eyes said it all!

Norris returned again and again to try to catch the big fish, but it was not going to fall for a spinner a second time. Fortunately, though, on the third night Norris spotted the beast lying off the side of a gravel bar. He knew it was the same fish because he could see the red Colorado spoon still hanging from the pike's awesome jaws. This time, looking carefully and sheltering behind the riverside trees he could see its full size and it was at least four feet long, probably at lot more. With recharged enthusiasm Norris rushed home and broke the news to Tom about his sighting. Tom said nothing, just studiously filled his pipe with tobacco and mentally started to plan a new approach. Norris realised from that point forward, the pike was as good as caught.

The next day both Tom and Norris set up their pike gear, complete with float and snap tackle. Before going to the river, they visited the trout hatchery to get some live bait. Tom said it was tragic to use trout in this way but was best in the long run as such a big pike would eat more fish if left unopposed. The walk to the river was over half a mile so they shared the task of carrying the heavy live bait tin. Once at the river they set up their pike rod and sent out the trout to do its vital work. Nothing happened for about an hour, but then the float began to nod its way slowly to the riverbank not far from where they were sat waiting. The trout bait could be seen right at the side of the river in about five feet of water. A few minutes later the familiar shape of the silver Colorado came into view, still hanging from the huge jaws. In an instant the trout was inhaled, and the float started to cruise its way back into mid river where it disappeared out of sight. The ratchet on the Allcocks reel was switched on by Norris and a firm strike sealed the fate of this biggest ever pike. After a long struggle, the giant fish succumbed to the gaff and using both hands it was lifted onto the bank. Norris said its huge size was almost too much to take in, its dimensions were so much bigger than any other pike they had both seen. The fish was too heavy for one man to carry so they cut a ten-foot-long staff from the wood behind them and tied the fish to the stick with binder twine threaded through the gaff hole in the lower jaw. They then each put the pole on their shoulder making it possible to walk back with the pike balanced in the middle of them. Even with this arrangement the pike's tail was still trailing on the floor, it was so long. They took their prize straight to the stables at the Bruce Arms Coaching Inn. There were some heavy scales there used for weighing up sixteen stone bags of grain. One sixteen stone bag of grain was checked by four 56lb weights. When the pike's full weight was laid on the scales it easily counter balanced one of these weights indicating the pike was well over 56lb.

Both my father and I have known about this for over forty years. Was it just another big fish story? We know of no photos of the fish. Tom and Norris would not wish to publicise it because coming from their trout fishery it was more of an embarrassment than an achievement. It could have been implied they were not in control of the pike. Pike control was their ultimate responsibility and with their jobs on the line discretion was the better part of valour. What put me off this claim was the fact that this fish was almost twice the weight of most of the largest known pike from the River Ure. Also, with no photographic evidence it is difficult to support such a claim. Just recently though two factors have made me review my doubts. Firstly, in May 2020 a well photographed and witnessed 53lb pike was found dead in a riverside lake just a mile or so down stream of Norris's catch. Secondly, the thing which really haunts me is the fact that Norris made it clear the fish was very long, six inches of its tail was dragging on the ground, even when it was suspended on their shoulders. That means it must have been well over 48 inches long. This alone combined to the pure integrity of Norris the man, makes me think it probably was every ounce the 56lb claimed. Knowing Norris though he would probably prefer to keep it quiet, just sharing the truth with his close friends. If only we had a good photo that would make Norris (a very reluctant) new British rod caught, pike record holder!

Tom and Norris needed a long staff to carry their biggest ever pike catch. Even then the pike was so large that its tail was dragging on the ground as they carried it back to the Bruce Arms stables for weighing. There was no photographic evidence of this pike. This line drawing is the next best visual aid, drawn from the exact details given in Norris Sturdy's testament. Its weight, over 56lb, just a few pounds heavier than the 'Belflask Beast' a fully authenticated 53lb pike taken in May 2020 just a couple of miles downstream from Norris's mammoth pike.

By the time Norris finished telling us about his giant pike it was about Ten o clock and we were all working the next day. It was a very enjoyable evening, good company all round with special thanks also to Dorris for being such a wonderful hostess. Norris had just retired at the age of sixty-five and had purchased a brand-new Austin 1100 motor car. His aim was to spend more time fishing and I met up with him for several fishing trips. I knew some great pike lakes and rivers in the area. Norris was becoming a little frail due to his ill health so when we went fishing, I gladly carried all his equipment and he provided the transport. It really was a great arrangement and we caught lots of pike together. I learnt a lot about river piking from Norris, knowledge which would have taken me years to learn without his help.

Another vivid account Norris gave me, again of interesting historical importance, was about Max Walbrans last day fishing the River Ure. The day in question was in February 1909 and Max Walbran was fishing right opposite Norris's riverside cottage. Tom Sturdy could see Max wading out to get a better trotting position in the river. Tom knew the river was fast rising by the huge number of floating logs and debris which always precede a flood. Knowing all this Tom shouted across to advise Max to return to the safety of the riverbank. Max just laughed and carried on fishing. Tom shouted again desperate to get him to safety. Max was on the far side of the river, so even Tom could not help him if he fell in. Then in an instant Max was swept off his feet, almost certainly by being hit by a floating log traveling at speed downstream. Utterly shocked and frantic with fear Tom grabbed his rope from the garden shed and sprinted down Church Street towards the river. Poor Max was already well ahead downstream but still in view. Then he just disappeared, probably sucked under by one of the many whirlpools in the river. Sometime later, Max was found dead floating in quiet water about five hundred yards downstream. Still in shock, Tom returned to the Bruce arms stables to get a horse to carry Max back to his lodgings at the Bruce arms. He was then laid out on the table in his favourite Inn where he was so well known.

    Max Walbran, one-time secretary and founder of Tanfield Angling Club was only fifty-eight years old and his tragic death saddened the whole angling community. Max was a highly regarded contributor to the Fishing Gazette and the Editor gave him a good write up out of recognition for all he had done. Tanfield Angling Club, who owed Max so much for his far-reaching innovations started to build up a fund, not only to support his widow in Leeds, but also to build a very impressive monument to honour his massive contribution to his colleagues and friends. This memorial is very impressive indeed and can still be admired standing proud in the St Nicholas Church yard in West Tanfield. At the base of the monument there are beautifully stone carved fish, a rod and net and beautiful words also carved in stone. To the best of my knowledge no other northern angler in British history has been so honoured in this way ever before. The memorial really is worth visiting and it leaves you in no doubt that Walbran stands tall as one of our most important founding fathers of the sport. If you do want to pay your respects, park your car in the Village Hall car park, it is only 50p to park, walk up Church Street passing the house Norris lived at on your left. Then, approximately 100 yards towards the Church you will see a narrow path along the church yard to the right. Halfway down the small path the Memorial can be seen to your left.

West Tanfield was my place of birth in 1954, so forgive me if I am biased. This Yorkshire village situated as it is on the banks of the glorious River Ure, with all its fascinating angling history and culture makes this place, for me at least, the spiritual home of angling. Not just in Yorkshire, but in the whole of England. If you would like to truly enjoy the river atmosphere, choose a sunny warm day in June, order a lunch at the Bull Inn and select a table right next to the river in the beer garden. Do this and you will enjoy the timeless sounds, scents and balmy atmosphere of the riverside. The exact same atmosphere enjoyed by our angling friends Max, Tom and Norris, a truly timeless experience.

Max Walbrans memorial. A lasting tribute to Max Walbran and paid for by voluntary donations from his many friends. The beautiful stone carving showing his creel, net and fishing rods is unrivalled in northern England and stands tall as a tribute to probably the greatest Northern Angler of the Victorian and Edwardian Era.

John Eastwood 1887 - 1952

In any discussion on the founding fathers of British Angling over the past hundred years the name of John Eastwood should be at the top of the list and known to every angler in Britain and yet to the majority he is a completely unknown figure.

As recently as the early twentieth century most of the great northern rivers were full of salmon, trout, and coarse fish. In Sheffield local workers complained about their constant diet of salmon, all caught from the local rivers which were so clean migratory fish were thriving in abundance.

It was not to last though, with the industrial expansion of the 1850s onwards large northern cities like Leeds, Bradford, Sheffield, and Manchester became overcrowded, new industrial processes like the dying of fabrics required lots of water, and some of the rivers turned different colours overnight. Sewage was also a problem with the massive increases in populations. Owing to all these factors rivers like the Rother, the Don, the Calder, the Aire, the Wharfe and Ouse were all polluted causing widespread fish kills.

In the upper river courses, places generally upstream of the industrial city's conditions remain tolerable and viable fish populations continued to flourish. In the river Ure for example, local inhabitants can remember good runs of salmon right up to the 1930s and of course locally spawning trout and grayling went on breeding without many interruptions.

Unfortunately, migratory fish almost died out from the 1930s onwards. This was because of all the pollution from various rivers in Yorkshire which collected in the tidal Humber estuary.

All the industrial waste from the whole of Yorkshire collected just upstream of Hull. When the tide came in each day the pollution was pushed back upstream. Then when the tide went out not all the waste was washed out to sea. This process of tidal shunting meant there were no periods at all when the Humber was clear of pollution which prevented salmon returning to their spawning grounds.

The pollution problem was at its worst during the second world war when factory output was working flat out in our massive war effort. For example, in Sheffield munitions were desperately needed to supply not only our own army but also our Russian Allies. Massive quantities were sent to Hull to be shipped onto Arctic convoys to help our Russian friends. At these desperate times river pollution was not a top priority at all. One unfortunate consequence of this was that the Humber estuary was badly polluted and Hull city was practically raised to the ground by continuous air raids throughout the war.

Under the desperate struggle of the war years, it was perfectly understandable all stops had to be pulled out to support Britain's huge war effort. Companies were given Crown Protection allowing them to pollute at will, factory output was the only thing which mattered. Things were so desperate that our coal miners were sometimes not allowed out until their quota tonnage for the day was achieved. These were indeed desperate times. Once the war was over though there was no further excuse to use our rivers as open sewers. Things needed to be tidied up.

It was just after the war in 1948 that one of the most important bodies in the history of angling was formed. It was established by John Eastwood, O.B.E., K.C. and it was called the 'Anglers Cooperative Association'. The purpose of the A.C.A. was to stop water polluters and restore rivers already polluted back to their natural state of purity.

Every angler and club in the country was encouraged to join. In this way the cost of prosecuting offending polluters could be spread out across the whole angling community. Most of the A.C.A. work was done by angling volunteers, but legal costs had to be paid for as well as some central administration.

Thanks to John Eastwood, who supported a network of thousands of voluntary workers, hundreds of court cases have been won and polluters prevented from repeating their mistakes. Now, over the last seventy years or so many rivers and lakes have been returned to their natural state of purity. Even once badly polluted rivers like the Aire, Don and Calder have been brought back to life after many years of being quite literally, dead rivers.

A nostalgic milestone in the progress of the Anglers Cooperative Association, a badge made to commemorate fifty years fighting water pollution. John Eastwood was the driving force who masterminded the founding of the ACA and is almost certainly the most important single reformer in the history of Angling.

Just over a decade ago the good work of the A.C.A. has been continued by the new Angling Trust which has successfully taken over the responsibility of looking after the health of our rivers and lakes and done great work bringing polluters to task. The Angling Trust has also focused a lot on improving the rivers to facilitate healthy salmon runs. As a result, we now have increasing numbers of Salmon returning to spawn naturally in the headwaters of our primary rivers.

It is particularly important that we all support the Angling Trust and its Fish Legal department to fight water pollution. By doing this we place ourselves at the very forefront of the conservation vanguard. Fighting water pollution as we do is the ultimate justification for our sport. This is important in a society which values clean rivers and lakes. The problem we face though is that we are not recognised for all the good work we do. Few other so-called conservationists can boast a seventy-four-year record of fighting for clean rivers. Anglers are the original true conservationists with a proven strong track record. Furthermore, it has taken a very long time and a lot of hard work to arrive at the marvellous results we anglers enjoy today.

The comparatively clean rivers we enjoy today did not just happen by accident, anglers have had to fight and donate millions of pounds out of their own pockets to pay for this privilege. That is why we need to continue to protect our right to fish clean waters by supporting the Angling Trust which is specialised and funded specifically to guard anglers' interests.

Any let up on defending our rivers will result in a fast return to polluted waters as farmers and industrial interests would return to polluting if they thought they could get away with it. Thanks to current strict enforcement rules polluting can be an expensive mistake which is why our rivers are now generally so good.

The name of John Eastwood today is an unknown figure to most modern anglers. Yet, in the fullness of time he is probably the most important Angler that ever lived. After all he found a way to unite the angling world which has always been something of a sleeping giant. He organised the Anglers Cooperative Association into a very efficient pollution fighting machine. The key word in his organisation, and the key to its great success was the word Cooperative. He forged a force where millions of anglers cooperated in the worthy fight against pollution, and he succeeded year after year in the protracted struggle which continues. As recently as 2021 one of the largest fines ever was delivered to Southern Water for continued pollution of rivers and the sea. The record sum amounted to £ 90,000,000! This just shows that the fight to protect our rivers is as important now as ever. Private companies are still prone cut corners to save money, but with a fine of this size must surely act as a serious deterrent!

Bill Winship

Barrie Rickards – 1938-2009

Here we discuss the long journey from pike killing to pike conservation on the Northern Rivers.

In Victorian and Edwardian England most communities still lived very close to the land and were used to eating locally caught game from the countryside. As we have seen from our Victorian review of Walbran it was customary at that time to bag both trout and coarse fish for the table. Hunger was still common amongst ordinary country folk and people were less fussy about what they ate. Hunger was a constant companion for many, any nourishing food like fish or game was a godsend. Remember, most Victorians had no old age pensions to look forward to, no unemployment benefits and the mortality rate was just forty-five. In the average village about half the population were continually hungry. Even the lucky ones like Tom Sturdy, with a regular salary and good house only just got by. Tom Sturdy collected firewood on his daily rounds and stored it in his back garden ready for winter. He never allowed a fire in the house until the first of November to conserve precious stocks. Even he, one of the lucky ones, could not afford to buy fuel. During the social conditions of Victorian England fishing for the table was not simply good sport but had a practical communal survival purpose of providing food for the table.

    Somewhere back in the mid twentieth century attitudes towards killing and eating coarse fish gradually began to change and in the case of pike the changes came roughly after the second world war, when food rationing was stopped in the 1950s. Food shortages were worse just after the war than they had been during the war, so any form of protein was much valued well into the 1960s. Having been a river angler for almost sixty years I have witnessed these changes gradually over my lifetime. We have already seen that in traditional trout streams pike were caught and killed for the table. The same anti pike policies were practiced in the lower river sections where match fishing was popular. Some of my first river pike fishing experiences occurred on the river Swale near Sand Hutton. I will never forget catching pike one after the other on Devon Minnow and Mepps spinners. Although these early captures were only small pike, mostly between one and four pounds in weight. The sheer number of catches was encouraging, especially as a twelve-year-old beginner using light tackle. The fishing rights on the far bank were owned by one of the big match fishing clubs. On several occasions I was observed by club members and when they saw me returning pike they were infuriated. I received several verbal death threats shouted over in unrepeatable Anglo-Saxon language, after all, like the trout anglers thirty miles upstream, they believed the only good pike was a dead pike because of all the cherished trout and roach they were eating.

Anti-pike feelings were the status quo on the northern rivers until the 1980s. This meant that on most rivers in the north, pike did not get the chance to live for long enough to grow big. Amazingly though they still seemed to proliferate in great numbers. This was because even three-pound pike can spawn, and all the jack eating big pike were missing, so this allowed the numbers of jack pike to just multiply. This for me at the age of twelve provided great sport when fishing rivers like the Swale or Ure which were just alive with jack pike. On good days I could bag six or more each day, a great start to my pike fishing career. The basic problem was that both match and game fishing clubs were still convinced the pike needed culling to keep predation levels down. On the lower river sections match anglers were incredibly good at catching pike and it was common to enter a new swim to find dead pike in different stages of decay slowly rotting in the undergrowth. The smell was unbearable and on a hot day blow flies were everywhere making it unpleasant to fish. Back in Edwardian England or through the inter war years this waste did not occur because any pike caught would be valued as food hence, nothing was wasted. In the 1960s though such killing could not be so easily justified, almost everyone in Britain was well fed by then and affordable processed food became popular and widespread, few were motivated to cook coarse fish anymore. Killing pike to protect other species was an argument which was beginning to wear thin too, but it continued because it had always been done that way in the past. As a result, the big pike fishing potential on the Northern rivers was generally poor and the capture of a twenty-pound fish was rare indeed. For me, a river twenty was still a full decade away. It took this amount of time for the pike to grow to full size.

In the mid-1960s I looked on with envy at the numerous giant pike featured in the Angling Times weekly paper, many of them caught by pike champion Dennis Pye who out classed everyone with his big catches during that period. If proof were needed to verify this point just read page 188 of the 1966 Allcocks Anglers Guide where Dennis Pye was hailed as the number one Pike Angler of his time, there was no denying the fact. With the benefit of hindsight, I now realise the Norfolk Pike scene was about forty years ahead of us here in the north as they were already practicing catch and release. Part of the reason Norfolk was better for pike fishing was that a lot, though not all pike, were released after capture and hence some pike had the time and opportunity to grow big. Thankfully, Dennis Pyes big pike catches were fully reported by the Angling Times and were read by fishermen all over the full length and breadth of England. There were a few jealous men of the time who tried to de bunk Dennis, people who should have known better. They just could not stomach the fact that a seemingly ordinary uneducated man like Dennis was so brilliant at catching big pike. He was anything but ordinary though, he had fought for us on the battlefields of Europe, and it is thanks to men like Dennis who put their lives on the line that we can enjoy our freedom today. Yes, Dennis was indeed woefully wronged in an act which probably marks one of the lowest points in pike fishing history. Derrick Amies wrote a full chapter on Dennis Pye in his book 'Pike Fishing on the Norfolk Broads' anyone who reads this book will be left in no doubt that Dennis Pye was one of the most highly skilled pike fishermen ever. Furthermore, his catch reports in the Angling Times, all fully illustrated with authentic big pike photos, created a huge appetite to catch pike with anglers all over the UK. Anglers who often, like me, openly tried to emulate his successes. As a result of this more and more anglers became interested in the sport and dedicated enthusiasts began to feel something had to be done to improve the lot of their favourite fish. Generally, most angling publications were supportive. Publications like the Angling Times, Anglers Mail, Coarse Fisherman, and the Daily Mirror all supported the drive to conserve our valuable pike stocks. In this way a groundswell of 'pro pike' support began to develop thanks to all the positive national publicity.

All this new energy was harnessed successfully in 1977 by Dr Barrie Rickards and friends who set up the Pike Anglers Club of Great Britain. This new club was established in a similar way to the Anglers Cooperative Association by John Eastwood in 1948. Like the A.C.A. a network of regionally based officers was set up to cover the whole of Britain. Regional meetings were held where local members could deal with their own parochial issues. Also, like the A.C.A. a national newsletter was published regularly to highlight all the good work going on, in this way we could all learn 'Best Practice' from each other. As a regional organiser for the Pike Anglers Club for the past thirty-eight years I still look forwards to my quarterly copy of Pikelines which still acts as guide to good practice and over the years has developed from a thin flimsy newsletter to a glossy world class magazine second to none.

When the P.A.C. was first set up in 1977 the challenge was daunting. The task ahead involved convincing the whole angling world that pike deserved a place in modern fisheries and should not be killed indiscriminately. Try selling that concept to those match anglers who threatened to kill me if I returned any more pike! Or in fact to my friend Norris or his father who spent a lifetime in the pursuit of pike removal from his trout fishery! To be honest, at the start I thought our chances of success were about nil. Yes, we may make a bit of progress locally here or there, but I could not have imagined the scale of success achieved over the past forty-five years.

Thankfully, Barrie Richards was not only physically and mentally brave (he had to be to face the approaching challenge) but he was also scientifically trained and could get to the raw facts of any issue by weighing up and interpreting scientific evidence. This unusual combination of qualities gave him the powerful wattage needed to tackle the task ahead. Remember at this time in the late 1970s about 90% of the angling world honestly believed 'The only good pike was a dead pike'. The central issue revolved around the fact that most angling decision makers genuinely believed pike needed to be eradicated. By using the latest scientific evidence Barrie formulated a case to strongly argue the need for pike conservation. Barrie was also incredibly good at public speaking; his steady reasoned northern accent came across as very reassuring. Barrie addressed many of the match-based clubs in Birmingham and the north and lobbied for pike protection measures. Using his scientific training, Barrie highlighted pike studies on lake Windermere by Dr Winifred Frost. In these studies, it was shown that killing big pike caused an explosion of the number of smaller pike whose numbers were not being checked by the best pike cullers of all, the big pike. In a similar way he drew reference to the work on pike carried out by Professor Crossman. In his studies he also found evidence to suggest that the removal of big pike was a gross ecological error. In fact, the removal of big pike caused the total tonnage of predators to increase through an explosion in the numbers of trout eating and fertile jack pike. The bottom line was the fact that by culling pike it increased predation levels and at the same time also increased the actual weight of pike in any given water. The solution was quite simple and inexpensive to activate. Just leave the pike alone to restore their natural ecological balance.

Early in the development of the P.A.C. this scientific knowledge was copied and distributed to all regional organisers, so we all had the tools to spread the word to all the clubs in our own geographical areas. In my Ripon region I contacted my local trout clubs as well as the local match clubs. I can well remember in 1980 addressing an audience of about 500 trout anglers in Harrogate, after my speech the audience was dumbstruck, you could have heard a pin drop, they simply had no notion of any need for pike conservation. Most of these clubs allowed us to attend their meetings to present our case which we did. Not much happened at first in my own area, I never expected it would as Ripon, being close to Tanfield had long established methods of dealing with its pike! On one local trout water the pike had been culled in the traditional way. The manager, Jeff asked me to help remove some pike. One Sunday morning I arrived with a bag full of sardine baits and caught pike one after the other ending up with seventeen fish and counting. It was a classic case of a trout water overrun by small pike. In previous years they had used netting to catch the pike, but weedy conditions made it difficult, they did catch some big ones up to 28lb which were removed. A year or two later Jeff moved to a new house in Southern Ireland and with the consent of Mr Ramsden the fishery owner I was granted permission to look after the trout fishery. From that point onwards we practiced catch and release for both trout and pike. Now twenty-one years later we hardly see any pike at all. We fish for pike only between October 16th and February the 28th. It is difficult pike fishing, but we normally catch one or two twenty pounders each year. We retain a very small number of big pike which rule the roost and ensure there are no jack pike at all. The trout fishing remains consistently of the finest order. We had the great privilege to invite our late great P.A.C. Founder, Barrie to the fishery for a day's pike fishing and he was suitably impressed. Unfortunately, though we both blanked but at least this was proof that the P.A.C. 'Catch and release' medicine was truly working well. Barrie and I had a great laugh at the rich irony that we were glad to blank as it proved his theory to be correct. Barrie always like to be proved right and had a wicked sense of humour.

Here we had a perfect case study to show other local clubs who were still killing pike. Again, we visited various local clubs and presented not only the science as highlighted by Barrie Rickards, but also our own local home-grown case study. This latter local case study made the difference, and we persuaded several clubs to change their rules to return all pike over 5lb. This, halfway house measure was not ideal, but at least it was a step in the right direction. In our effort to get new changes we secured a lot of unexpected support from the trout anglers themselves on our own water. Not only did they notice a steep decline in pike 'bite offs' (showing there were less pike) but equally good they also noticed that their club subscriptions fell from £400.00 per year, to just £125.00 and we supplied three free boats too! This change in subscription charges was made possible because winter pike fishermen were paying for the privilege to catch pike hence making it a lot cheaper for the trout men. The free boats were donated by both pike and trout anglers whose wives were fed up with their fibre glass boats taking up room from their suburban gardens! Another powerful effect came from the fact that many of our trout anglers were also members of various river trout fisheries in the region. In this way the good news story of our 'Put pike back campaign' diffused into all the surrounding areas without us having to lift a finger. I think this is a case of 'Success breeds success'. A few years later we managed to get all pike and coarse fish to be returned on our local river which is a mixed fishery. This was written into the rule book of this local river fishery. Hallelujah! Job done, or so we thought.

Two full years after the new pike protection rule was written up, we discovered one angler, a retired policeman, with two dead pike next to him as he was fishing the river Ure. Both dead pike were upper doubles, and we could not believe what we had just witnessed. "You are supposed to return all pike its written in the rule book" I said. This character claimed he did not realise and upon reading his rule book openly apologised. We did not take the matter further and just trusted he would obey the simple rules. As it was, I am incredibly pleased we were patient because the poor man died just a year later. Since then, the pike now live long enough to grow big and now there are pike well over twenty pounds taken each year. The lesson here was that even on a river section seven miles long, it only takes one pike killer to ruin the whole fishery, not just for pike fishermen but for trout and match fishermen too. It takes about ten years for a pike to reach a weight of 20lb on our local river Ure but less than ten minutes to kill one.

The struggles just highlighted above provide a flavour of the kind of changes we were implementing on the northern rivers in my local region. However, thanks to the nationally based pike club similar struggles were also going on in hundreds of waters all over the UK. This spanned a period running from the nineteen eighties right up to the present day, covering over forty years and it was all set-in motion primarily by Barrie who made up the blueprint for the PAC. From time-to-time new PAC committees consider ways of improving the club involving changes in the way it is run. The PAC Committee is completely changed every three years so when a new set of managers take over there is a natural urge to change things so they can make their mark. Tinkering with a system which runs well is a dangerous game though. My advice to these well-meaning innovators is 'If it isn't broken then don't try to fix it'. Barrie had it right first time!

It is now just ten years since Barrie died, I can clearly remember the first issue of Pikelines after his death, the editor Steve Ormrod gave Barrie a true hero's send-off second to none. It naturally focused on Barrie's achievements, not just in the angling world but also his life as a lecturer at Cambridge University where he achieved the title of professor. It was interesting to see Barrie dressed in his cap and gown rather than his usual fishing clothes!

Barrie brought an air of respectability to the world of pike fishing. In his book 'The Ten Greatest Pike Anglers' co-written with Malcolm Bannister, Barrie and Malcolm have catalogued our shared cultural heritage of Pike fishing and traced the very foundations of our sport. This included early writers from the Victorian period like Cholmondeley Pennell, Jardine, and Senior. In addition to all this he wrote numerous other books on fishing and managed to fit in catching over two hundred and forty-three pike of over twenty pounds too! I do not think anyone has ever or could ever make a bigger contribution to the sport of pike fishing and its cultural history than Barrie. Rest in peace my dear friend, your legacy lives on in your unrivalled contribution to the sport of pike fishing.

Bill shares breakfast with the great master himself. What a great honour it was to not only fish with Barrie but also to share a fried breakfast too! Barrie's cooked breakfasts are now world famous. Bacon was his favourite morning feast. I have since taken up Barrie's taste for quality food, but my guilty pleasure is taken on an early morning drive through the Golden Arches!

THE MAIN SIXTEEN NORTHERN PIKE RIVERS

MAIN PIKE RIVERS IN NORTHERN ENGLAND

The main Northern Rivers of England. All these rivers contain pike which have lived in balance with trout, salmon and other fish species for thousands of years. Big river pike over 20lb are shy, wild and very elusive, but they can actually be caught! Pike are generally more numerous in the southern half of the map, but good salmon fish counter readings in the Tees, Wear, Tyne and Tweed give the northern rivers good odds for producing a new giant pike or salmon of over fifty pounds, just as happened in the 1920s before the ecological collapse of salmon runs.

For the purposes of this book the northern rivers of England are defined as the rivers which flow within the latitudes bound by the Yorkshire Humber in the south up to the river Tweed in the north which forms the northern border of England with Scotland. These are a unique set of spate of rivers and have their origins high up in the Pennines and North Yorkshire Moors and flow from upland fells, many of which are over two thousand feet above sea level.

These northern rivers drain a huge area of the High Pennines so during periods of heavy rain large volumes of water cascade downstream into these river courses. For this reason, river levels can fluctuate drastically within just a few hours. These are true spate rivers and create ideal conditions for salmon, eels, flounder, lamprey and coarse fish to move up and down the river course. Ideal also for the pike too who look out in wait for these seasonal visitors to bolster the background ecology with protein direct from as far as the Greenland shelf in the North Atlantic Ocean, and the Sargasso Sea beyond Bermuda.

The map shows the main rivers, mostly flowing from west to east towards the mighty Humber and out into the North Sea. On this map we have identified just sixteen rivers known to hold big pike. Only the lower half of each river holds pike as the upper reaches are mostly too fast and only suitable for trout and grayling. The pike only take up residence generally below the five-hundred-foot contours where the rivers run in a series of rapids, fast glides and intermittent pools. These are truly wonderful places to fish and spend time in. The prime rivers shown on the map constitute well over three hundred miles of viable pike fishing bank space or six hundred miles if you count both banks. To put this in perspective, this is more than enough space to run a line from Horsey Mere in Norfolk to Loch Ness in Scotland! In terms of pike fishing potential, the Northern Rivers have been overlooked for far too long and another reason this book is long overdue. In addition, these main rivers shown on the map have many very interesting tributaries. For example, the River Swale has several small rivers and becks which are productive mixed fisheries and regularly produce big pike over the twenty pounds mark. Also, the River Derwent whose chalk stream tributaries rise on the North Yorkshire Moors also support rich mixed fisheries which again in turn provide good feeding grounds for both game and coarse fish alike.

Many of the tributaries of the River Derwent are less than ten feet wide and yet have still produced big pike which makes them challenging and very interesting places to fish. All the rivers shown on the map have a network of tributaries with countless miles of good fishing much of which is never or seldom fished. I can well remember prospecting one part of the River Ure and asking local farmers about the possibilities of fishing. A dear old Farmer called Mr Isles, now sadly deceased, allowed me to fish for free on his riverside meadows. He told me that because of the distance from the road no one ever fishes for pike and very rarely for trout or grayling. However, during most winters after the floods have subsided, he said he often found big pike stranded in the fields, some of them almost four feet long. Often they were only found after the crows and rooks have done their scavenging, but the pike sculls remain, sometimes connected to their tails via a long gruesome skeleton revealing their full length and size.

The remains of a pike stranded after the floods have subsided. This is good evidence showing the potential of the adjacent river. The carrion crows and rooks make fast work of de fleshing any stranded fish.

After these vivid descriptions I became extremely interested and was soon a regular visitor, always taking Mr Metcalf and his wife a large box of Chocolates for Christmas! In time I saw a few of the stranded giants, some must have been over twenty-five pounds and even pushing thirty pounds, in their prime. My own personal best from this fishery has so far been a twenty-six-pound beauty caught just before Christmas, a fish which was returned immediately as an investment in our future pike fishing. This is just one example of how 'Pike Heaven' can be discovered on the northern rivers. We continued to fish this section for over fifty years, gradually discovering that the fish in this small river section were directly influenced by a system running the full seventy-three miles of the river course and even beyond into the North Atlantic Ocean. This knowledge told us that the river's potential was far greater than we had originally realised, and with good river husbandry the fishing potential could be second to none. As it has proved repeatedly whenever conditions allowed its full potential to be reached.

From the sixteen rivers highlighted we have allowed ourselves the luxury of describing each one separately. Most of the rivers discussed are truly wonderful places to fish for pike though there are a couple which are best avoided, they are only included because they do contain big pike and one day may become viable pike waters. The individual characteristics of each one is dealt with in alphabetic order and we briefly discuss the potential of each river, what fish they contain and what makes them so special. The marvellous thing about these rivers is that each one has its own unique strengths, weaknesses and above all charm. All of them just waiting to be discovered and to reveal their secrets to us.

Huge areas of these rivers can be fished by joining the local fishing clubs for a small annual fee which is generally about the price of a single meal out, with drinks. A very modest amount considering you can fish several times and be privileged to fish dozens of miles of pristine riverbank. These clubs provide exclusive access for anglers, so really do deserve support for providing these special privileges. Do not forget though, on river stretches not affiliated to clubs, private owners often allow access if approached in a courteous and friendly manner. When such access is granted in this old-fashioned way it is particularly rewarding because these areas are mostly completely unfished for pike at all.

THE RIVER AIRE – THE MIRACLE RIVER

Firstly, and in alphabetic order we start with the River Aire. This is a very large and important Yorkshire River which has its source near Malham at a height of 1,329 feet above sea level. From here as a small stream, it flows east through the beautiful valley pastures of Airedale past Gargrave and Skipton and past Bingley and Leeds to meet up with the river Ouse near Howden, ninety miles to the east. As recent as 1995 this river was so polluted that fishing was not advised below the Leeds area. In fact, for almost one hundred years it was seriously polluted as it ran right through the centre of the industrial West Riding of Yorkshire including towns like Keighley, Bingley and Leeds. Many industrial mills used the river as a dumping ground for waste materials and thus all life in the whole lower section of the river died. The good news is that over the past thirty years the river has once again returned towards its original pristine state for the first time since 1850. This is partly owing to industrial decline in the West Riding, but also due to tight water quality standards demanded by the Anglers Cooperative Association, (Heavily funded by the big city Angling Clubs in the West Riding.) and more recently Fish Legal who have kept a close eye on would be polluters. As a result of all this, plus enormous efforts from the West Riding Angling Clubs re stocking activities, the river is now a very good quality mixed fishery. A section of the river Aire in the Leeds area has been canalised and offers valuable fishing along its banks. Indeed, great shoals of bream roach and perch now haunt the deeper sections towards Ferrybridge. In fact, from Skipton downstream all the way through to Howden now offers not just good fishing but mixed fishing of a very high standard. This is because the river Aire has something very special in its favour. In the upper reaches of the river the water flows through carboniferous limestone geology. This special limestone is formed from the shells of millions of sea creatures which make up the geology of the area. The nutrients of this bedrock are dissolved into the river Aire providing the whole river with very fertile conditions for growth, not just the fish, but the whole biosphere making both plants and animals grow bigger and faster. What then does all this mean to the pike angler? For well over forty years when travelling south to work I have passed over the old A1 Road bridge at Knottingley and looked over at the scenic river Aire and considered what a great pike river it would be if only it was not polluted.

I often thought what a great pike sanctuary the lock cutting on the right-hand side of the river would make in times of flood.

The modern face of the River Aire. Wide, deep but with shallow weedy shelves. Teeming with fish fry, clean water and now at last big pike too! Fed by feeder streams running over limestone geology the river Aire has it all. Generations of Anglers in the West Yorkshire Clubs have worked tirelessly to achieve this revival from what not long ago was a dead river.

In my mind the whole scene just screamed 'Pike'. For a big part of those years, I knew of course the river was polluted, but not now! For me this is nothing short of a miracle and a dream come true. Never in my wildest dreams did I think this great river would come back from the dead in my lifetime, well it has! I know already that quite a few very big pike have been taken in recent years, pike well over the twenty-pound mark. As a result of this the river Aire is now a regular destination water for us and we have already caught several big pike. From our very first visit we were very impressed at how lush the river weeds looked and by the teeming fry fish which could be seen as soon as we arrived. The river Aire is obviously still in recovery but in time, and if the pollution does not reoccur the river Aire is set to become one of the top three waters in the north, it has the size, it has the water quality, and it has a good stock of fish which are becoming bigger and more numerous as time goes on. As a result of all this I would not be surprized if it became the Number one top river destination in the north within the next ten years or so. This really is amazing when you consider it was mostly a dead river just a few years ago.

THE RIVER CALDER – A RIVER SAVED BY THE ANGLING COMMUNITY.

To the south of Airedale lies the beautiful Calder Valley and the sparkling River Calder. The River Calder rises in Lancashire on Heald Moor which is 540 feet above sea level. It is only half the length of the River Aire which it joins at Castleford after a journey of forty-five miles from its source. Like its sister river to the north the Calder has suffered badly from pollution as it runs right through the old 'Heavy Woollen District' of Yorkshire around Huddersfield, Mirfield and Wakefield. Of course, like most of our northern spate rivers the Calder was once a prolific salmon river but until recent times the last salmon was caught in Wakefield in the year 1850. Thankfully, again owing to over sixty-two years of work done by the A.C.A. and our new 'Fish Legal Group', salmon are now gradually returning as the old pollution problem is thankfully becoming a thing of the past.

The road to recovery has been a long and hard-won battle though. Back in the nineteen sixties the river was just beginning to become fishable again. Local angling clubs and especially 'Bradford Number One Angling Club' spent thousands of pounds in re stocking, but they were still plagued by intermittent fish kills. On some days, the water would be blue, on others orange and pike anglers needed to use extra-long bite indicators on top of their floats to cope with the multi coloured foam. Thankfully, a big improvement came about in the sixties when an electricity generator was built at Elland. The cooling towers provided warm clean waters as a by-product of the process and this helped water plants and insects to thrive and mitigate the organic pollutions in the river. In turn the fish grew faster and were more robust. The roach gudgeon and pike thrived which was great for the match fishing circuit of the time. Dave Thomas the famous match angler of the 1970s won the Calder Championship in 1974 with a bag of over eight pounds of roach. Then the very year after in 1975 a huge pollution wiped out most of the river and tons of prime roach had to be removed from the river at Brighouse.

Thankfully, through all these difficult times local anglers have been relentless in fighting for a clean river Calder and now the eco system seems to be much more stable. Good trout and grayling fishing can be enjoyed in the upper regions whilst in the lower deeper stretches around Huddersfield, Mirfield and Wakefield there are now good stocks of roach, dace, chub, minnows, gudgeon, tench and of course pike. Fishing for pike on the River Calder in these areas has a unique charm of its own. A lot of the river is canalised, and big pike move up and down the river with ease. One feature I particularly enjoy are the numerous lock cuttings which give huge character to the place and provide great shelter for all fish species during those frequent winter floods.

As is obvious from this section on the Northern rivers the river Calder has a dark past and this obviously gives this river a bad reputation. As such it does not attract too much attention from modern day pike anglers. Remember though, pike thrive on neglect, so the Calder's murky past is as we speak effectively working in its favour now! Do not forget too, it only takes about ten years for a young Jack pike to go from nought to twenty pounds. In a very well stocked river like the Calder possibly a lot less. Local anglers are fully aware of the exciting potential and big pike to over twenty pounds are regularly caught. The Calder pike I have seen are very well conditioned, and I know for a fact that there will soon be a few pleasant surprises coming from this now promising pike river. I strongly advise all fishermen to not only join the big clubs like Bradford number one and Leeds clubs, but also crucially, do join the Angling Trust which is an organisation which specialises in fighting river pollution. They employ some of the finest specialist Lawyers in the land to prosecute water polluters, which is particularly important. The Angling Trust needs all the funds they can raise to provide a good service for us. To the best of my knowledge there are few other specialised services which provide anglers with this kind of protection.

RIVER DERWENT

The River Derwent rises on Fylingdales Moor not far from the sea near Scarborough. It springs from the ground at about 800 feet above sea level and flows south for over ninety miles where it meets the River Ouse at Barmby on the Marsh. On its way south it is joined by a network of smaller rivers which mostly drain the south facing fringes of the North York Moors. This is another Yorkshire River whose tributaries flow over both chalk and limestone geology which sweetens the water making it particularly beneficial to both plant and animal life. Just like the River Aire, the fish consequently do very well and have impressive growth rates. In the upper reaches of the River Derwent and its tributaries trout and good-sized grayling abound. Salmon also run up the River Derwent to spawn in the various headwaters to the north of the catchment area. Lower down the main river has a very rich range of fish species too including minnows, dace, chub, barbel, grayling, perch, pike, roach and tench. Up until about 1920 burbot were also present in the lower reaches but these seem to have died out now.

At the young age of fourteen our family moved from the Bedale area to live at Bubwith on the banks of the Yorkshire Derwent. During the first year we lived there I grew a good twelve inches. I often wonder if it was as a direct result of living in a high PH area! (Only joking). I was over six feet tall at the age of fourteen. This meant I was over eighteen inches taller than my classroom friends at School. "What's the weather like up there"? was the ever-recurring joke! At least the big fish in the River Derwent was good compensation for all the good natured but irritating ribbing. We lived just on the outskirts of Bubwith which was within casting distance of the River Derwent, and I was glad to be living so close to some incredibly good fishing. This was during the late 1960s and at that time the River Derwent was fully tidal with a daily tidal pitch of about seven feet. This made the banks very slippery and treacherous to fish from. This did not prevent my new local friends and I from fishing regularly and catching lots of fish though. Our main catch was eels and flounders, lots and lots of them which were fresh from the Humber estuary. We also fished for pike, mainly with spinners which suited the restless impatience of our adolescence. As a result of this we only caught lots of small pike during that time. If I could just turn the clock back, I would now cut one of those lovely fresh eels into sections for dead bait and ledger it in the slack waters below the dense bankside willow bushes. I knew there were big twenty-pound pike there for the taking at that time. The trouble was I was just too impatient to sit it out for long enough to get the results. I did catch a nineteen-pound pike though from Castle Howard. My Uncle Ron took a lovely photo of me holding that pike. I kept it safe in my hymn book which lived permanently in my school blazer pocket. I took great delight in showing it to my school friends. Of course, those cheeky fourteen-year-old girls made a great Joke out of it. At the most unexpected times one of them would shout out loud, "Can I have a look at your big Pike Bill?" that was a request I became accustomed to, it was a great laugh, especially when the teachers were near bye, they wondered what on earth all the commotion was about!

A few years later in the 1970s a tidal barrage was built at the very point where the River Derwent meets the River Ouse. This barrage blocked out the tidal surges from racing up the river Derwent so overnight the whole character of the lower Derwent was changed. Fresh water was needed for Hull, so it was decided to extract it from a treatment works at Loftsome Bridge on the lower Derwent. These works were only about two miles from where the Derwent joined the tidal River Ouse.

A young Bill at the age of fourteen. This is the photo of the 19lb pike which was kept safe in the hymnbook inside my school blazer pocket. The teachers at school never understood how important this pike was but my fishing pals did. This was in 1968 a period I spent a lot of time fishing on the tidal river Derwent at Bubwith. Photo taken and developed by my late dear Uncle Ron from Leeds.

From here the water was purified and pumped into the water grid bound for Hull.

Bill holds a low twenty pounder taken from the river Derwent just a few miles from his childhood home in Bubwith.

Thankfully, the barrage gates at Barmby are left open during the low tide, so once a day the eels, flounders and salmon do get a chance to enter the lower Derwent. Also, another huge improvement from building the tidal barrage was that the riverbanks had time to dry out making it much safer to fish. Living and fishing regularly on the banks of the Derwent has left me with a strong connection to the river. This kind of familiarity gives you a feel for the place and the fish which live in the river. Since those happy days, together with my friends I have fished various parts of the river from one of its many small tributaries the River Rye at Nunnington Hall near Helmsley, down to Kirkham Priory, Stamford Bridge, Elvington and Wheldrake too. All these wonderful places contain big pike. In the middle reaches near Sutton on Derwent the river, though narrow compared with the lower River course, is surprisingly deep, in some stretches it is up to twenty feet deep. Great places to try in the very coldest weather. Big pike can also be taken in very shallow water too. We have taken twenty pounders in water no deeper than three feet deep in some parts. What I can say with certainty is that wherever you fish on the Derwent you will never be too far from the pike, big pike too. The Derwent has the double benefit of high P.H. water as a result of its chalk stream groundwaters combined to its regular influx of sea fish from the Ouse and Humber Estuaries.

Before the tidal barrage was built the lower ten miles or so of the river was constantly coloured due to the ebb and flow of the tidal driven waters. Now though the water tends to be much clearer, except of course during high rainfall when coloured waters again fill the whole river length. Having fished in all conditions we have found that falling flood levels combined to the gradual clarification of the water is on balance the best conditions possible. Yet we have still done well on a rising river, especially in Summer after a prolonged dry spell when new fresh waters infuse the river with higher oxygen levels. One thing to take great care of on the River Derwent is stealth. Most of the river is very narrow, in many parts no more than twenty to forty feet wide. This means you tend to fish close to your quarry. Any banging about on the bankside will certainly be detected by any fish in the area, and of course at such close range they can see you too. One can of course fish at greater range downstream, but there is no need to if you keep still and out of sight. Quite often and especially in Summer the riverbanks are lush with thick vegetation, so this provides ideal cover, but in open pasture extra care needs to be taken.

Thanks to Natural England the river Derwent has been given a Triple-SI status which is good as it helps to provide protection of the river from damaging external activities. This is all for the best and certainly helps to protect our Angling interests. Of course, as highlighted in the introduction of this book we anglers have been guardians of the waterside and working towards what Natural England call 'Biodiversity Nett Gain' for over one hundred and fifty years, as illustrated in our chapters on Francis Walbran, John Eastwood, founder of the A.C.A. and Professor Barrie Rickards, founder of the P.A.C. With all this support the future of our northern rivers looks secure indeed.

RIVER EDEN AND LEVEN – WHY SO FEW PIKE?

The Rivers Eden and Leven are not in our opinion viable pike rivers. Yes, they both turn up the occasional big pike, but their presence is so intermittent that we would not recommend fishing for pike on these two rivers. We were going to omit them from the map of pike rivers altogether but decided not to as their inclusion illustrates an interesting imbalance between the northeast of the country to the northwest. If any local anglers to these rivers know better and believe good pike fishing is available on the Eden and Leven, please do not hesitate to contact us (preferably with convincing evidence) as we would love to be proved wrong! If we are, we would be happy to update this book with your help in future publications.

After constructing the map of pike rivers in Northern England, I was immediately struck by the vast imbalance between good pike rivers in the northeast compared to the very poor showing in the northwest of England. One reason is of course that the east flowing rivers take up about 75% of the map as they reach further west. Even so, the rivers in the northwest, fewer and smaller as they are, do not seem to match up in proportion to the northeast rivers. If the pike holding lakes in the lake district like Windermere, Esthwaite and Bassenthwaite were counted as rivers that would help to some extent, but they are large lakes so cannot be included. Whenever I drive over the River Eden on the motorway heading north, I often think what a great looking pike river this is, and yet all my contacts in the area tell me it is not worth a light as far as pike fishing is concerned. Could we blame game anglers for killing all the pike in a systematic way? You could argue this, but we have even more game anglers in the northeast too and they have not caused a significant effect here so game anglers cannot be blamed.

I do have one pet theory as to why pike are more established in the east. Go back about twelve to fifteen hundred years and the river people from Scandinavia colonised eastern England mostly via the Humber estuary giving access to the whole river network shown on our pike map. At first of course they came in small numbers as hit and run raiders and ruthless pirates. Later though, they slowly settled in their thousands as traders and then farmers and fishermen. These were river people who knew how to net freshwater fish and pike were an important part of their diets. This has been proved by archaeological evidence unearthed at the Coppergate site in York. As highly mobile boatmen and river people it would be quite easy for them to seed the River Ouse tributaries with small pike which would multiply quickly within about ten to fifteen years creating a bountiful harvest of easy to net pike, just as commercial nets men do now on the Irish Loughs. Much to our annoyance! Of course, the western rivers of the north also attracted northern invaders, but more of the hit and run pirates than the farmers who settled in the east. This theory may also explain why so many of we northern Englishmen have such a love of pike fishing; we were born with it. It is in our very DNA! How else could you explain why we are so happy to sit out in all weathers to catch pike. No, we are not mad, we were just born that way. The River Leven is another river in the west which is not considered viable for pike fishing. The River Leven flows out of Lake Windermere in Cumbria for eight miles where it meets the sea in Morecambe Bay. Most of the river is tightly controlled by game angling interests who target the dwindling numbers of salmon and sea trout. It does contain a small head of pike and occasionally big ones too, but according to local fishermen, not sufficient to make it worthwhile.

THE RIVER HULL IN EAST YORKSHIRE

The River Hull catchment is fundamentally different in its makeup from most of the other northern rivers featured in this study because it is not a spate river. Instead, it draws its waters from a network of streams which drain the relatively low-lying chalk-based Yorkshire Wolds which lie like a giant sponge to the north and west of Driffield. Thanks to this the river Hull is probably the richest water for plant and invertebrate growth out of all the northern rivers. Many of the waterweeds and insects are the same as those found in the rich chalk streams in the south of England like the River Test and Itchen. Thanks to all this the upper stretches of the water course have been designated as sites of special scientific interest and hence protected from unauthorised developments. The whole river length is just over thirty miles starting about ten miles north and west of Driffield and ending up in Hull where it meets the tidal Humber estuary. At this point the river is protected from tidal shunting by a massive tidal barrage at the mouth of the river Hull. This barrage is particularly important as the land in the lower part of the River Hull is very low lying and vulnerable to flooding. With global warming and the resultant increases in sea levels some experts believe it is only a matter of time before the Hull hinterland is completely flooded. Just across the sea near Amsterdam the Dutch engineers have been struggling with the same dilemma for over two hundred years and have succeeded in keeping the sea back perfectly well so perhaps there is hope for us too!

When we first fished the River Hull, we were amazed at how rich the water plants were in comparison to my local spate rivers in North Yorkshire. The flat low-lying meadows were also somehow more luxuriant than those at home in North Yorkshire and the slow steady pace of the river was very relaxing after the swift waters of the River Swale and Ure. We found the water to be visibly teeming with small fish fry and full of very well-conditioned pike. Other coarse fish were also much bigger too and the trout and grayling from the upper reaches of the Hull catchment have always been known to be the largest grayling and trout in the north. Even as far back as the Victorian period our angling champion Francis Walbran made a special visit to the Driffield area to impress his famous southern friend William Senior to sample the best fly fishing available in the north. Senior was not disappointed thanks to Walbrans skills as an expert angling host.

A very well-conditioned River Hull Pike caught by guest writer Mr Adrian Brayshaw. A casual check on the condition scale shown in the appendix of this book shows it must measure high on the scale, perhaps as high as 0.8 or even 0.9! In over fifty years fishing the northern rivers the author has never seen a Northern River Pike as fat as this! (Photo courtesy of Adrian Brayshaw).

After a lot of research, we now believe the River Hull has produced the second largest Pike from the Yorkshire rivers at the massive weight of 37lb caught by pike expert angler Adrian Brayshaw who lives close to the river Hull near Beverley. The largest pike from the northern rivers is of course the 56lb pike taken from the River Ure. Full details of the capture of this pike have been fully chronicled in the chapter on the one-time river keeper and trout protector Mr Norris Sturdy. From first impressions the river Hull is far more capable of producing a very large pike, so how, one may ask has the Ure produced a fish so much bigger than the Hull? The only rational explanation is we believe that in the 1920s the river Ure was a dominant spawning ground in Yorkshire for migrating salmon. First-hand accounts and primary witnesses of the time can remember how the River Ure at Tanfield "Turned Black" with the number of spawning salmon heading upstream in both spring and autumn. The implications of this will be discussed in more depth later in the book, but as things stand in modern times and until the massive runs of salmon return to the spate rivers, we believe it is safe to say the River Hull is the number one big pike river in the north for modern day anglers. Furthermore, in modern times I think it is safe to say Mr Brayshaw holds the record for a modern time big pike capture with his 37-pound fish. This is not the only pike in the thirty-pound category Mr Brayshaw has caught either, he has a further three thirty-pound fish to his name from other waters. Again, later in this book Mr Brayshaw has been asked to provide his own account of his experiences fishing the River Hull as a local expert pike angler.

THE RIVER LUNE IN CUMBRIA AND LANCASHIRE

The River Lune rises in the Cumbrian hills at a height of over 2,100 feet in the Ravenstonedale highland fells. This is a true spate river and flows towards Lancaster over fifty-three miles to the south. The upper two thirds of the river provide superb trout and salmon fishing in some of the most spectacular scenery in the north. There are also strong seasonal runs of sea trout and salmon have been caught up to over thirty-nine pounds in weight! Once the river reaches low lying section downstream of the village of Hornby coarse fish start to complement the trout stocks making for some excellent mixed fishing. Further downstream in the Halton area roach and bream inhabit the river and though few, there are pike and like the salmon they have been caught well over twenty pounds in weight. The largest Lune pike we know of was twenty-eight pounds in weight and is probably the river record. Most of the River Lune is too fast and rocky for coarse fish so pike fishing is extremely limited. Yet in the lower course of the river pike with good numbers of roach, bream, trout and sea fish too there is the opportunity for some quality pike fishing, and the river certainly has very good past form. In the 'Red Letter Days' section our guest writer Dave Holden contributes a nostalgic account of how good the river Lune really is.

THE RIVER NIDD

The River Nidd rises just one mile south of the famous Great Whernside at a lofty 1952 feet. At this point the fledgling river is aptly called 'Nidd Head Spring' forming the beginning of the water course which runs for over fifty miles eastwards until it meets the River Ouse in the vale of York. On its course east the river flows into Angram reservoir, then later into upper Nidderdale where it flows into Gouthwaite reservoir which not only holds brown trout but also a natural breeding colony of grayling making it the only reservoir in England with self-sustaining stocks of this species in still water. From Patley Bridge downstream the river is a top-class fly fishery catering exclusively for our game fishing friends until the river flows through the Nidd gorge, a steep sided valley formed by fluvio-glacial activity about twenty thousand years ago.

From Knaresborough downstream the river becomes a mixed fishery full of trout, grayling, chub, dace, barbel, and of course pike. There are plenty of very accessible local clubs who allow fishing for a very reasonable fee. The river is quite narrow even in this lower stretch, but in the case of the river Nidd size is very deceptive. Here double figure barbel have been caught along with chub over five pounds. Several pike over twenty pounds are caught every year too. The river here can be quite fast and runs in a series of deep glides broken up by deep slower pools. The banks are well covered with willow and lots of cover in the form of long grass and bushes. The river itself is also very weedy with long streamer weeds being quite common. For this reason, noticeably big female pike nose their way upstream from the mighty River Ouse to spawn in the spring. The shallow weedy clean water is ideal for spawning so although it is only a narrow river its pike can be surprisingly big!

The actual Nidd mouth is probably the best-known pike fishing place on the whole river. For that reason, we seldom fish there, it is not that we are anti-social, it is just I prefer the virtually unfished narrow upper sections where the big pike live and thrive on neglect. It is also good for plug fishing in summer when pike explode out of the shallow clear water in a very dramatic way. You do not need to worry too much about high summer temperatures either as this fast water, coming from hills over 2000 feet high normally guarantee a cool high oxygenated water source, ideal for summer pike fishing.

THE RIVER OUSE

Working our way downstream to the mouth of the River Nidd brings us neatly to the mighty Yorkshire Ouse. We say mighty because it is of course made up from seven of the rivers covered in this study. I must start off by saying that the one thing we love about the Northern rivers of England is the tremendous contrast in the type of river fishing available. For example, one day you can be trotting a dead bait downstream in only three feet of water in a river like the Nidd which is so narrow that willow bushes on opposite sides of the river meet in the middle! Then the next day you can be fishing the broad acres of the River Ouse where a spinner can be cast a good sixty yards towards the far bank sixty or seventy yards away in water as deep as twenty-five feet in some places. Knowing also that our Yorkshire River pike are known to haunt both venues at differing times of the year. The River Ouse starts officially about two miles downstream from Aldwark Bridge. It is just a continuation of the river Ure on its way south. There is a tiny stream which starts in the village of Ouseburn and where that stream meets the River Ouse there is a big sign which clearly defines the exact point where the River Ure changes its name and becomes the River Ouse. The river then runs south for over forty-five miles to where the River Trent joins to meet the River Humber near Goole. Before the construction of Naburn lock the Ouse was tidal right up to Aldwark bridge. In the year 1741 a large weir was built near the village of Naburn on Ouse below York and this blocked tidal surges further upstream. As a result of this the River Ouse is no longer tidal upstream of Naburn providing more stable and slightly deeper water upstream from the lock.

Downstream of Naburn lock the River Ouse is of course still tidal, but the pike fishing remains good. In fact, the river here is enriched with large numbers of sea fish like flounder, eels and lamprey which add an extra dimension to the pike's menu! Further downstream still at the village of Riccall the river is known for large barbel and pike too. This is also where Harald Hardrada tied up his giant fleet of war boats a week or so before the battle of Stamford Bridge on the River Derwent. They were called dragon ships and there were over three hundred of them. What an amazing sight that would have been! Harald was of course making a bid for the English crown and in the process the river ran red with blood. Sometimes whilst quietly fishing on the River Ouse one can reflect on such amazing historical events which have taken place on these very same riverbanks. That is one of the great things about fishing, it gives you time to reflect on our rich local history, and to know it all happened in the very place we now enjoy our fishing.

The River Ouse below Naburn lock is tidal, the water is deep, and the current is extraordinarily strong. The banks are also very slippery thanks to the constant tidal movements. In short this is a very treacherous place to fish and even if you find a safe swim to fish it is best to wear a life jacket as a safety precaution. We have fished in the tidal section of the River Ouse, but it really is extremely dangerous. If you fell in the strong currents would immediately carry you off downstream. Even with the benefit of a life jacket it would still be very difficult to climb out on the very steep and slippery banks. For this reason and with so much relatively safe fishing available above Naburn Lock it seems foolhardy to choose this hazardous section. I would not be at all surprised if this lower tidal section contained some of the largest pike in the north, but many people have died on the lower Ouse section and no pike is big enough to risk your life for!

The river above Naburn lock is much more accessible and a lot safer to fish. From here the Ouse runs for about four miles upstream into York town centre. This stretch is deep and has a relatively gentle flow and its banks are adorned with beautiful trees and willow bushes. There are also plenty of safe fishing positions. We have caught very big pike in this section a lot of it which is controlled by the big city clubs. By joining these clubs, you can have full access to many productive miles of fishing. The city centre stretch seems an unlikely place to go pike fishing, and yet this can be one of the best places of all to catch pike. It was here that my good friend Lee Maloney who lives in York caught his thirty-pound pike, I say thirty which is an understatement. His scales only went up to thirty pounds and when he bottomed out his scales there was still a lot of weight not registered so who knows how heavy it was. This fish was properly witnessed, and Lee managed to get a good photo too.

My own deep winter efforts in York town centre were also very productive with lots of doubles up to eighteen pounds. I fished one dead bait rod in settled water about fifteen feet out and a second rod only three feet out from the stone wharf. Just about all the action for me came from the rod which was fished only three feet from the riverside wall. What I found particularly interesting was how fat the pike were in comparison to the fish caught in the faster upstream river sections. This showed how rich the feeding was. On further trips I began to fish one rod for pike using suspended dead baits and a second rod float fishing maggot for perch and roach. This was very enjoyable fishing, and I kept my silver fish in a long keepnet suspended deep into the marginal water. I found the keepnet full of six-inch perch and roach was like a magnet for the pike. It was laughable to see the pike butting the net trying to grasp the fish safely inside. A suspended sardine was all it took to catch these hungry pike. I could have used live bait, but it was completely unnecessary, in any case I find using live bait is unpleasant and seems to attract too many unwanted jack pike. There is no doubt that a keepnet full of small fish acts like a magnate to pike of all sizes. I now believe it more than compensates for using just one rod instead of two for pike. I really love fishing the town centre of York for pike. The only trouble is though that the fishing is right on a public foot path and after about ten o clock well-meaning members of the public repeatedly ask, "Have you caught anything mate?" This is fine for an hour or so, but after about the fiftieth time the same question becomes very demoralising. We would never want to be impolite to the public, some of whom may live on their own and are just wanting some friendly banter. The polite way round this problem is to be very selective about the kind of weather you fish in. We have found that the River Ouse in York town centre often fishes well when it is coloured and running high. By a happy coincidence, these conditions are often linked with wet windy weather. The kind of weather too inclement for the casual walkers, and those who do venture out are not in the mood to stand around making small talk. The colder the weather, the more this solution works, and in the York area cold weather is certainly conducive to good pike fishing.

From York the river continues upstream for over ten miles where it reaches its starting point near Ouseburn. Again, access to almost the full length of this stretch can be obtained by joining the big city clubs of York, Bradford and Leeds. If we wish to retain our wild river fishing in Yorkshire it is vital to support these clubs who provide us all with privileged access to top quality coarse and game fishing at a very reasonable rate. Certainly, the quality of the fishing on the River Ouse is first class. Not only for pike, but also for perch, bream, barbel, chub, dace, roach, tench and increasingly even the chance of a salmon. All this can be accessed for around £ 50.00 per year. We are members of six different clubs which grant us access to most of the rivers in the North and a lot more fishing we could ever do justice to.

The River Ouse is of course navigable and several good pike anglers prefer to fish from a small, motorised fishing boat. Of course, a boat gives access to several places unreachable from the bank and this is where the advantage lies. Various friends have taken me boat fishing in the past and on those days, we did catch plenty of very small pike. It was extremely dangerous though, even more risky than even I had anticipated, not only from the large pleasure cruisers which run at high speeds up the river, but also from unforeseeable things happening like boats getting caught up in currents and being dragged under waterfalls. This has happened several times with tragic results. Also, the anchor rope being trapped by a fast-moving five-ton log floating downstream pulling the boat under. There are a hundred other unforeseeable things which can happen in an instant too which you simply cannot plan for. Therefore, we would advise anyone to stay safe on the bank. Also, after an hour or two on a boat one can begin to feel very confined, especially after being trapped behind either a car screen or computer screens all week at work. Despite my own prejudices I do realise boat fishing can open new areas to fish so do not let me put you off boats. One boat fishing friend I know argues that those willow tree bound banks which cannot be reached from land suddenly become available from the boat. This is very true in the short term in that the boat allows instant access. However, my personal preferred method of reaching those 'hidden' pike is to fish upstream for the full day, let the concealed pike smell and taste those delicious dead baits free offerings. Eventually, and it may take three hours, three days or even three weeks, but if you stick at it, and if they are present, they will eventually come upstream to you where they can be landed in perfect safety from the bank. By the way, I think a lot of big pike are put off when they can hear all the banging and knocking sounds coming from a boat only a few yards away. Far better I would argue to let the pike come to you of their own free will, drawn upstream by the irresistible scent of your favourite pike attractant. This is safe pike fishing at its best, but you need the confidence in your tackle and methods to see it out.

Finally, as a result of the sheer acreage and the prodigious food chain of the River Ouse I believe it probably holds more big pike than any of the Northern rivers dealt with in this study. The River Hull is more fertile, but it is a lot smaller so just lacks the capacity. In the next twenty years the river Aire could possibly out strip both the Hull and the Ouse as it is both very fertile and occupies a massive acreage, but at this stage it is still in recovery from over a hundred years of pollution. It will be all very interesting to see what the future brings.

THE RIVER RIBBLE

The beautiful River Ribble on a fine July day. Deep pools flanked by lush weed beds. The kind of scene which makes you glad to have been born an angler!

Another beautiful Northern River, again with a unique and indescribable charm of its own is the River Ribble. It rises in Yorkshire at a height of over 1,000 feet not far from the famous Ribblehead Viaduct and runs for over seventy-five miles west to meet the estuary at Lytham in Lancashire. The head waters of the river near Horton and Helwith Bridge are of course trout preserves. Below Settle the river deepens and becomes a good mixed fishery. Further downstream between Sawley and Chatburn the river forms the boundary between Yorkshire and Lancashire and once again is primarily a trout and grayling water. Some very large salmon and sea trout are caught on the river and this can have the effect of limiting access on some stretches. Below Clitheroe the river once again offers good mixed fishing including some very interesting fast water pike opportunities. Access here is available on local club waters and several day ticket venues are available. From Salisbury downstream to Preston good quality mixed fishing for dace, roach, barbel and pike can be secured. River improvements have recently been undertaken at Samlesbury by removing the weir. This man-made feature was obstructing the upstream migration of endangered species like eel, lamprey and smelt. During periods of low water, the weir was also causing a build-up of these fish making them vulnerable to cormorant predation. Now, with the removal of the weir there will be a free and natural movement of fish which will increase biodiversity of all life in the river. The lower region of the river provides top quality coarse and game fishing with lots of barbel to double figures, perch to over three pounds and pike to over thirty pounds. Such large pike are very rare though, yet a recent pike of thirty-four pounds was reported which is probably the river record for this species on the Ribble. Make no mistake thought, for big pike the river Ribble has good form, and is probably the best pike river in the northwest as well as being a very beautiful place to spend time pike fishing.

Pike Fishing a deep bend on the River Ribble. In the foreground Bill basks in autumn sunshine whilst at the same time a dark weather front rolls in from the west.

THE RIVER SWALE - THE FASTEST RIVER IN ENGLAND.

The River Swale runs through a classical glacial valley within beautiful Swaledale. The river starts off in the hills over 1200 feet high which surround the small village of Keld. From here it runs a good seventy-three miles into the Vale of York where it meets the River Ure just below Myton on Swale.

The name 'Swale' comes from the Anglo-Saxon word 'Sualuae' meaning 'fast and Likely to flood'. It would be difficult to find a more appropriate name as I know from personal experience. Whilst fishing the mid-section of the river near Morton on Swale I have seen the river rise as much as four or five feet in just half an hour. Of course, all the northern spate rivers tend to flood but when it comes to fast rising water the Swale comes at the top of the list, which is why it is known as the fastest river in England. To guard against this natural feature high levees have been built at each side of the river to help prevent flooding the adjacent fields and pastures. During the second world war large gangs of German prisoners of war were employed shoring up the high flood defences using wheelbarrows, and shovels and these features are still very much in place today. They still provide protection from flooding during the high spate periods which often only last a day or two.

From upper Swaledale near Keld down to Richmond the river has a reputation for good trout fishing with wild brown trout averaging about three to the pound. What they lack in size is more than made up for with their sheer beauty. Then below Richmond the river widens and becomes a series of fast streams followed by intermittent deeper pools. This is where the river starts to become a good quality mixed fishery with chub, barbel, perch and of course trout and grayling. Pike also show up in the Catterick area. I know this because we were once fly fishing for trout and grayling in summer wading in the shallow water. On that lovely warm day, the trout were rising well to the fly, I was positioned in a perfect swim where I could fish the fly past some willows on the opposite bank. The trout were coming every ten minutes or so. It was such a productive position I did not move an inch. The water was only about a foot deep and I was stood over a lovely clean gravel bed. After about an hour or so I thought it time to move on but before I did, I just looked down, and to my astonishment there below me was a big pike, at least three feet long sheltering between my legs! Fortunately, I managed to stay calm, and it stayed there for another few minutes before swimming upstream into deeper water. It was not at all concerned about my presence (It probably saw my P.A.C. Logo!) and was only interested in the trout which kept coming to the small net. I will never forget that River Swale pike, it was about fourteen pounds or so, but I know for certain that pike in the Swale reach at least as far upstream as Catterick. In the northern rivers we have caught the same pike in different parts of the river sometimes several miles upstream. These, upstream catches are usually made in the summer period, on several instances we have caught the same fish much further downstream in the deeper stretches in winter. We know the fish are the same thanks to their unique markings which can be checked on photos. Not that photos are required really as we can usually recognised individual fish by various characteristic features which we remember. For example, perhaps a red spot on the body, or in one case a tiny deformity in the caudal fin. I caught this fish when it was 6lb, then again, several years later at twenty-four pounds, I recognised it instantly from the same tiny deformity on its tail. On the second capture it was only fifty yards from its capture when it was only a jack about five years before… Happy days!

The experiences we have had above prove that our northern river pike move several miles up and down stream, yet at the same time have one favourite 'home venue' which they like to return to. This is not guesswork, but rather fact gleaned from a lifetimes pike fishing on these rivers.

Mr James Taylor from Redcar displays his magnificent 22lb 8oz River Swale pike. Although the photo is a little grainy there is no disguising the spectacular markings and the sheer size of the fish. The fact this fish was taken from a snag ridden swim flanked by very steep banks earns James extra congratulations on its capture. (Photo courtesy of Mr Jim Taylor).

On the River Swale pike can be found in good numbers downstream from Catterick all the way to Myton on Swale near to where the Swale meets the larger River Ure, this is over twenty miles and most of it is easily accessible by joining the big city club waters or day tickets. Having fished the river Swale for over fifty years I have many fond memories catching pike on spinners as a young ' Jack catcher' in my early teens. Then, as now it would not be too difficult to catch half a dozen small pike on plugs and soft baits in the warmer months. In winter though I prefer dead baits fished in both fast and sheltered water. If you are unfamiliar with fast water pike your first instincts will probably be to fish all the slacks first. On the River Swale though, big pike can often be taken in deep fast water which is running at ten miles per hour or so. A lot of the prey fish tend to feed in the fast sections where they lie in wait for food items to drift downstream. The faster the water, the more food drifts past and if that is where the prey fish are then so too are the pike. In the lower reaches of the River Swale the barbel fishing is particularly good especially in the vicinity of Topcliffe Weir which has always been a magnet for big barbel specialists. Downstream from Topcliffe big chub, perch, barbel and pike can all be caught with a bit of skill, stealth and patience. The river here is particularly rich with streamer weeds and insect life and it is of goodly proportions, as are the pike. Fish of ten to fifteen pounds can be caught most seasons and for the lucky few even a twenty pounder is a real possibility. To keep one's expectations in proportion though it is worth remembering that many pike anglers' fish all their lives without taking a twenty-pound northern river pike. One of my best friends had caught over two hundred pike over a weight of twenty pounds in his life, yet not one from the northern rivers. That is because there are twenty pounders, and then there are northern river twenty pounders, there is a vast difference between the two!

When fishing the lower sections of the River Swale in the Helperby and Myton regions there is some water sharing between the Ure and Swale pike. Indeed, at certain times of year the river Ure pike swim upstream to take advantage of higher oxygen levels and better still, easy to catch prey fish which become very vulnerable whilst spawning in the weedy shallows. The lower Swale is densely weeded in the early summer months making it a good venue for tiny pike to hatch and develop during summer, so the area has multiple advantages. Pike have evolved to spawn slightly before other coarse fish giving the tiny two-to-three-inch pike hatchlings a head start for catching the slightly later and hence smaller minnow, dace, and chub fingerlings. Later, in the season the pike fall back to their deeper winter haunts to shelter away from the strong currents of England's fastest river.

THE RIVER TEES

Only ten miles to the north of the River Swale lies the River Tees which rises on Cross fell at a height of over 2,400 feet. The Tees is a substantial river flowing a good eighty-five miles east where it meets the sea between Redcar and Hartlepool. On its journey east it flows through limestone beds down to Barnard Castle where it becomes a very fine trout and grayling water with, as time goes on, an increasingly good chance of salmon and sea trout. By the time the river gets to Darlington it becomes a very fine mixed fishery producing good quality brown trout, grayling, dace, chub, barbel, perch and pike. From Darlington downstream to Stockton, it provides very accessible fishing through various of clubs based in local towns like Darlington, Stockton, Thornaby which all provide top class coarse fishing opportunities at a very affordable annual fee.

The River Tees Barrage which was completed in 1995. This structure includes a salmon ladder and fish counter to monitor salmon numbers as they make their way upstream to spawn. The barrage also prevents the tidal shunting of sea water upstream creating more stable conditions for both coarse and game fish. Photo courtesy of Mr D.R. Winship.

Akin to some of the West Yorkshire rivers the Tees has a dark past with bad pollution from heavy industrial activity, especially in the lower tidal sections. The lower Tees was once so polluted that it prevented salmon and sea trout from making their annual runs. However, the good news is that the pollution has now virtually disappeared, thanks partly to the closure of the heavy steel industries in Teesside, but also thanks to the tidal barrage which was opened in April 1995 to prevent tidal shunting. This barrage is built near Stockton and holds back the tide with its giant steel lock gates and concrete structure. The barrage was designed to allow the free passage of migratory fish like eels, sea trout and salmon. Since June 2011 there has even been an electronic fish counter installed which monitors the number of salmon moving both up and downstream. This enables these fish to once again complete their life cycle and fish numbers are steadily growing. Spring runs of Salmon have been very modest but runs for August and September have been steadily rising into several hundreds of fishes each year. The more stable and now unpolluted lower sections of the river are ideal for coarse fishing and good consistent results are now more attainable than before the barrage was built. The lower twenty miles of the River Tees meanders through rich meadows and farmlands and is now the haunt of some particularly good pike which now grow to well over twenty pounds in weight. As the river continues to develop, thanks largely to the protective barrage at Stockton, the quality of the mixed fishing can only get better, and of course the pike fishing will continue to improve too.

Pike conservationist James Taylor from Redcar displays an immaculate River Tees pike weighing 15lb 6oz. At the 2021 P.A.C. convention near Newark James raised over £ 900.00 selling raffle tickets in aid of pike conservation. (Photo courtesy of Mr James Taylor).

THE RIVER TYNE – SLEEPING GIANT

No book on Pike rivers in Northern England would be complete without some mention of the mighty River Tyne. Why? because from time to time some very large pike are caught in its powerful east flowing currents. The River Tyne is a very substantial river rising high up in the north Pennines and flowing from two rivers, the North Tyne and the South Tyne which meet near Hexham. The river is seventy-three miles long and is mainly fast and very turbulent until the two rivers meet and then flow in a series of fast glides and deep pools until they meet the Tyne estuary below Newcastle. One of the Tyne tributaries is the River Derwent which flows to the south of the main river in county Durham. Before the 1890s the River Derwent only contained small brown trout and was controlled by the Consett steel workers. When they wanted to stock with grayling, they consulted with fisheries expert Max Walbran before investing in grayling fry. These wealthy steel workers paid for Walbran to travel by train from Leeds to Newcastle to give his advice on whether the river was viable. After a full guided tour Walbran found the river perfect for grayling and recommended they proceed. The river has been a good grayling water ever since! This is just another example of the wide-ranging influence the great man had as a result of his burning passion for his sport. The river is exceptionally beautiful in the Lintzford area just upstream from the Tyne. Visitors to Lintzford Garden Centre can enjoy the beauty of the riverside from the cafe. There are some lovely deep pools full of trout and grayling. Big Pike are also rumoured to haunt this lower section of the Derwent but tend to be persecuted by game anglers. Another tributary of the River Tyne is the River Rede most notable for its trout and salmon, but it also has also produced pike too. The size of its pike would be far bigger if trout anglers could refrain from killing them and hence causing an explosion in the number of jack pike which then seed the whole river length. On the River Tyne itself coarse fish and pike can be found below Hexham especially in those very deep reed fringed pools in the Mickley, Prudhoe, and Wylam sections of the Tyne. The deep pool below the bridge at Wylam is a particularly lovely stretch of water. Again, providing a beautiful backdrop and atmosphere unique to the River Tyne.

From time to time some very large pike are reported in the local press, fish in excess of thirty pounds and more, leaving us in no doubt about the true potential of this great river. The Tyne Valley Regional Organiser for the Pike Anglers Club, Mr Damian Mc Hale, kindly sent me a news report with a photo of a 25lb River Tyne Pike caught on a fly very near Hexham. Thankfully the captor returned the pike unharmed. The fish itself was very large indeed and judging from the photo it would register a reading of about 0.4 on the condition scale. Very similar in look to the River Ure Pike but was obviously every ounce a twenty-five pounder! The only problem with the Tyne is that the Game fishing interests are strong indeed. Just recently I was travelling over the Tyne Bridge on the old Roman Road, the A68 just east of Hexham when I witnessed an incredibly sad event. I watched as a twenty something salmon angler ran up onto the road bridge holding a gasping salmon gaffed through its chin and flapping helplessly. I felt so sorry for that poor salmon, it should have been either returned, or despatched quickly if wanted for the table but no, the man was so callous. This made me realise the PAC catch and release credo is about fifty years ahead of the anglers like this. Thankfully though, a new breed of salmon anglers is coming to the fore with a responsible 'Catch and release' credo. Long may it last! I think it is time we took a leaf out of the Loch Lomond Angling Improvement associations book and simply ban all fish being killed. Thankfully, the River Tyne is one of the few rivers where salmon numbers seem to be holding up well. For example on the salmon and sea trout fish counter at Riding Mill May 2021 was 319 fish, June 2,108, July 6,507, August 6,735 with an annual number of 20,462! The actual figures were even more impressive though as some of the counters were temporarily not working making these figures smaller than they would otherwise have been. With large numbers of sea trout and salmon running through the river there is every chance of some amazing pike being caught on the Tyne and its tributaries. I think the River Tyne is a true sleeping giant as far as both its pike and salmon potential is concerned, if all its fish were returned on a catch and release basis the whole river could move towards its full potential, not just with its salmon, but with all other species too.

The River Tyne has always contained a good head of pike which are sometimes taken unintentionally by game anglers spinning for salmon.

THE RIVER TWEED – BORDER COUNTRY

The River Tweed forms the border between Scotland and England and has tributaries which blend the two countries perfectly in the form of one of the United Kingdom's best Salmon fishery, namely, the beautiful River Tweed. The rivers source is at Tweeds Well, over ninety miles upstream from the river mouth at Berwick upon Tweed. It is a very substantial river and of course world famous for its Game fishing. Interestingly, the Celtic meaning of tweed is border.

Whenever I travel north on the train bound for Edinburgh, I always feel a little uneasy crossing the Berwick viaduct. The bridge itself is a magnificent piece of engineering but looks very precarious and I always breathe a sigh of relief when we reach the far bank! This bridge looks too much like the old Tay bridge for my liking which collapsed causing the train and all its passengers ending up at the bottom of the River Tay. In the same way I also feel a little uneasy mentioning pike and River Tweed in the same sentence! I would like to make it clear from the start that I would not recommend anyone travel to all the way to the River Tweed to fish for pike, unless of course you have an invite from one of the locals 'In the know' and with authorised access. The only reason I have included the river on the map of Northern Pike Rivers is the fact the River Tweed is in Northern England, and it does contain natural stocks of big pike and it always has.

When traveling north up the A1 trunk road on the way to Scotland we love to call in at the shop run by Hardy's of Alnwick. With the Angling Museum combined with the shop itself I always stock up on fishing tackle. Most of the products are aimed at the Trout and Salmon Fishermen but it does not matter, the cultural history of our sport is intoxicating, even for an angler like me who fishes mainly for pike... better known in these parts as the poor man's salmon!

I have huge respect for the way the salmon fishing industry along the River Tweed has developed over hundreds of years to be a world-famous destination for its salmon fishermen. There are many hotels along the river course which specialise in providing an all-round service for Anglers. Not just with accommodation, but also the provision of traditional fishing guides who provide a gillie service. In ancient Scotland, the highland Chieftains employed gillies or male attendants to help whilst fishing or hunting. To fish the Tweed properly from a boat an attendant is more of a necessity than a luxury so a whole industry has been set up in the area to cater for this high-end market. When guests are paying anything from £ 500 to £ 1,000 per day for this kind of service, they naturally expect to have the best possible chance of catching their target fish, the salmon.

It is not often you get reports of big pike catches from the Tweed, this is understandable too, if your livelihood depended on salmon and trout fishing you would not want to advertise the presence of trout eating pike! Science does not come into it, its image that counts here, and an international image carefully cultured over many years. All this brings us back to Tom Sturdy the river Keeper on the West Tanfield Estate on the River Ure. Their 56lb pike was hushed up for all the right reasons and with their livelihoods at stake it was the right thing to do. At that time, in the 1920s the River Ure was full of salmon, even more so than the Tweed is today. For this reason, I would not be at all surprised if the River Tweed produced another very large pike or two, it has happened before, and it will certainly happen again.

THE RIVER URE

Hewick Bridge on the glorious River Ure. This is Yorkshires premier salmon river. Thanks to the Yorkshire Salmon Trust all salmon must now be returned and numbers are gradually starting to increase. Not so long ago the river Ure "Turned Black" with the sheer number of fish running upstream to spawn. It is also the haunt of some very large pike.

The River Ure rises high up on the Pennine moorlands and is fed from feeder streams running off Lund's Fell and High Abbotside at a height of over 2,000 feet. The river then flows east to meet the Ouse seventy-four miles downstream. Salmon run as far as Aysgarth falls which block further upstream movement whilst pike can be found as high up as Middleham, but the presence of pike is very intermittent until the river flows past Ripon. Below Ripon the River Ure becomes deeper and from here their presence is continuous right down to Ouseburn where the Ure meets up with the River Ouse.

The River Ure has an extraordinarily rich angling history and was once recognised as Yorkshire's premier salmon river. As we have already mentioned earlier Norris Sturdy had witnessed how every year around August the River Ure below West Tanfield bridge turned black with the sheer number of salmon running upstream to spawn. Also, Lord Bolton, further still upstream, once caught thirty hundredweight of salmon in just one year. This amounts to over one and a half tons of fish! Furthermore, salmon were so plentiful they were used as agricultural fertilizer by local farmers. All this was taking place just after the first world war in the 1920s. This was the same time period Norris, and his Father Tom landed their fifty-six-pound pike. During and before this period salmon over fifty pound in weight were regularly caught too! With an annual harvest of salmon on this scale it is clear how a river pike could reach such a massive size. Up in Scotland similar salmon and pike relationships were in evidence too as was shown by the discovery of the Endrick pike where a truly huge pike estimated to be well over fifty pounds was found near the banks of the Endrick river and fully chronicled in Fred Bullers great pike books.

Only fifteen years or so later in the late 1930s the salmon runs suddenly came to a halt as pollution from the industrial west riding of Yorkshire poisoned the lower reaches of the Ouse and Humber making it de oxygenated thus preventing the salmon returning to spawn. For the next sixty years the River Ouse tributaries were dead as far as salmon were concerned. During the second world war years industrial polluters were given Crown immunity to go on polluting the rivers during the war effort but continued for some time after the war too. As we have seen in the chapter about John Eastwood the Anglers Cooperative Association was formed in 1947 to combat water pollution. From then onwards river polluters were not only prosecuted for illegal polluting but were also responsible for paying for re stocking waters they had destroyed. The A.C.A. was heavily funded by all anglers, especially the big city clubs who invested millions of pounds, in the fight for clean rivers.

A 24lb specimen pike from the River Ure. An immaculate streamlined pike typical of these Northern River Pike.

Finally, after sixty-two years of campaigning and donations from ordinary anglers the Yorkshire rivers are now beginning to see the return of the salmon. The Angling Trust and Fish Legal are continuing the good work of the A.C.A. and making a special effort to remove river obstructions in order to help salmon and all migratory fish like eels, lamprey, sea trout to complete their natural spawning life cycle.

More recently and encouraged by the success of the A.C.A. the Angling Trust has made a concerted effort to clear our rivers of any unnecessary obstacles like redundant weirs which made it difficult for salmon or eels to move upstream to spawn. A very interesting article titled 'Fish highways created in 12,500 miles of rivers to help migration' appeared in the Daily Telegraph on 21st May 2016. It reported that 'Fish passes, or weirs have been removed in almost 200 obstructions which were hindering fish as they struggled to complete their life cycles to spawn'. Furthermore, on the River Ure an organisation called 'The Ure Salmon Trust' has been set up to further build on the seventy-year effort invested by the A.C.A. to purify our rivers to such an extent that they can now support Salmon runs through the whole river course. The really encouraging thing about the U.S.T. is that they insist that any salmon caught must be returned so they can breed and thus actually complete their life cycle. Equally good is the fact that the U.S.T. are fostering the development of young salmon to re seed the River Ure system, hopefully to further enhance salmon numbers for the future. It is an exceptionally long process though as it took the A.C.A. over sixty years to clean up our rivers to pave the way for salmon runs. I suspect it will take another long period to truly realise the dream of self-generating salmon stocks the likes of which Norris and Tom Sturdy enjoyed in the glory days of the 1920s. One of the main problems is that salmon are traditionally killed for the table, and whilst Ure Salmon are now protected it will still be very difficult to stop such a long-established tradition. Perhaps one very straight forward solution would be to ban killing any migratory fish in all our rivers, that way it would allow all fish the chance to recover to natural stock levels.

THE RIVER WEAR

The River Wear is a sizeable river rising at a height of over 1,100 feet at Weirhead and flows for sixty miles east where it meets the tidal Wear Estuary in the Sunderland area. The upper reaches are of course mainly trout and grayling fishing as the river flows through Stanhope, Wolsingham, Bishop Auckland down to Durham. Once at Durham, the river flows through a beautiful, wooded gorge. The river is held back in Durham by the weir which has a salmon leap and fish counter. Thankfully, in recent years both salmon and sea trout have made a big come back on the river and thousands of fish have been recorded on the monitor. This fish monitor which is situated at Framlingate weir in Durham has recorded some very satisfying results over the years as shown below.

Recent Annual Fish Counts at FramwellGate Weir on River Weir at Durham.

Salmon and Trout Monitored Travelling Upstream Over Last Four Years.

2018	Fish Recorded	8669
2019	Fish Recorded	4704
2020	Fish Recorded	5462
2021	Fish Recorded	13051

As can be seen above the best of all recent years is 2021 (Despite Covid) the recordings were a very satisfying figure of 13,051. These are wonderful details provided by the environmental agency and give us all a very useful concept of what is going on within the river both day and night. Again, as on the results provided by the Riding mill counter on the River Tyne these figures are slightly on the conservative side. There are also many cormorants around the weir which are seen to play havoc with fish of all species but especially the trout.

Nigel Winter skilfully pays out line to a very big pike which is not at all ready for the net!

Special efforts were made here by the Pike Anglers Club to create non-lethal underwater deterrents to which were designed to frustrate the cormorants' underwater activities. Above the weir at Durham the river meanders for mile after mile through beautiful rich water meadows which provide deep bends and weedy shallow areas which have provided good conditions for pike through the ages, back and well beyond the time Duke William of Normandy built the giant Castle and Cathedral which still command a dominating position over the river weir below. When Duke William the new King of England visited Durham all those year ago I would wager that the evening banquets would feature not only Venison and Hog roast, but equally essential the traditional Norman pike platter. Not Salmon or Lobster, but a proper pike served in Norman tradition with a red sautéed apple held firmly between the pike's jaws! The pike was a symbol of power, sometimes ruthless power, just like the giant dominating Castles they built. The sheer brute size of the pike combined with its legendary ferocity symbolised all the qualities the Normans valued. In later centuries as Bishops and Monks took control of the land and rivers the pike lost favour; its blatant ferocity did not go down so well in ecclesiastical circles where it was too satanical for its own good! Only recently in the past thirty years or so has the pike been rehabilitated as science has overtaken centuries of ill-informed dogma. Below Durham the river flows into a low-lying valley and meanders through lush green meadows for many miles until it finally reaches the outskirts of Sunderland. In this low-lying area, the River Wear is very scenic and there are plenty of opportunities to catch some good quality coarse fish including dace, barbel, chub, roach, bream, perch and of course pike. I certainly know of pike up to twenty-five pounds being taken in these lower regions of the river and with the increasing numbers of game fish running through a thirty pounder or even bigger is a distinct possibility. There are at least five local clubs which offer members access to this part of the Wear, all at very affordable prices.

THE RIVER WHARFE – ONE OF WALBRANS FAVOURITE RIVERS.

The River Wharfe has its source near the tiny hamlet of Beckermonds which is situated high up in Langstrothdale at an altitude of over nine hundred feet.

As with most other northern rivers the Wharfe is a spate river providing top class trout and grayling fishing in the upper reaches. It also benefits greatly from its Limestone geology as a booster for its fish and plant life. The River Wharfe lies within a classical u-shaped glacial valley and there can be few places on earth more beautiful to practice the art of fly fishing for trout and grayling. There are opportunities to fly fish, but you may have to wait a short while before a new place becomes available. It is generally fly fishing only in these upper reaches and I know of no pike this far up on the River Wharfe. The river runs quickly down to Kettlewell, Ilkley, Otley and then Pool. This is the village where Francis Walbran once lived and not surprisingly was one of his favourite fishing venues. Further downstream near Collingham and Wetherby the river offers good mixed fishing for trout, grayling, dace, chub, barbel, perch and pike.

Mark Green displays his twenty-pound river Wharfe pike. A great achievement from a water more famous for its specimen barbel and chub than it is for pike. The river Wharfe is another water which has a history of serious pollution but now seems to have recovered well.

In the Wetherby section our guest writer Nigel Winter has taken several pike in the twenty-pound class, not to mention specimen sized chub and barbel. This part of the river is heavily match fished on weekends, so for pike fishing we would advise to visit mid-week. Further downstream at Tadcaster the river continues to get even better with long deep stretches broken up by weedy fast shallows. In this section pike can be caught anywhere along its length. Pike of all sizes do move up and downstream often daily, so wherever you fish you are certainly in with a good chance of meeting some good pike. Further downstream the river becomes tidal at Ullerskelf and then flows further to meet up with the River Ouse near Cawood.

CONCLUSION TO THE NORTHERN RIVERS SECTION.

In this section we have given brief details on the various prime northern rivers, details which could if required form a starting point for river fishing in the north of England. Remember though, it takes a whole lifetime to truly understand a river. However, I believe there is no harm done by fishing some other rivers in the meantime! There is a delicious contrast for example in fishing the River Ouse one day, then fishing the fast River Swale the next. Both part of the same river network, yet the pike look and behave in different ways. We were tempted to include the mighty River Trent in our list of northern waters but decided against because although it runs into the River Ouse, it primarily drains the West and East Midlands of England making it basically a Midlands water of course.

Fishing for river pike is a very interesting and rewarding sport, it is also very complex and is affected by a multitude of geophysical, and social traditions which all influence what we can achieve. I hope after reading this we have made it clear that most of our rivers, good as they now are, are still in a state of recovery from widespread pollution experienced over the past seventy years or so. Thankfully, our rivers are becoming much cleaner, and this is shown by a steady return of our salmon stocks. Yet we are still a long way from realising our full potential. Before the industrial revolution, our rivers were teeming with salmon fresh from the Greenland Shelf in the North Atlantic Ocean. Our rivers were also full of eels from the Atlantic too. To make a meaningful contribution to restoring our rivers back to full health we need to support the Angling Trust. Every angler needs to be part of this as it is the only agent capable of really continuing the fight against water pollution. If we just continue as we have it will only be a matter of time before fifty-pound salmon and pike once again swim in our northern rivers. That is surely a worthy aiming point.

ALTITUDE, ATMOSPHERICS AND THE ALTOSTRATUS

Atmospherics and the Roof of England.

As those atmospheric depressions we all see on the weather charts come bowling in from the North Atlantic it usually means one thing, rain, rain and yet more rain. To most people such a forecast can be dispiriting as the rain often continues for days on end. To the northern angler though this weather can herald good fishing opportunities for those in the know. The Pennine chain of hills, known as the 'Roof' or 'Backbone' of England have a trigger effect on those moisture rich altostratus clouds condensing them and giving us the highest rainfall in the country and most of it feeds directly into our northern rivers making them very efficient distributors of not only water, but also oxygen and temperature change. This beautiful and vast network of tiny feeder streams and gills can act as a giant heater in winter and can similarly operate as an oxygen rich cooler in the dry periods of Summer. In both these instances and many other weather combinations, the great air masses can carry with them exciting opportunities for the angler. Only though if you know what to look out for and the exciting opportunities they bring.

Timing is the key to getting it right. It is worth remembering that there is a time lag between rain falls on the upland fells to when it takes full effect within the whole river system. In a very heavy summer thunderstorm, the time lag to get water to the middle river reaches may be twenty-four hours or less. In winter, with heavy snow falling the lag time may be eight weeks during periods of cold sub-zero conditions. There have been many very interesting articles written about weather and atmospheric conditions and the effect they have on our sporting prospects. Some pike anglers recommend fishing the first frosts, others prefer warm sunny days whilst others swear by a rising barometer and keep an eye on air pressure changes in the atmosphere. All this is interesting reading and we keep a keen record of the weather in our fishing dairies. On the northern rivers there are other related conditions we record too. For example, whether the river level is rising or falling, temperature changes in the water and visibility too. All these factors do affect the way our fish behave, and it is interesting and helpful to know how these weather variables may affect one's fishing.

The critical factor in applying this knowledge lies in selecting which rivers to fish the day before you venture out, then when you arrive it helps you decide how to fish. Most importantly we recommend not to use weather forecasts as an excuse to stay at home! On so many occasions we have heard anglers' remark. "I didn't bother fishing this weekend because the rivers were in flood". Another reason for not going is "It's too wet and windy". This kind of fair-weather approach is not something we would recommend at all as some of the best possible fishing can be missed by adopting this 'Weather shy' approach. The happy irony is that we 'discovered' our favourite fishing conditions by just fishing in all conditions. As workers, my fishing partner Nigel and I have had very limited time to go fishing, a Sunday *day off* is like gold dust. Therefore, whatever the weather we just go anyway, even when it is forecast for storm force winds and driving rain. One thing we have found from this is that once you get out into the countryside the weather is rarely half as bad as forecast. We just take sensible safety precautions like avoiding parking under trees or powerlines and not fishing on river stretches likely to be cut off by rising water. By adopting this safe all-weather approach, we can say without any doubt that very low atmospheric pressure accompanied by strong winds and rain are fine for catching big pike, as are floodwater conditions too. In fact, more than half of our big pike have been taken in exactly these conditions. The most important thing to know about weather is to choose the right venue to get the best out of the day. This is something which should be a lot easier after reading this chapter and relating it to the water's you fish.

In this photo the author can be seen stood on 'The Roof of England' To the right of the scene is Abbotside Common and the source of the River Ure. To the left, just a few hundred yards away lies the source of the River Eden. This area is just a small part of the giant Pennine watershed. It has the highest rainfall in England and is what makes the Northern Rivers totally unique. This really is where river conditions are shaped, sometimes for the better, at others for the worse.

From where Bill is standing here on the Pennine watershed there are no river pike for about a twenty-five miles radius, and yet it is here that the weather magic happens which determines the mood and flow of the rivers and all the fish contained in them. The fells on the horizon rise to over 2,000 feet in height and it is this highland which causes the orographic uplift where moisture laden clouds cool quickly to condense as rain. The rainfall on these hills is often sixty to seventy inches per year compared to under twenty inches in lowland regions like York in the east and Southport in the west. For these reasons, the highland fells or the 'Roof of England' really are most important in providing the 'trigger factors' which shape what conditions are like further downstream. Warm air masses can hold much more water than cold air. For this reason global warming is causing much more torrential downpours of rain which has led to more frequent flooding. In winter, such warm floods often get the pike into a feeding frenzy and provide opportunities too good to miss. The opposite conditions come about when cold air masses grip the country often causing a winter drought, but still pike can be caught even in sub-zero conditions.

River Pike in Northern England

On the 10th of January 2010, Great Britain was held in a frozen airmass which was reported by weather forecasters as the deep freeze with the coldest conditions for forty years. The roads were still passable so Nigel and I went pike fishing to our favourite haunt on the River Ure. We normally drive the car down the farm track to the river, but with over a foot of snow in the fields we decided to park the car in a local village where the council had cleared parking space for cars. It was a good mile walk down to the river so we used the wheelbarrow to carry all our cold weather equipment. In places the snow was over two feet deep and we used the barrow as a sledge man hauling it over the deepest areas. We took turns to reserve our energy for the cold task ahead. Our humour took on a 'Scott of the Antarctic' theme, and we joked about how we could use a team of huskies to haul our tackle. Our cheerful mood soon changed though when we reached the river to find it frozen right across making fishing impossible. We walked further upstream and thankfully found some clear water just below the rapids with a deep pool just big enough for two anglers.

Sub-zero piking. After about six hours the cold started to get to us despite our warm clothing but catching this pike really got the circulation working again.

We could see all manner of footprints from ducks, mink, and foxes too. For the first four hours we were as warm as toast, but after about six hours the cold was really starting to get to us. In turns we went for short walks to get our circulation going. Then, unexpectedly, we both started to catch, Nigel had a four-pounder followed by an eight-pound fish. Then I had a sixteen pounder which warmed me up very quickly indeed. All our pike looked lovely in the snow, the primrose flecks contrasting warmly with the pure white freezing snow. The air temperature was minus five degrees centigrade and the pike were noticeably lethargic with the cold. The water temperature registered zero degrees centigrade on the thermometer. The line was freezing in the rod rings towards the end, so we packed up and called it a day. Our sub-zero fishing experience had taught us it is possible to pike fish even when most of the river is frozen over. To catch though, we had to fish a completely different way in a place never fished before. The river had been frozen over for weeks and was very low and clear. The water level was also very gradually falling in the winter drought causing the river to groan and crack in a way we had never known before. Also, the ice in the edges had morphed in a downward slope as it slowly became shaped by the falling water level. The upland fells were frozen solid and began to take on characteristics of permafrost causing a winter drought. There was also a sense of desolate desperation amongst the wildlife. Robins came in close for food, which we gave and so did other birds including ducks and coot. They were all suffering after the big freeze and were clearly desperate. We got back to the car, it struck up first time and on came the heater. After a full day in minus temperatures the warmth of the car brought on an overwhelming tiredness. It was a fight to stay awake, so we stopped for a half hour break to refresh, then we were fine. I fully realize that our Russian and Canadian friends will laugh when they read, 'we were cold in just minus five degrees centigrade.' I have seen Russians on You Tube walking round in T-shirt's when it is minus ten, but we are just not used to it, especially these days with central heating in almost every home!

In winter, our favourite conditions for catching river pike take place when it is unseasonably warm. A summers day in winter with air temperatures of between twelve and fifteen degrees centigrade invariably get the pike feeding. A very warm Atlantic front from the Bermuda area causing warm rainfall high up in the Pennines in winter can be transmitted into the whole system within one to three days. When this takes place suddenly the pike and other fish can really start to feed well, until of course the reverse conditions come into play and turn the feeding switch back off. Similarly, after a long dry, hot spell in Summer a sudden down pour of cool oxygen enriched water can do the same. Fresh August floods again trigger great conditions for pike fishing with artificial lures. In fact, these provide the best lure fishing we have ever experienced. In both these scenarios the catalyst happens up on the high fells. This is where the 'weather magic' happens which trigger off all the changes which can suddenly transform the fishing possibilities throughout the whole river system. When looking at factors affecting pike fishing prospects there are many things to consider, but the most important consideration is what is going on up on the high fells. All other factors like wind direction, air pressure and so on are still important, but just secondary to sudden weather changes delivered up there on the roof of England.

Several people have also suggested that Moon Phases can affect the feeding habits of pike too. Our findings bear this out, in fact we have had many good pike fishing days which coincide with full Moons including a twenty-two-pounder taken under a full Moon at midnight. There are several convincing theories why this should happen, but our theory is quite simple. On a full moon light conditions are incredibly good making it easy for pike to see their prey, as old 'Esox Lucius' lie in wait beneath the shoal fish, they get a particularly good silhouette of their prey above them. The additional light levels of a full bright Moon get them started on a good feeding binge which can last for several days. Pike have huge eyes in relation to the size of their body, so sight is obviously a key part of their hunting repertoire. What could be better for them than a full moon in clear water in summer? The opposite scenario is of course slightly muddy water in the dark depths of winter. In this situation hunting must be done in the pitch black using smell and vibrations, plus of course their ability to pick up minute electronic pulses from their prey. All these factors are linked closely to the weather and atmosphere and help make the subject of pike fishing such a fascinating and broad field of enquiry.

As described, our understanding of how our northern rivers operate as a system has been found out through fishing these rivers for over fifty years and the information gained has been like rocket fuel to our fishing results.

Summer double taken in fresh cool floodwaters. Before the flood water temperatures were in the seventies Fahrenheit but the floods brought fresh cool temperatures in the 55-degree mark. When summer water temperatures rise over sixty-two degrees Fahrenheit or about seventeen degrees centigrade it is best to stop pike fish fishing as heat stress can kill pike very quickly in such high temperatures.

Let us not forget that it is the Pennine Hills which make our chosen rivers so special and unique. These northern hills can be so grim and threatening in winter and yet so beautiful and inviting in summer. They effectively give birth to our rivers through the process of Orographic Uplift. This process takes place when warm moist Atlantic air masses reach the Pennines and are lifted as they move over the hills. This causes the moist warm air to cool and condense, often, continuously for days and even weeks on end. In effect you could say the Pennine Hills are a rain making machine which work in close unison with the atmosphere to produce regular and powerful pulses of water. These in turn create the spate conditions so important to our game fish, which, under natural conditions will provide marvellous pike fishing possibilities.

Once again, our angling future can be seen to rest in our own hands. Fishery scientists have already identified that our rivers can be improved a lot further by simply allowing our rivers to return to their natural pure state. The Angling Trust have already cleared hundreds of obstructions in our northern rivers to allow the natural processes of regeneration to take hold. They are also continually fighting water pollution. As a result, salmon and sea trout are already returning to their natural spawning grounds thanks to the combined benefits of the Pennine Hills and our water rich atmosphere. These natural conditions have just been waiting for the return of the salmon to their ancestral home in the northern rivers. Make no mistake, these rivers have the full potential to produce salmon and pike second to none. That is why it is good to support the various modern river agencies who are working hard in various ways to improve and protect our rivers. In particular the Angling Trust and of course the Yorkshire Dales Rivers Trust.

Fishing When the River is in Flood

It was 31st December 2021, the last day of the year and the final day of the warmest December on record according to the Met Office. It had also been very wet, there had only been twelve minutes of sunshine recorded in London over the past two weeks and news broadcasters were calling it the most miserable December ever. Not for us though, in fact the mild conditions created the perfect conditions for pike fishing the Northern Rivers giving us the best possible chance to catch one of those elusive twenty pounders. Let me explain how and why.

On this warm December day I set up my fishing chair next to the point where the main river joined to the canal cut. From where I was positioned I could cast one deadbaits to the left into the calm canal then a second to the edge of the current of the main river at a point where the canal waters joined the main river, right in the crease of the current.

The main river was eight feet above trim level and was in a very dangerous and angry mood. The water was coloured and still rising fast. The first job was to put a marker peg on the water line to record the changing water level conditions. Then out went some ground bait in the form of old chopped up sardines and trout. Finally, the landing net and rods were set up and I sat back in the chair to savour this very special time of year.

Out in the main river the water was flowing at about fifteen to twenty miles per hour, it was boiling and tumbling along in a very chaotic way. There were rafts of sticks and every ten minutes or so whole trees went belting downstream, some over thirty feet long weighting several tons. An excited dog walker rushed up to me and said, "Did you see the size of that tree which went down stream?" I confirmed I had and added I had seen several other even bigger ones too. Our friend shot back to his car; he was heading downstream to the road bridge to see how the bridge stood up to these fast-moving battering rams! Pure drama! A dull December? Not a bit of it.

A very angry river in flood. A huge tree limb over thirty feet long can be seen floating downstream at approximately fifteen miles per hour just one of many similar logs passing by every ten minutes or so. The writers float can be seen anchored in the crease of water between the main river and canal. The new rod performed perfectly when it was called on to turn a big pikes head just before it crashed in the willows to the right. On this day the river was rising fast, the pike were looking for shelter, ideal conditions for selectively catching big pike.

Floods like this make it difficult if not impossible for pike to stay in their normal haunts. They need to shelter from the chaos in canal cuts or other backwaters which afford shelter. In some river sections there are no canal sanctuaries at all, but there are always the sheltered margins of the river which though often very shallow, do at least provide a temporary harbour. During very high floods when the river can burst its banks pike and other species spread out onto flood meadows to escape the adverse conditions. In this way they can become too comfortable though and become stranded when the rivers return to normal. These fish soon fall prey to the crows' rooks and jackdaws which are the anglers' constant companions, at all times of the year. The relationship between pike and crow is a two way one though, when crows form an ideal prey for the pike when they venture too close to the water and are engulfed by hungry pike. (See photo).

Par digested crows' leg. These grisly remains were coughed up by one of the authors pike proving crows do feature on the pike's menu of delights from time to time. The writer also knows pike regularly feature on the crow's menu too when pike are stranded helpless in riverside meadows following floods. Of course though they wait for the pike to expire before taking advantage.

After fishing without luck for over two hours I cast my left rod further into the mouth of the canal to the left. The water visibility in front of me next to the river was only twelve inches, but ten yards into the canal the suspended sands had fallen out giving much clearer water with a visibility of approximately three feet. I therefore repositioned the left-hand rod to try the relatively 'clear' water. Once the float ledgered sardine was anchored mid canal I catapulted a dozen or so bait chunks around the float to create an interesting carpet of fish chunks around the main bait. Within only ten minutes I had a run and landed a lovely plump eight-pound pike which was quickly unhooked and returned.

I returned to the chair full of renewed enthusiasm. The float set up in the 'river crease' swim stayed in position. Long experience had taught me this was a good place to catch the bigger fish. Over the years I have caught more really big pike in floodwater conditions than any other, and although there are many favourite conditions in my ever-increasing list of favourites, I think on balance floodwater conditions are my favourite of all, especially for selectively hunting down very big pike in the twenty-pound plus bracket.

For a pike to grow to become a twenty pounder on the Northern Rivers it needs to live relatively undisturbed for at least ten years or so. To do this it may have a safe lair beneath a jumble of underwater logs, completely safe from anglers fishing from either boat or bank. The great thing about the turbulent floodwaters is that such fish are literally flushed out of their normal hides, they venture out to seek calm safe waters which can be easily identified by those in the know.

Fishing in a relaxed position and in complete safety next to the tumultuous river a rare shard of sunlight broke through the relentless cloud cover. At the same moment the right-hand float bobbed gently and disappeared out of sight into the cloudy water. Not leaving anything to chance I wound down firmly and bent the rod into a heavy fish. Was it a snag? Had I got tangled on a log? No, a big slow frequency head shake confirmed a fish was hooked, and all the omens pointed to it being a big one too! My brand-new rod was put under pressure as the pike moved slowly but very deliberately into the fast water of the main river. The new rod handled the fish perfectly and stood the test, in fact the rod did all the work really, providing a firm cushion on the long runs, and holding firm when the pike made a rush for the overhanging willows to my right. Now that fish was swimming blind. The water visibility was still only twelve inches and the river was still rising, and yet that pike still knew exactly where the willow snags were, and it headed straight for them! There was no choice but to hold firm to avoid a snag up and the new strong fourteen-foot-long rod passed the test. We managed to turn her head just in time even though the stress in the line guards made the line sing like piano wire. Soon though she came into the net. I had deliberately used the full extension on the landing net handle so I could keep well back from the river's edge. I netted her on the first attempt and gently eased her out up the slippery bank. This fish was too heavy to be lifted out with the net handle so great care was taken to lift holding the net itself so as to avoid breaking the frame. What a beautiful pike, on the chubby side with very distinctive markings. She weighed in at just over sixteen pounds. Caught just as the sun finally broke through, yes, the Northern Gods were truly shining down on us that day.

Now I have shared one of the top secrets to catching big river pike I feel duty bound to give a warning that floodwater pike fishing is a very dangerous activity. It is impossible to overestimate the very real hazards faced when fishing the angry flooded rivers in winter. Please find below some suggested precautions which will all but remove any danger you may face.

(1). Make sure you are familiar with the geography of the river before wintertime fishing. In particular ensure you can walk back uphill to safety when the river levels come up quickly.

(2). Even when you are familiar with the river do not go wandering around up and down the bank, a moments lapse in concentration can land you in very deep treacherous fast water in no time at all.

(3). Find a nice slack piece of water which will provide a safe harbour for both you and your pike. Once found, set up your chair and relax behind your two pike rods. Once you are sat in comfort you are safe and can fully relax and enjoy the sheer drama of both the river itself and the big pike which it produces. Think positive, set up your camera in readiness and feed the swim with groundbait every half hour or so. The flooded river is a dynamic system. Pike will be nudging up and down stream in search of both shelter and their prey, they will soon enter your haven without the need to expose yourself to the dangers of slippery unstable soggy banksides.

(4). If there is a vertical drop of over twelve inches from your pitch into deep water you must stand well back from the edge at all times as it would be almost impossible to get out if you fell in. Far better to fish from a gentle slope into the water so you could crawl out if the worst happened. Dozens of people are drowned each year in our rivers both in summer and winter. Always have full respect for the river and you will be as safe as anywhere. Take chances and you will never get a second opportunity if you fall in! No pike is big enough to risk your life for.

Jackdaws and crows have a close symbiotic relationship with the pike. When the floods recede stranded pike are regularly eaten by the carrion crows and Jackdaws. When Crows venture too close to the river they in turn feature on the pike's menu as witnessed in the previous photo. This particular Jackdaw came close to the author tempted by bread crumbs.

EQUIPMENT AND METHODS FOR CATCHING NORTHERN RIVER PIKE

Landing Big River Pike With all Round Safety

Way back in the mid-1960s my school pals and I often went on long fishing trips to various rivers and streams in the Yorkshire countryside. Before these long trips, my dear Mother always ensured we had a good pack up and plenty to drink. I will never forget the one thing she always emphasized was. "No matter how thirsty you get, never ever drink water from any streams or river no matter how clean it looks". It was good advice too as even the cleanest looking stream is full of harmful bacteria, far too small to see with the naked eye, yet big enough to make you very ill, and sometimes capable of killing you in a short period of time.

All the rivers in Great Britain carry a certain amount of sewage and toxic waste, often at its worst just after floods when untreated waste finds its way into our rivers. On one occasion on the River Ure the field we intended to fish was full of sanitary towels spread out very evenly for hundreds of yards across the whole field. Each one about eighteen inches apart and had been stranded on the meadow as the floodwaters subsided. Someone upstream had 'unintentionally' allowed the flood to empty his septic tank in the high water. The debris stranded in the field soon rotted down though, and the following spring produced a particularly lush crop of grass! The generally small amounts of material involved do no harm to the ecology of our rivers, but if ingested or injected directly into our blood stream a heavy viral load can prove fatal within a short time. Diseases like Cholera, Typhoid or Weil's disease are a constant danger to the river angler so certain precautions need to be taken from the start.

One of the most important and often underrated pieces of equipment needed by the serious pike angler is a forty-two-inch landing net, either round, rectangular or triangular, they all do a great job in safely landing your fish which are dangerously unpredictable when first landed. Some anglers without nets often try to land their fish by lifting them out of the water from under the pike's chin. One real danger when landing a pike by hand is the sudden spontaneous head shaking which often takes place. This can result in loose treble hooks becoming deeply embedded into one's hands or even worse into your more vulnerable wrists. With the use of a large net such sudden movements remain within the net and are no problem at all. But if the net is not used and the fish is chinned out by placing the hand under the pike's chin, not only do you ensure you have a good source of toxic water on your hands, but you also run the almost inevitable risk of being injected sooner or later by your own treble hooks as your pike thrashes about because of being lifted under its jaw.

The practice of chinning pike is like driving at fifty miles per hour in a thirty miles per hour zone, you may get away with it ten or twenty times, but sooner or later you will be caught off guard when least expecting it and as we all know the results are often fatal. In the case of chinning pike, lifting pike from the water by the pike's chin, large treble hooks frequently become deeply embedded in unsuspecting hands as soon as the pike jumps. When it does happen, and I have seen it happen many times, there is nothing to do but to check in at the nearest accident and emergency facility to have your hooks removed. This often involves a wait of several hours and then taking a massive anti tetanus jab! The size of those needles is more than enough to put anyone off the chinning practice, it must be seen to be believed! The dangers are even worse though, if you contract Weil's disease you could be in hospital for three months and several people die from the illness each year.

Way back in the 1950s and 1960s pioneering anglers like Richard Walker, Barrie Rickards and Ray Webb went to great lengths to demonstrate it is possible to catch and land big fish safely providing the correct tackle is used. Back then it was difficult to purchase a net big enough for pike because the gaff was always used so there was no real market for large nets. During this period Barrie Rickards wrote articles to show how a simple bicycle wheel could be converted into a perfect landing net for pike at minimal cost by removing the spokes and spreading a large net round the rim. This was the perfect solution for a short period and was one of the first steps towards banning the gaff which was a tool most used at a time when almost all pike were killed. Soon though, in the late 1960s good quality pike and carp landing nets became available at very affordable prices and Neville Fickling called to ban the gaff once and for all. By the 1980s I thought the war against the gaff and other cruel landing methods was well and truly won, sadly though it seems not.

Over the last ten years or so, a time coinciding with the advent of worldwide networking of fishing videos a lot of the early good work in pike conservation seems to have been completely undone. I have recently noticed a lot of anglers landing pike by lifting them out of the water by their eye sockets or by chinning them, again by lifting them bodily from the water supported only by their delicate gill covers.

Few people can enjoy watching angling videos more than us and there are few better ways of broadcasting the joys of our sport than by this medium. The problem is though that a lot of unbelievably bad practice is also broadcasted. For example, lifting pike from the water by their eye sockets, or by lifting them bodily by their gill covers as highlighted above. This constant exposure of bad practice subconsciously advertises and normalises these habits, especially to youngsters who have not had time to become aware of good practice. To illustrate just what can happen when fishermen choose to use the chin method of lifting pike from the water, please read on.

Just recently I watched in disbelief as I saw a young man lift his newly caught pike into the boat by the chinning method. It was a big pike, probably about twelve pounds and it protested by violently shaking its head in panic. As this happened our hapless friend lost grip and a large treble hook went straight into his thumb. Fortunately, he managed to snip the barb off the hook and freed his thumb by forcing the hook back through the same way it entered. The pike fell to the bottom of his fibre glass boat which was now covered from the blood which was gushing from his badly lacerated thumb. The smooth plastic boat hull became so slippery he could not even stand up and he fell awkwardly into the hull of his boat. His coat and trousers were thus covered in blood, and he had to be rushed to hospital as his thumb refused to stop bleeding.

Barrie Rickards told me an even worse story about a young man who also lifted a big pike by the chinning method and as the pike jumped in panic both his hands became handcuffed to a big pike still frantically thrashing around to get loose! All this is the stuff of nightmares, yet the chinning method of landing pike it is being broadcasted on a global scale. There are many other even worse practices being circulated which could fill a whole chapter in themselves. In the meantime, all we can do is report these mal practices and try to get them taken down. What worries me is that all this can be seen by the anti-angling brigade who could easily use these examples to help ban our sport. There certainly are many people who would like to ban angling so its best we watch out for the offenders and 'Educate' them before they cancel out all the good conservation work, we have achieved over the past hundred years or so. Yes, modern social platforms are a wonderful thing, but in the wrong hands they can unintentionally broadcast awfully bad practices.

Back to northern river pike, it is important to realise that by using the correct equipment it is possible to land big fish safely and return them back to the water unharmed in a safe and responsible way. We use three main different types of landing nets on the northern rivers, firstly a forty-two-inch triangular net which is big enough for any pike, and strong enough to lift a fifty-pound fish safely from the water. If only! This net was amazing value at only thirty pounds.

The Authors three favourite landing nets all of them perfectly good for netting big river pike. They all have their differing strengths and weaknesses, but they are all equally good. The important thing is to use them!

It has a nice fine mesh, strong handle and pop out arms which enables one to disconnect the net from the handle in seconds. This is very handy if you need to weigh a big fish quickly. Just use the net as a weighing sling, no messing about. Of course, after weighing, the weight of the nets needs to be deducted from the total weight to get the actual pike weight. The important thing here is to work fast so you can return your pike to water quickly. We have a target of getting the fish back to the water in under two minutes, which is about the same time we can hold our breath without fainting. Two minutes is an exceptionally long time when you are holding your breath! This needs to be considered every time a pike is out of water. The fine mesh on this landing net can be a problem when treble hooks get enmeshed. For some anglers, the answer has been to use a net with wide mesh of about four inches diameter. We have used these in the past, but they split the rays of the pike's caudal fin which does permanent damage and makes them look very ragged. Also, the pike's caudal fin is where all its power is generated, a split caudal fin causes a serious loss of power and acceleration in the water. Imagine how bad it would be for us to enter a one hundred metre swimming contest but only allowed to swim with your fingers spread open, it would cause a serious loss of traction and acceleration, and for the pike acceleration is the key to its survival. For this reason, we prefer to use finer mesh sizes of about one or two centimetres as it is far gentler on the pike, and in any case, once the pike is returned you can untangle the hooks at your leisure once the bait has been cast out again. Should another run occur before the untangling has been done then a shout to one's fishing partner will always provide a second back up net. Yet another advantage of fishing with a good friend! One highly successful angler recently published an article in 'Pikelines' magazine explaining that he always carries two landing nets to cover the exact circumstances just described. This is a great idea and especially when fishing alone. It just goes to show you are never too old to learn from others which is one of the massive benefits of being a member of the 'Pike Anglers Club of Great Britain'.

There are several different types of landing nets available to the pike angler. The circular net with at least thirty inches diameter frame is extremely popular. The beauty of the round net is that it can be used instantly regardless of whether the pike comes in sideways, at an angle or straight. This is an important advantage, especially if you can see your hooks are holding the pike by a very precarious position. The downside of the round net is that it rarely folds down neatly and is hence more awkward for transporting. In contrast, the triangular net fold away beautifully in a very compact way, ideal for transport in the car or carrying for miles across water meadows. In recent years we have started to use the large rectangular landing net produced by Savage Gear, again this is a wonderful net with rubber netting and is delightfully light in weight yet has a strong extendable handle. This feature is valuable when fishing the northern rivers which often have high banks. In this situation the long strong handle is a real advantage.

There are different ways of landing one's quarry. My favourite method is to have the net ready sunk in the water about one foot deep. Then you can draw your pike slowly over the net. Once you are satisfied the full length of the pike is over the net all you need to do is lift gently but firmly and then, if it is a big lady and the net is fully round your prize just sigh a breath of pure relief! Of course, this approach can be used with triangular, round, or rectangular nets all to great effect. I have noticed that in Sweden and on the continent a slightly different netting technique is sometimes used. Here I have seen the anglers often draw the pike close in, then holding the draping net in their hand, suddenly jab the net frame into the water under the pike in an extremely fast scooping manoeuvre. Of course, to do this you need a partner to net your fish. I must say they do it so fast and efficiently it always seems to work very well, but to use this method you need a very stout frame to stay rigid during the lunging process. When fishing from a rowing boat the rectangular net seems perfectly stable for hanging the net over the side whilst resting the fish before getting the unhooking equipment organised. On reflection then, perhaps the rectangular net with its heavily engineered frame and very deep net is best for boat fishing. Whilst, for landing awkward big pike from the bank the round net is best. Whilst the versatility of the triangle net is great for both landing, weighing, and transporting your net. It all comes down to personal choice and the local function you have in mind. What I do know for certain is that all these large nets are perfectly suitable for northern river pike. The important thing is to possess one, always keep it with you and always use it to land your pike, small or large.

From time-to-time treble hooks can get caught in the landing net and become seriously snagged up. This is particularly true with some of the fine mesh nets used. The best way to avoid this problem is to buy one of the new green rubber coated nets, the mesh is spaced at about one-centimetre intervals making it fine enough to avoid damaging the fins of your catch, but wide enough to avoid serious tangles. These new nets are a little more expensive but well worth the money in the long run. Of course, using barbless hooks makes it much easier to remove your hooks from the net and If using single hooks, they are even less prone to getting snagged up.

Here an Upper Twenty has plenty of room to recover in a 42-inch Triangular Net. Head upstream.

The important thing here is to get the pike back into the water right away and clear your hooks from the net after the fish has been returned. If the tangle is particularly bad, I have no problems with cutting the net to remove the hooks. A hole in the landing net can easily be patched up with half a dozen half hitch knots using fishing line or cotton if you want to be posh. Mending nets is a thousand-year-old tradition with professional fishermen so we are in particularly good company doing the same.

On most reputable club waters, it is a set requirement of members to carry a large frame landing net for pike fishing. A lot of good clubs also require an unhooking mat too. Quite often though I have seen pike anglers fishing with their nets but seemingly too lazy to use them when they land their fish. Again, we suspect that these anglers are just unaware of the dangers surrounding them which is why we have tried to emphasise the importance of using nets in this work. It is a point of particular importance when river fishing due to the unpleasant reasons as mentioned in the introduction to this section. If the new wild swimmers of today knew what we know about our not quite so pristine rivers I think they may think twice about making the plunge!

Upon returning home a wet net is always a good sign of a successful day! To avoid an unpleasant smell in the garage its best to lightly disinfect the net in a bucket of water, then hang up the net in the green house to dry out completely before storing. In summer, the net will dry within a couple of hours, but in winter it may take a couple of days to dry into a safe and wife friendly format!

Gently does it! Nigel lands a good pike 'Textbook style'. Safe for the Pike and safe for the angler too. Note how Nigel keeps a low profile whilst netting his fish to avoid spooking it.

Finally, on steep riverbanks it is very wise to wear a life jacket especially in wet cold conditions. A steep grassy bank which in dry weather is safe can become a death trap when it is wet and slippery. Another good safety precaution is to carry a twenty-foot length of rope and peg it into the bank at the top and throw the rope down the slope into the riverside. Such a rope can be a real-life saver if you become trapped on a ledge with fast rising water. The rod and net can easily be thrown upwards onto the bank above. Then, with both hands free it is so easy to get the traction needed to climb out of trouble. Such places are best avoided though, but this can be difficult if you know the swim is full of big pike.

Reels Suitable for Northern River Pike

CHOOSE YOUR PLEASURE

As a boy of about ten years old my first reel was a small three-inch centrepin. It was a sturdy little reel made from heavy alloy and was quite solid and reliable. At that time most of my fishing was for minnows, perch, and wild brown trout. I knew I needed a spinning reel as soon as possible to start lure fishing for pike. All the best advice on the which reel to get was to "Just get the most expensive one you can afford". The cheapest option in Wrights tackle shop in Bedale was a small light alloy reel and it cost fourteen shillings; it took about six months to save up to get it so that is the one I chose. At the age of ten life just wasn't long enough to wait any longer despite all the good advice! I soon loaded my new reel up with twelve-pound line, made some wire traces from single strand alasticum wire and I was in business. Now I had the tackle to catch one of those Dennis Pye sized pike shown every week in Angling Times. By good fortune I caught my first ever pike on this new spinning reel on the first day out, it only weighed about five ounces, and I knew John Garvin's record pike weighed 53lb, so I was aware there was room for improvement! At least I had caught my first ever pike and it was marvellous, I have been catching pike on spinners ever since. I still used my centrepin for perch and trout fishing using worm, but as an active and restless youngster it was the spinning reel every time for pike fishing during this junior period. It would be many years before I came to realise that for selectively catching big pike, the underrated centrepin reel was in fact the superior tool for me.

There can be no doubt that the modern fixed spool spinning reel is a most efficient and user-friendly method for casting artificial lures and playing hard fighting fish. Firstly, and most importantly long-range casting is easy compared to the centrepin. Provided the line is loaded up to the edge of the spool long range casting becomes effortless. Secondly, for the novice, playing a big difficult fish on a spinning reel is made as safe as it could be. Once you set the slipping clutch at the correct drag level a running fish can take line off the spool without fear of line breakages and fish of any size can be played out with minimal risk. Even when your fish take off on those violent unstoppable runs the spool just pays out line at exactly the required rate, all one needs to do is make minor corrections to the drag with your finger if deemed necessary. For example, if a fish is running towards a sunken tree, then extra drag is necessary and appropriate finger pressure on the spool can be added to divert your fish away from the obstacle. Also, when netting your catch, the spool can be held firmly by just one finger on the spool to get the fish over the rim of the net. All these benefits and more add up to the reasons why spinning reels are the most popular choice on the market today.

Despite the multiple advantages of the spinning reel, there are still one or two qualities which are peculiar to the centre pin reel which for many anglers make them indispensable, and new models continue to be made. But why?

For me, the main pleasure of using the centrepin comes when you are playing big pike. As soon as one's pike makes that first energetic rush the power of the fish can be felt directly as you check the drum as its backwinds. With small jack pike the reel can be braked satisfactorily by the reel check which will have been turned on before striking. However, with bigger pike upwards of about seven pounds, the reel, if only braked by the check tends to overrun risking a serious bird's nest, this is easily avoided by gentle finger pressure on the rim of the reel to prevent over runs. When you do apply finger pressure on the running reel drum you get a definite sense of the sheer power of the fish. Then, most exciting of all, when you get an even bigger pike upwards of around sixteen pounds, then finger pressure on the rim of the reel becomes insufficient to make a proper brake. With bigger fish one needs to check the inertia of the spinning drum with the whole palm of your hand. If you relay on finger pressure only, the concentrated friction and heat will burn the skin from your finger making you realise like nothing else just how powerful your newly hooked fish is! All this activity makes the whole experience of playing and landing pike so much more vivid and exciting than with the super-efficient spinning reel. In short, it just makes the experience much more tactile and rewarding. At the end of the day reel choice is all about personal subjective preference. There is no right or wrong, I am just grateful we have such a wonderful range of options, in the end it is all up to you to choose your pleasure.

Choose your pleasure, this is mine. This photo shows a mid-twenty-pound pike taken on the Shakespeare Piranha reel. Catching big pike on the centrepin is so much more rewarding in our experience.

It seems fair to say all pike anglers have one thing in common, we all strive to catch a big one, and on most waters a ten or twenty-pound pike is a satisfying achievement and is still for most of us the catch of the year, or even the catch of a lifetime. The reality of pike fishing though is that most of the pike we catch will inevitably be between about three and ten pounds in weight. I find the centrepin reel gives even the smaller pike the chance to show its worth and hence more enjoyable to catch. I was really saddened recently when I heard one pike fisherman land a fifteen-pound pike and say out loud "Oh, it's only fifteen pounds" in a disappointed tone. If that fish had been caught on a centre pin reel, I am sure our fine friend would have been happier to land his very noteworthy catch. On the northern rivers pike in the twenty-pound category are few and far between, if you get one or two each year you are doing well. Therefore, it is important to get joy from the smaller fish too and that is the main reason I always like to fish with at least one traditional centrepin reel on the rod rests.

There is however a further reason why the centrepin can be advantageous, especially when selectively fishing for big pike. It took me several years to realise that one of my biggest barriers to catching excessively big pike in the twenty-pound class was impatience and a misguided belief that the more area covered the more and bigger pike I would catch. This belief was partly fuelled by fishing articles written by authors who were more of the armchair theorist's club than experienced bank side anglers. The result was that I tended to move my pitch too often if I had not had a run for two or three hours. This meant that I would move all my rods, banging about on the bank to move lock stock and barrel to a new swim perhaps only three hundred yards away. I fully realise that rod hopping every hour or so is a respectable strategy for catching lots of pike and I have done it myself regularly and caught hundreds of jack pike as a result. Not twenty-pound pike though except for one occasion which I will relate later. We have found that to catch the bigger pike its best to choose your swim very carefully, bait up your chosen area, set out the rods and wait patiently until you secure one of those bigger fish. By moving on every hour or so you are effectively starting from zero on each new move. Yes, you may catch a bigger number of smaller fish by covering more ground, but generally you will miss out on the bigger more cautious twenty pound plus pike. This has been our experience anyway. I think it is a bit like the race between the hare and the tortoise where the tortoise wins the race...but by running slowly! In a strange way I think the centrepin reel helps you to fish more slowly, but and in so doing fish more thoroughly and effectively.

    Over the years in my role of Ripon Regional Organiser for the Pike Anglers Club I have had many friendly phone calls from anglers who typically proclaim. "I have been pike fishing on the Yorkshire rivers for over twenty years but never caught a pike over the magical weight of twenty pounds, please could you advise". All these anglers had perfect gear, good baits, and a good basic knowledge of river craft. What they did not have though was the self-confidence to settle into a swim, bait it up and just stick it out until the correct results materialise. I am pleased to say that most of those friendly souls now have a list of twenties notched on their rod butts, thanks to just a few simple adjustments in tackle and approach as fully covered in this guide.

    When fishing seriously for big pike I have found the centre pin reel has one perverse advantage over the fixed spool reel in that casting the bait into the right position is much more involved. You need to carefully pull the required amount of line off the reel before casting, and then position the bait exactly right where it will stay for perhaps two or three hours in a well baited position. This involves a few minutes care and attention. Therefore, once the bait is positioned correctly you are more than happy to just leave it to do its magic. In contrast, the fixed spool rod can be repositioned at the drop of your hat almost instantly, and because you can, you tend to do it. In this way one can scare the living daylights out of that big fish which was just contemplating your carefully prepared offerings.

Young pike anglers with only ten- or twenty-years' experience of pike fishing rightly regard themselves as highly experienced pike anglers. However, twenty years pike fishing is not a long time really. Yes, such an angler has a good basic knowledge, but a lot of what I know now makes me realise that when I was thirty, with only twenty seasons behind me, I was only just beginning to really learn. Now, at the age of sixty-six I can look back over the detailed angling diaries and pick out successful methods and patterns which have only just emerged over that long period. One thing which has emerged, is that most of my largest pike have been taken on the good old centre pin reels and I believe for the particularly good reasons just expounded.

I should add at this point that although we love our centrepin reels we also love our spinning reels too! For this reason, most of our pike fishing career we have fished one rod on centrepin and the other second rod with a spinning reel. In winter I normally start off the typical day with both rods fishing static dead baits. Then, if by mid-morning no runs have materialised, we will use the spinning reel to do a little mobile lure fishing to stimulate some interest with artificial baits around the dead baits. Then after say twenty minutes I will resume fishing with static dead baits with both rods. By using this approach, it is amazing how often pike can be coaxed to take the natural baits by I suspect being woken up by the passing spinners. In this way one **can** have your cake and eat it, that is, fish with both favourite reel types, after all we only live once! We have not mentioned using the bait casting reels, often known at this side of the Atlantic as multipliers. We do own three bait casting reels and love to use them for plug fishing in summer. We have caught River Ure pike up to sixteen pounds on those long summer evenings and I really enjoy using them for spinning and plug fishing.

This photo captures the excitement of the spinning reel which is matchless for lure fishing for pike. This makes them an indispensable part of our pike fishing repertoire.

Multiplying reels are very much in vogue now with the You Tube pike fishing broadcasters; not sure this is because they are sponsored to do so but they certainly are put to good use.

If you are about to purchase your first ever fishing reel, we suggest you buy the most expensive one you can afford! My first reel which I bought for fourteen shillings did not last long at all, so I had to buy a new one after only about twelve months, if I had just saved up a bit longer, I could have bought one which would have lasted for years and in the long run would have worked out much cheaper. There are dozens of wonderful spinning reels available from your fishing tackle shop, the bait runner type reels are incredibly good for static dead baiting. I have a pair of Mitchell electronic reels which my boss at work bought me on my fiftieth birthday over a decade ago, they have an audible alarm as well as a flashing red light as a bite alarm which is perfect for bait indication for both day and night fishing. Modern spinning reels are like modern cars, they are built so well it would be difficult to make a bad choice. Remember though that the bait runner type reels with extended spools are more for fishing with static baits, whilst those tagged up as spinning reels are better suited for continual casting of lures when seeking out for pike over a large area. My advice here would be to buy both types, they are wonderful to use and if well maintained they will last for years. I still own a beautiful sleek black Mitchell 300, one of the original ones with an attractive green handle. Norris gave it to me before he sadly died, it still works well, and it even came with a match spool in a black case for light fine diameter lines. I only use Norris's reel now and then; I do not want to wear it out so for everyday use I have a modern mid range Ninja spinning reel. I love this reel as it has a lovely sleek black and silver finish with a striking red spool. It is quite a solid reel weighing 0.42 kilograms of aluminium and just like my first ever spinning reel has frontal drag which is second nature to me.

There are also some lovely centre pin reels available on the market too. The most modern versions are wonderfully crafted with highly decorative spokes, ideal for pike fishing and available in a good range of prices. My most expensive centre pins are the two Allcock Aerial reels which again Norris kindly left me. One is an old large version owned by Norris's father Tom; this is the very reel which was used when they landed their 56lb Yorkshire record pike on the River Ure at Tanfield. The second is the black Allcock Aerial purchased by Norris for his own use. This reel is featured in the 1966 Allcocks Anglers Guide and is on sale for 127 Shillings plus 21 Shillings purchase tax! I have included a photo of this black Aerial next to a twenty plus pound Pike I caught on it. That was before I realised how valuable these Allcock reels were. Indeed, my two vintage reels are together worth well over £ 1,000. Now I only wheel them out for special ceremonial occasions! I believe the Allcock Aerial reels mark the peak of precision reel manufacturing in Britain and they are in great demand, even for people with no angling interest but rather for their solid investment value. For me they are a reminder of my friendship with one of Yorkshires finest anglers. I would not sell my pair of Aerials for anything, some things in life are much more important than money!

The main 'Workhorse' of my centre pin collection is my trusty Shakespeare Piranha centrepin. To date I have caught well over fifty twenty-pound pike in various rivers and well over half of them have been taken using the Piranha centre pin reel. I have also caught literally hundreds of double figure pike on it too, so it has certainly proved its worth as a big fish reel. I continue to use it even though the ratchet brake is just about worn smooth, and the central brass pin is heavily worn. Yes, it does wobble a bit now, but so do I, so I am not about to complain. Provided I regularly grease the pin it still works well! The drum of this reel is quite wide with a diameter of over four inches giving good line retrieval speeds which is handy if ever the pike suddenly runs towards you unexpectedly. However, most big pike run away, and this is where the fun starts. Just about every twenty plus pound pike taken on this reel has really tested the reel and operator to the extreme with quite dramatic recollections of long truly searing runs where I have had to carefully break the drum with the palm of the hand. It is difficult to describe the sheer force generated by a big running twenty pounder on a centre pin reel. It is both unnerving and extremely exciting at the same time. It is easily ten times more exciting than playing a big fish on the fixed spool reel which does all the work for you. I can always tell by the sheer inertia if it is a twenty or not, the sheer force is so impressive, every single time! Another thing I love about my Shakespeare reel is that when casting you can take the drum off and attach it to a forward-facing pin which enables you to cast any distance just as you do with the spinning reel. My only regret about this reel is that I did not buy two whilst they were still available in stock. I do not know who invented this reel, but whoever they were its 'Hats off' to them, they really knew how to put a good reel together. From memory I purchased this reel in about 1993 in Ripon and I have never seen them for sale before or since.

Another lower twenty-pound pike taken when using the centrepin fishing reel. This reel has been used to catch well over half of the big river pike the author has taken on the Northern Rivers.

For some reason I seldom see anyone using the centre pin reels for pike fishing these days. That to me is a great pity, but at least the reader of this will get some idea of how good they are. It is true that some of the most successful anglers from the past used them to great effect, not least the great Pike Angler Alfred Jardine himself. He had his own centre pin reel designed in his name and marketed accordingly so he was naturally a great advocate. I also know that Norfolk Pike Expert Dennis Pye was a remarkably successful centre pin exponent too and he caught 316 pike over the weight of twenty pounds on his local waters making him a legend his own lifetime. Dennis Pye had something else in common with Alfred Jardine too: both men shared huge pike catches which were so far ahead of their contemporaries they both became targets of malicious envy. In effect they became victims of their own success, a phenomenon common in all high-level sporting activities to this day.

Another mid twenty 'Pike on the Pin' This time taken on the legendary Allcocks Ariel reel, undoubtingly one of the finest centrepin reels ever made. This reel was given to me by my old friend Norris making it a priceless piece of tackle. The rod it is matched with is the famous mark four carp rod. A truly wonderful combination steeped in a rich angling heritage. This big twenty-pound northern river pike tested both rod, reel and angler to the very limit!

Rods Suitable for River Pike

A variety of different rods are needed for effective river piking so here we discuss some of the different qualities we look for to meet our specific needs on the riverbank.

As a boy of ten back in the mid-1960s my first fishing rod was a six-foot solid glass spinning rod with a solid wooden handle and a test curve of about half a pound. A lot of my early pike fishing was done on the River Swale which was full of jack pike and the occasional double figure fish. On this light rod a four-pound River Swale pike felt like a monster, catching pike on this rod was so exciting and each pike presented a fresh new challenge. Then I acquired a new seven-foot hollow glass spinning rod with a posh cork handle. This was a real luxury, and it was slightly stronger than my first rod but not much as the test curve was still only about one and a half pounds, yet it was and still is very robust and light to use. Owing to its sensitive nature it was a delight to play any sized pike on it, again even a small jack pike gave great sport in a very enjoyable way only possible on this kind of light tackle.

Then during Christmas 1967 at the age of fourteen Santa brought me a very special rod indeed: an ABU Atlantic 405 Salmon and Pike spinning rod made in Sweden. This was a superb rod capable of playing and landing pike of any size. It had a lovely cork handle, huge eye fittings designed for long range casting and screw lock reel fittings. Built from hollow glass it was and still is both light and strong. Now after over fifty years I have just recently caught another twenty-pound pike on this rod, and just as it said in the sales brief it was "Built for life". It certainly has kept its promise having lasted over half a century. I think if I were forced to use just one rod for the rest of my life, I would choose this rod as it has such good all-round capability. However, for casting large dead baits it is not quite strong enough, for this task I needed something with a bit more length, leverage, and backbone.

I purchased my first heavy duty pike rod in 1979. Designed by Fred Buller himself and crafted by Hardy's of Alnwick it was aptly named the Endrick. The River Endrick flows into Loch Lomond and has an important association in our shared angling heritage. It was here the famous Endrick

Pike Skull was found. This pike skull almost certainly came from a pike weighing a good fifty or even sixty pounds or more in its life. This skull is now displayed with full honours in the Kelvingrove museum in Glasgow. I measured the test curve of my Endrick rod at about three pounds, it can launch a ten-ounce dead bait to the horizon with ease. Fred's rod design was based on the philosophy that a sixty-pound pike has not been caught yet because no one used tackle strong enough to cope with such a big Pike. I fully bought into Fred's ideas and now I have the tool to do the job! Unfortunately, that longed for fifty-pound pike still eludes me but no matter, this strong eleven-foot rod has been ideal for heavy river piking and particularly helpful for persuading those big and very strong river pike out of those deep tree root swims which are so prevalent along our rivers. With the publication of Fred's Mammoth Pike book, it was perfect timing to produce a rod strong enough to handle such big pike. I have no regrets; Fred's rod has earned its keep on the riverbank over the last forty years and I still live-in hope. Indeed, the Yorkshire waters have produced pike well over the fifty-pound mark as recently as 2020 and the fifty plus pounder as described earlier by Norris Sturdy from West Tanfield. I just wish there was a huge skull to record the evidence of it in York Museum! Again, no matter as the full details of Norris's giant pike are finally documented in this book, better late than never and at least it was caught on rod and line.

Even Fred Buller's powerful Pike hunting rod did not fulfil all the requirements for a perfect river rod. What I was looking for was a much longer rod which could reach out over the river and trot floats down past over hanging willows without the float edging into the tree branches. Also, a rod which when held up on first contact had a much higher upward angle for 'Lifting' big fish upwards and out of the riverbed snag zone. To do this I built my own custom-made river rod. I acquired a strong fourteen-foot general purpose rod and removed the eye rings and replaced them with larger rings more suitable for pike fishing. When I first hooked a big pike on this new customised rod, I discovered it had a very progressive test curve. As the pressure increased the more powerful mid-section of the rod came into force with a test curve of about four pounds or more. This really is a very strong rod yet very forgiving at the same time. When you first hook a fifteen-to-twenty-pound river pike, especially in the early part of the season when they are still very active, the speed and acceleration of the first run can often lead to trouble if you are not ready for it. That dreaded first explosive rush which can sometimes continue for five or ten yards is largely absorbed by the progressive spring effect. This is very reassuring and allows a lot of force to be absorbed at least initially by the rod. It also allows a couple of seconds to double check the reel settings are correctly positioned. Best of all though, when stood up by the riverside with a fourteen-foot rod in hand the angle of line entry is very high indeed giving so much more control over a large wayward fish. There are certain reels which help even more in this process and in particular the direct drum pressure of the centre pin design as already recommended in the previous chapter.

As for the casting qualities of this extra-long rod there are also many mechanical advantages which come into play. Firstly, if an overhead cast is required then a half pound sardine can be cast very easily to the far bank, even on the lower Ure or Ouse which can be over fifty yards wide. On most rivers this is not even required though as a gentle underarm cast can reach halfway across the river. A simple quiet swing of the tackle is all that is needed. What is even more pleasing is the way you can float paternoster baits under willow bushes on the far side of the river. On some of my favourite pike hotspots on rivers like the Swale, Derwent, Nidd and Ure there are extensive willow bushes on the opposite banks which run wild for five hundred yards or more. Owing to their inaccessibility from the far side these areas are virtually untouched and make ideal pike holding areas. By using a large float held in place by a two-ounce flat lead paternoster a bait can be positioned craftily between willow bushes. Once the bait and tackle has been placed into the ideal position the long rod can be supported on a firm rod rest at an angle of about forty-five degrees. Thanks to the high position of the rod tip, and the fact it is already reaching well over the river, the line can be held above the central current almost directly to the float. This means the presentation will not be disturbed by floating debris catching on the line. With shorter smaller rods the line is unable to reach so far and hence becomes snagged up with those annoying clumps of weed and dead leaves which are a constant feature in any flowing water.

Another very pleasing quality of the longer rod is that you can trot dead baits downstream in a very effective way. Since the rod tip can be held well out in the river the float can be fished downstream in the current far enough out from the bank to keep the float out of the willows. The bait can be fished at a set depth just off the riverbed in a very enticing way. Furthermore, if the bait is not taken after trotting for half an hour or so then the bait can be stopped downstream just off the willows and just held in place by the rod tip in the right position. Again, the rod can be held firmly by two rod rests holding the tackle in place. If the riverbed is ten feet deep along the margins the bait can be fished in a horizontal position with a large single hook.

Figure 1 From left to right (1). A.B.U. Atlantic 405. Over 50 years old. Truly a 'Rod for Life' (2). Hardy built Endrick Pike Rod. Built to handle a 50lb Pike. (3). Home-made 14-foot river rod. Very lucky with over 25 twenties and counting. (4). A.B.U. Salmo seeker. Light travel rod for spinning. These are four very different rods each one with its own purpose.

I only possess one fourteen-foot river rod for pike fishing but on it I have caught almost half of my big pike over 20lb and literally hundreds of doubles. Whenever my fishing partner Nigel and I fish for pike together it is amazing how often out of four rods in action it is almost always the fourteen-foot rod which gets the most and biggest pike. This has become so apparent we have christened this rod 'Magic Matilda'. It has even become a long running joke that as soon as we get a run we say. "Oh, its Matilda again" and have a good laugh as it is so very often true. The fact is that this favourite old rod, which was bought for next to nothing, has so many small advantages over the other rods which results in catching more fish. Hence its winning qualities.

On reflection and when I see those expert match anglers bagging up on their very long fishing poles it all makes sense. The long pole enables the match anglers to ground bait with precision exactly where they are fishing. Then they can place their baits quietly in exactly the right spot. Yes, it is all about presentation and that is where the longer rod can be more effective. You may not realise the benefits over a short couple of weeks or even a couple of years but in the long run the benefits show up a clear pattern of success and this is a big advantage when you have years of experience to call on. It is the kind of thing you cannot often learn from reading books, but more a matter of something you learn from hard won experience at the riverside, or by carefully reading old fishing diaries which record recurring successful practices.

As already mentioned earlier I recently retired from work after over forty years working in sales in the fast-moving consumer goods sector. Working in this high-pressure environment has been likened to living in a bath full of sharks, a very appropriate simile and especially for one who spends his spare time fishing for pike! Before I left my boss explained the company normally buy a carriage clock as a final present for retirees. However, as he knew I was a fisherman he very kindly gave me the option of buying fishing tackle instead, as he knew I would get better use from it. I decided to get a good spinning rod for pike and chose the ABU Ten foot 'Salmo Seeker' which is a four-piece thirty-ton graphite rod with a lovely AAA cork handle. I have already field tested this lovely rod several times and I can confirm it is a very good rod for pike spinning. For one thing it is incredibly light in weight and yet has a strong crisp action. Using an ABU Killer plug for bait I had a strike from a twelve-pound pike which really put my new rod under testing pressure. The light weight of the rod combined to its latent strength proved a very satisfying combination of qualities. I can only describe it as the pure delight of playing a pike on the light spinning rods I used as a boy and mentioned at the beginning of this chapter yet with a seemingly hidden back up strength of the powerful Endrick rod produced by Hardy's of Alnwick. The rod also came in a classy looking Cordura Tube, ideal protection for this very light rod and ideal for anglers who travel a lot for their pike fishing.

Rods suitable for river pike fishing therefore come in a whole range of options from light spinning rods mainly for spinning for pike in summer running to heavy dead baiting rods used mainly in the colder winter months. We also like to spin for pike in winter, so rarely go out without the ABU Atlantic spinning rod as a third rod. We normally set up the heavy dead bait rods in the early morning then if nothing has happened by say 11.00 am, we have a cast around with the spinners. This often results not in a take on the spinner itself, but often prompts a run on one of the dead bait rods, usually on Magic Matilda! This is something that I found Barrie Rickards did regularly when we fished together in winter. We both instinctively knew why we did it and never even discussed it really, but the idea was to just get the pike moving about a bit, not so much that they had the energy to chase after spinners, but rather to just nudge them towards our baits where they could indulge their appetites in their own slow motion winter fashion. On the Northern rivers I would say spinning for pike in summer is about twenty to one times more effective as opposed to winter. Therefore, spinning for pike in winter is just about enabling us to dead bait more effectively. It may seem illogical, but it works and that is all we need to know.

I probably do about ninety per cent of my summer spinning using the trusty ABU Atlantic spinning rod, as already described this rod is a medium strength rod yet with plenty of backbone to tackle a twenty pounder if required. However, just now and then I love to go back to my boyhood days and use my very light six-foot spinning rod. The excitement of getting a take on this light rod really is so much more dramatic. On rivers like the Swale or Ouse I love to fit in a few evening sessions in July or August and catch small pike in the extensive marginal weeds. Most of these pike are just three to five pounders but they hit the baits so hard they almost knock you off balance. Then as you are playing these on the light rod they shoot off into deeper water as if they were twenties. Just now and then a big double comes along and really gets the pulse racing. On one memorable occasion I had an eighteen pounder on my tiny rod, at first, I thought I was in serious trouble, but my line was twelve-pound mono of the best quality and after about five minutes of very serious rod bending negotiations, she eventually succumbed to the waiting net. All this brings back an interesting talk I had with my fishing friend Barrie Rickards. Barrie surprised me a little when he said that if he had to make a list of items of fishing tackle in rank order of priority then choice of rod would come low on his list. He went on further to say that provided you have a good reel loaded with good quality mono you could easily land a big pike effectively even if your rod had snapped! he was obviously talking from long experience, and I fully understood and agree with his argument.

Perhaps I should not encourage the reader to take up my self-indulgent fishing methods but just now and then it is good to regress using tiny baits on light tackle. On such tackle on a warm summer evening, I often catch at least half a dozen small pike on light rods, and it makes a very welcome change to the more challenging specimen hunting approach where you may only get one or two pike each session, even though the results are more productive in terms of sizeable fish. As a precaution though, and in the interests of safety the golden rule should be never use fishing line below twelve to fifteen pounds breaking strain.

When fishing for big fish and using big baits, one must use strong tackle with fifteen pounds breaking strain line to allow a margin of error for when the unexpected can happen. All the rods shown in the photograph are more than capable of handling any big river pike and certainly have proved their worth. Magic Matilda alone has been my most successful pike rod with over twenty-five pike over twenty pounds in weight to her credit, a very lucky rod perhaps? Probably, but over a long period of time I think there has been more than just luck in her favour. Some rods make their own luck by design and Magic Matilda is one of them.

Handling and Unhooking River Pike

The secret to easy handling and unhooking river pike is to strike early when you get a run. In this way the hooks will almost always be near the front of the pike's jaws and hence easy to see and quickly remove. The second important thing to do is have the unhooking mats and tools laid out ready as soon as you start fishing. In this way your pike will not be flapping around on the bank whilst you are looking for lost forceps. It has always been our stated aim to get the pike back into the water in under two minutes. On many occasions you do not need to remove pike from the water at all, especially when the hooks can be seen on the edge of the jaw, in this case just unhook the fish whilst still under water whilst resting in the safety of the landing net.

It is good to get in the habit of always carrying a spare set of forceps in your jacket pocket. By having the forceps 'ever ready' it is easy to remove hooks while pike are still in the net and saves the time-consuming job of climbing back up the riverbank to get your tools. Quite often when I net a big pike for my fishing friends, I quickly unhook them in the net to save the fish a trip onto the riverbank. When it comes to handling and unhooking pike less is always best so the fish can be returned as soon as possible.

With the best will in the world though there are times when the hooks go well into the mouth cavity. When this happens simply lay out the fish on the unhooking mat and open its mouth by gently inserting a hand under the gill cover and pulling down an inch or so, this simple movement often causes the pike to involuntarily 'Open up'. Once the mouth opens one can usually see the hook hold and quickly remove the hooks using a set of nine-inch forceps or long nosed pliers.

Open Wide please! This pike involuntary opens its mouth as the writer lifts gently under the chin. The main weight of the pike is held on the unhooking mat below. By using forceps or long nosed pliers the hooks can be removed in seconds. In this case the fish was hooked on a size two single hook. The shank can be seen in the top right of the photo. This hook was removed in under two seconds. The pike was back in the water in under two minutes.

From time to time the hooks may be down the throat and out of sight. Do not panic, this can easily be resolved. In this case when the hooks are out of sight one needs to work from behind the gill cover. If you have a friend with you just ask them to pull the trace very gently and slowly from the mouth entrance. Slowly, the shank of your offending treble will come into view and at the same time at least one hook point which is clear of the throat tissues. When you see the clear hook carefully clamp the forceps onto it and once clasped, then ask your friend to slightly reduce the pull pressure on the trace. This slight relaxation of the trace will help you to invert the treble. At this point, and once the treble has been inverted, the treble will simply pop out harmlessly causing no harm whatsoever. During these more involved unhooking procedures I prefer to use forceps, you never need to apply much force to remove hooks and forceps are more sensitive and gentler in this procedure. The key is to push gently towards the mouth opening from behind via gill covers. Very little pressure is needed to 'pop' out the hooks in a completely harmless way. Remember pike are constantly swallowing sharp objects like perch fins and crayfish and only yesterday a 12lb river Swale pike coughed up a set of razor-sharp claws from a par digested crow, so they are not at all unfamiliar with very sharp objects puncturing their throat cavity. After a few years pike fishing one does become something of a skilled surgeon through practice. However, this latter procedure only happens possibly once every three years or so provided you strike right away it will be a very infrequent procedure. When handling pike in this way it is helpful to wear a glove on the left hand to hold your pike carefully. This protects the vulnerable hand which is holding the pike under the jaw. The right hand needs to be free to allow full dexterity for hook removal using the long-nosed forceps.

We strongly recommend and endorse the use of unhooking mats; such items protect pike on their short visit to the bank. In some of the pike photos in this book pike can be seen laying on soft grass. These photos predate the modern practice of using mats and whilst the pike concerned were returned completely unharmed, we no longer photo pike without a protective mat. The photos are still used here to illustrate the specific context, but we would like to make it clear that we fully endorse the modern more pike friendly mats and aids available to the modern anglers.

This 22lb River Pike is shown resting safely on a modern proprietary unhooking mat. This one is a roll up model and is compact for carrying on long range missions. It can also serve as a very comfortable cushion to sit on when not in use!

There are now many unhooking mats available ranging from simple roll up mats to more elaborate trough like structures which contain the pike in a secure frame. If your pike starts to flip around a gentle reassuring hand over the middle of the pike will often calm it down so you can start to remove the hooks. Another very good method of controlling a jumping pike is to use the Martin Gay method. Martins' favourite method was to straddle the pike on the mat using his legs as a holding tunnel to support his fish in all directions. This really is a helpful tip with wild river pike which by their very nature tend to be very energetic on the bank. By laying the pike on its back one hand can be used to hold the lower jaw open whilst the other can remove the hooks. Again, I believe Martin's method is particularly helpful with wild river pike as if they start to flip around, they are safely but firmly restrained in all directions. When they realise, they are safely held they tend to calm down allowing the hooks to be quickly and humanely removed. With big pike I always use Martins 'Leg Tunnel' method with the pike on the soft mat and my aging knees cushioned on the mat too! Modern mats are very slippery, and without supporting the pike they can and do flap all over the place.

When removing plugs and spinners from the pike's jaws, we prefer to use light long nosed pliers as a gripping tool because the hooks used on artificial baits tend to be quite large when compared to baiting rigs. As such slightly more pressure is often required to remove the hooks quickly. For this reason, we always carry both pliers and lighter forceps on every fishing trip. Never use too much force though, I have seen some anglers being rough in their rush to unhook pike. If you hold the hook and push down slightly to undo the barb, hardly any force is required at all.

As mentioned at the start of this section it is good practice to set up the unhooking mat as soon as you arrive to fish. On the corner of the mat one can place the various tools at the ready. It also looks good if the river warden comes to check your tickets, on several occasions being fully prepared in advance like this has really impressed our local wardens, so much so they do not bother to check our permits or rod licences. In effect, actions speak louder than words, it shows you are fishing responsibly and with care. When fishing the lower lengths of our rivers there are many places where levees have been built along the riverside. Some of these are fifteen to twenty feet deep and the bank slopes at an angle of about forty-five degrees. On such banks it is impossible to use the unhooking mats, so it is best to unhook the pike whilst still in the water. If the water is not accessible for safe unhooking, then the pike can be lifted in the landing net and unhooked on the slope. To do this effectively though all the unhooking tools need to be kept in pockets at the ready. If deep hooked then a journey to the top flat part of the levee is the only option, but only if essential as it is often a struggle to reach the bank top. This is especially so when you only have one arm available as the other is holding the pike. Again though, an early strike usually ensures the hooks can be removed easily which immediately eliminates having unhooking difficulties of any kind.

Unhooking tools at the ready! We always aim to return our pike in under two minutes flat. It is a great help to have all the tools laid out on the unhooking mat in advance as illustrated here. Unhooking glove for the left hand to hold pike under the jaw leaving the right hand free to do the delicate unhooking work. Wire cutters helpful to quickly free wire entangled in net. Forceps for gently lifting out the hooks and long nosed pliers helpful for unhooking lures. Speedy unhooking is essential if we want our pike to live long enough to grow to a good size.

We generally return small single figure pike back to the river to swim free straight away. With bigger pike a quick photo may be required.

A very large river pike like this (48 inches long) is best retained in a large loose carp sack where it can stretch out in a comfortable posture whilst the camera is set up. Note how well the pike's markings blend in perfectly with the winter sunlight.

In this case the pike can be retained in the water's edge within the safe folds of the landing net whilst the camera is set up to take a few photos. With very large pike upwards of twenty pounds the landing net is too small for this to work effectively. Therefore for very big pike, which can be literally four feet long, we prefer to use a large carp sack which allows more space and is less restricting. This should only be done in winter though when water temperatures are low making it safe to hold pike safely in the margin. Again, when taking photos we always get the pike returned in under two minutes. With modern cameras you can take a dozen or so photos within thirty seconds provided you are well prepared to work quickly.

Having researched the progress and status of pike fishing in this book we are fully aware of how badly pike were regarded and treated only a matter of sixty years ago, within our living memory in fact. Therefore, whenever river wardens ask to check if we have the required unhooking mats for pike fishing it really gives one a sense that we have succeeded in the fight for pike to be rehabilitated into the modern world of Angling. It is truly amazing what progress has been achieved. We also feel it is important for all anglers, especially younger ones, to realise this and be proud of how far we have come thanks to generations of anglers who have literally ploughed in millions of pounds of cash in the cause of conservation and thus have won anglers the reputation of being the original guardians of the waterside. Recent television programmes in Britain portray anglers as a bunch of cranky individuals and make great comedy out of the whole sport. I don't think there is any malicious intent in what they produce, but this superficial coverage is not helpful for the public image of angling and always falls short of giving fishermen the true credit they deserve in the constant struggle to keep our rivers clear of pollution.

Float Fishing and Float Making

HOW TO FISH EFFECTIVELY IN OUR SNAG RIDDEN NORTHERN RIVERS

The northern spate rivers of England all have one thing in common, they can suddenly change from quiet pools of tranquillity to raging torrents of water carrying tons of tree branches, logs and boulders downstream. Then, as the flood subsides all the debris are just as suddenly deposited along the whole watercourse. Some of these logs become so stuck in the riverbed they remain for years as permanent obstructions. Most though are scattered at random along the full river length and can often be seen building up on bridge buttresses forming temporary log jams. These only last until the next major flood sweeps them further downstream where they are all finally swallowed up in the Humber estuary and washed out to sea on the tide.

As a result of this on-going process most of the northern rivers are festooned with snags which can make fishing very tricky and expensive if you use the wrong tackle. Thankfully, the careful use of well-designed floats and purpose-built rigs enables one to fish safely despite the ever-present obstructions. In the few places where the riverbed appears clear of snags, it is probably not, so it is still best to err on the side of caution and use a float to prevent your baits drifting into the nearest snag. It is best to fish defensively to avoid losing both fish and tackle.

One thing we are sure of is that river pike love to hide next to sunken logs and tree branches, it is part of their survival technique, they even look like sunken logs in the water, and they seem to know it too. Why do we suspect this? The answer is that when sunken logs lie parallel in line the pike often lie in line with them to blend in. What better way to catch an off-guard surface feeding trout than laying perfectly still on the riverbed, right next to a log and blending in with the natural underwater scene. Then, when the time is right, accelerate upwards in a flash, grab the prey which may be a duckling a grayling or even a small hunting pike which continually feature high on the menu of our bigger river pike.

Pike love to haunt the snag ridden riverbeds. All our Northern Rivers are festooned with waterlogged tree branches and sometimes whole trees. A pike float is the best way to keep the line safely above these obstructions.

Knowing then that pike love to haunt snag ridden areas as 'Living Logs' we need to become expert at fishing in snag ridden waters and have the tackle to fish safely in areas known to be littered with submerged obstacles, but not so snag ridden that it becomes reckless to fish. There is nothing worse in pike fishing than to be snapped off by a pike losing floats and tackle into the bargain. A degree of common sense needs to be applied to distinguish between a safe workable swim and one which is not safe. For example, your swim must have adequate access where you can land a big difficult fish in safety for the sake of both for you and your quarry. One needs room around you and above you to allow your rod to function properly and be able to reach the water safely with your net.

A good-sized float combined to a one-ounce ledger can anchor a float fished dead bait in position all day without any danger of snags but once a run is registered it is essential to pull your newly hooked pike upwards and away from danger. Once hooked the pike's natural tendency will be to make a deep sweep of the riverbed to snag the line on the nearest available obstacle. Fortunately, superior quality fishing line with at least fifteen pounds breaking strain is safe enough to guide almost any pike out of trouble and safely into the awaiting landing net. It does though require a high degree of skill and robust rods and reels are particularly helpful. Modern braid lines can be used which can have breaking strains of sixty pounds or more. By using such strong line, a snagged hook can be pulled out of any log, sometimes by even straightening the hooks. There are many good anglers who use nothing else and swear about using braids. My own personal choice is fifteen to twenty pounds high quality mono line and again, the hooks can be pulled out, but only as a last resort.

A useful range of popular floats including the famous 'Fishing Gazette' on the left and a selection of slider floats.

There are better ways of retrieving snagged gear which I will cover later in this chapter.

If the worst does happen and you do get a pike which runs into a snag it is best to just surrender to your pike and let the tackle go slack. This action is completely counter intuitive and takes some discipline but never just pull to break. If you let the line go slack your pike will certainly swim out on its own accord after five minutes or so thus allowing you to make contact again once it is free. It may take a few minutes for the pike to 'back out' of the snag, so one needs to be patient, but they usually free themselves in their own time. This has happened to me several times, including with one very big pike of 24lb which I was particularly grateful to land, but it was only achieved by knowing the right thing to do. If on the other hand your dead bait set up does become snagged on a log on its own, again just leave it, only this time for an hour or two. It is amazing how often a pike will come along and snatch your dead bait and hooks from the snag. This sounds too good to be true, but it does often work, and it is the hallmark of an expert angler to convert a serious snag up problem like this into an opportunity to net a big pike. Such a turn round of events deserves a good write up in the angler's diary, or something good to tell your friends about over a pint! It may sound like the tallest of tall fishing stories, but that is exactly what makes it so special, only it is not a tall story but a true one.

On a typical northern spate river, a good purpose-built pike float is one of the most important pieces of equipment in your whole tackle set up. A good pike float will hold your line safely above the snags all day making fishing perfectly viable and risk free. To serve this function I have always used a secret custom-built cork pike float specially designed for fishing snag ridden swims. As can be seen from the photo illustration these floats are ordinary looking egg-shaped designs, yet they are anything but ordinary. They are made in varied sizes ranging from about an inch in size for shallow water fishing with small baits up to over two inches in size for fishing large baits in water over fifteen to twenty feet deep.

These sliding floats are 'Snag Friendly' and are specially designed for fishing where obstacles may exist. They are made in assorted sizes but are all designed to serve the following functions:

1. They are slider floats so can be fished at any depth depending upon where you set the stop knot on the reel line.
2. They most importantly hold the line above and away from potential snags.
3. They function as bite indicators showing movement as soon as the bait is taken.

4. Normally set over depth they show which direction the pike is moving; we normally strike in opposite direction as run develops.
5. Specially designed to allow float retrieval. The four-millimetre gape on the lower attachment of the float ring allows it to be retrieved if the hooks are truly snagged up. This latter feature makes the float truly snag friendly.

The fifth point needs further explanation as to how it works. On normal sliding floats as soon as you pull for break on a snag the slider float is freed and floats downstream and unless you have a high-speed motor launch to chase after it your float is lost forever. This special float design can be retrieved though by the following method. Firstly, once you realise the tackle is firmly snagged and all efforts have failed to retrieve it just do as follow. Firstly, pull the reel line as tight as possible but without breaking it. At this stage, your float will submerge out of sight and when it slides up to the stop knot release the line, so it catapults back towards the float. Since the float ring aperture is large at four millimetres the stop knot will be forced to fly straight through the float ring. Once this has happened the stop knot will be below the float allowing the float to return towards the rod tip where it can be retrieved when it comes within reach of the landing net.

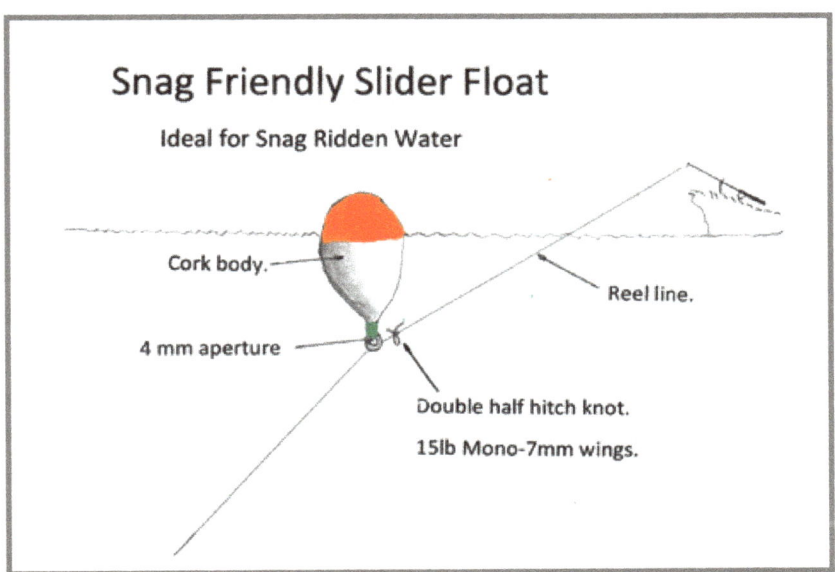

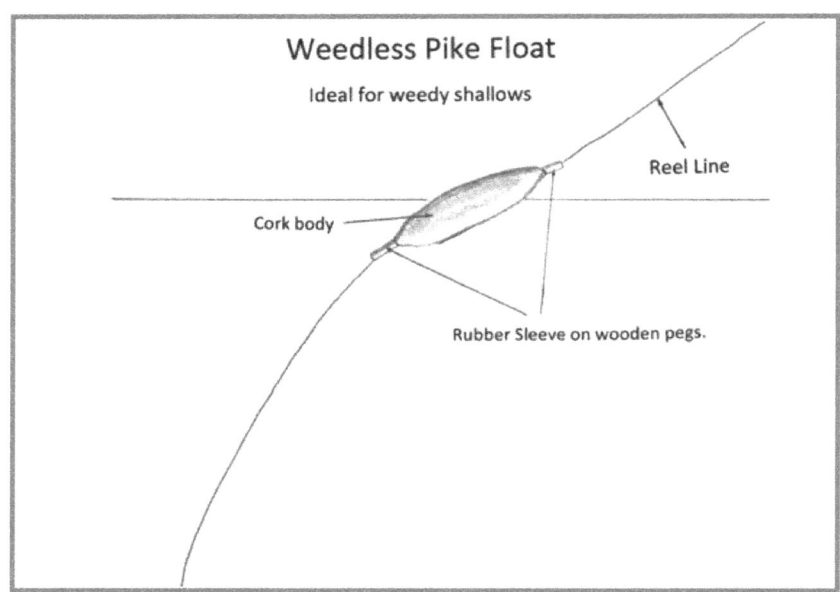

The 'Snag Friendly Float' above can be made in a variety of sizes, larger for deep water, smaller for shallows. Using this float, you never need to lose a float ever again. Below shows the weedless streamlined pike float. This float can be fished right amongst the shallow weeds with no fear of becoming snagged up.

Once the line is tight then suddenly release the line so the stop knot will be happily below the float allowing it to run back up the line.

During this straightforward process, the line must be kept slightly below the water to allow the buoyancy of the float to move it back towards you. This method works every single time and prevents losing your much treasured floats. Finally, an important note on the stop knot. The method I have used for over fifty years is a very simple one. Just clip off about two inches of fifteen-pound reel line and tie this short piece of line onto the main line, usually for me about fifteen feet from the terminal wire trace. Simply tie two tight half hitch knots to the line tightly. Then trim the stop knot so each length is about five to ten millimetres long. These dimensions are rigid enough to prevent the knot getting through the float ring when fishing, but flexible enough to be 'catapulted' through when you are snagged up. The double half hitch knot more commonly known as the granny knot allows for this to be achieved. We never use other kinds of stop knot though as it would catch in the ring every time preventing float retrieval.

Many of my home-made creations are over thirty years old and have a lot of sentimental value. I can remember the famous river piker the late John Sidley saying many of his pike floats were like "Old Friends" to him. I fully understand his sentiments, several of my floats have been instrumental in catching dozens of pikes including some very big and memorable specimen's. As John Sidley said, these are more than floats they are treasured items of sentimental value. I can also remember the author of one of my favourite pike books 'Pike Fishing' by Tom Seccombe Gray expressing similar thoughts advising us to take care of our floats and they will last much longer and be in with you at the end. Very fond comments indeed! The message is very clear here that our floats as well as other items of tackle do hold a special place in our hearts and the act of making them from scratch is very enjoyable in so many ways. In effect a hobby within a hobby.

To the best of my knowledge the home-made 'Snag friendly' float just described cannot be obtained commercially so this is another advantage of making home-made floats, you can tailor make them to suit your local unique fishing needs and gain huge satisfaction which comes from catching big pike on your own creations. There is a further advantage too in using cork floats. Recently, Sir David Attenborough has highlighted the severe problems caused by plastics collecting in the sea. By making our own cork floats we can choose to be more intelligent and mindful by using biodegradable materials such as cork. There are millions of anglers around the world so we can have influence and a move in the right direction. Indeed, as we have already seen in the opening chapters of this book, the angling community set out as the forerunners of the modern conservation movement, so it is important for us to stay in the leading vanguard and not be displaced by so many relative newcomers to the cause. Non angling newcomers who incidentally have contributed virtually nothing except verbal hype to conservation. In contrast, as we have seen from our study of John Eastwood and the A.C.A. The angling community have ploughed in countless millions of pounds of hard-earned cash towards creating and maintaining clean rivers over the last seventy years and more. The clean rivers we enjoy today are the legacy of all those millions of anglers who went before us and devoted time money and energy into the cause of conservation.

MAKING YOUR OWN CUSTOM BUILT PIKE FLOATS FROM CHAMPAGNE CORKS

Most of my floats are made from Champagne corks which are big enough from which to make a decent quality fishing float. For many years I have collected them from friends and family, and whenever I attend a party or works function, I always keep the wine and Champaign corks to supply my tiny float fishing operation in my garden shed. I will never forget returning from Miami airport with two Champagne corks in my trouser pockets. When I tried to get through the check in at the airport, I was stopped abruptly by a tall lady police officer. "What have you got in your pocket?" she asked. She had a loaded gun on her hip, so I thought it best to play safe! I humbly apologised and showed her my two corks, fortunately she saw the funny side and let me through without further delay. I was particularly glad to get back to the relative safety of my home and the unique tranquil atmosphere which can only be found in an English garden shed!

If you decide to make yourself a float collection it is best to start collecting your corks as soon as possible. Champagne corks are in a compressed deformed state when they are first 'popped' and it takes about a year for them to relax into their normal shape. If you make a float from a newly opened cork it will end up a slightly different shape to its original design. It will still work of course, but the shape will be odd, and the paint will also crack. It is therefore important to leave them in your float shed for a year or two to completely 'loosen up' before shaping them into your pike floats.

My good friend Nigel Winter caught the tackle making bug from me over thirty years ago and as an engineering buff he now makes precision-built floats on his lathe. Nigel did offer to make all my floats on his lathe, but I politely declined his offer. Pike floats are too personal for that and I would not want to miss the fun of making them. All my floats are made from ordinary tools which can be found in every home including the following.

Firstly, it is helpful to have a small shed where you can practice your skills without being distracted by the outside world. My private sanctuary is a small twelve by eight wooden shed my wife bought for me just before I retired from work at the age of sixty-six. (This may be a diplomatic way of saying she does not want me under her feet all the time!) It is now affectionally known as the Float Shed and is a place of great solace and calm! It is also nice if you have some sort of a chair to sit on and a flask of coffee and biscuits. Even if it is cold and raining outside you can focus completely on the job in hand. It is not as good as fishing of course, but not far off and the tackle you can make is perfect preparation for the fishing days ahead. Try to remember that tackle tinkering is not a chore to be rushed but a piece of artistry which is worth doing just for the pure pleasure it brings. To start off though you need a few basic tools to work with as follows. A Stanley Knife, or a very sharp pen knife. A few pieces of very rough sandpaper and a sanding block. Also, some fine sandpaper to use after the coarse sandpaper to give a much smoother finish. You also need a bag of skewer sticks which will last a lifetime. These can be bought for next to nothing from any good grocers' shop and of course a few small lengths of twenty-eight-pound wire and a spool of cotton thread. A small tin of talcum powder and a tin of yacht varnish and a range of tiny Humbrol paint tins in your chosen colours. After a whole lifetime float making, I now have a collection of at least fifty small tins of Humbrol paints ranging from bright red to olive green, they are so collectable!

It is helpful to keep all your float making equipment in a bag or a box as shown here. Champagne corks need to be stored away for a year or more to allow them time to relax into their natural shape. Float making is a very enjoyable activity, essentially a 'hobby within a hobby'.

For obvious logistical reasons I keep all my float making kit in one bag, this makes it easy to both start up and finish each session because to make a batch of say three floats together it is a multi-stage process where you need to re visit each stage after paints and varnish have had time to dry before moving on to the next stage.

The first stage is to take a Champagne cork and cut it into a rough egg shape using a Stanley Knife. Just whittle away the small pieces of cork taking care to cut away from yourself to avoid an accident. Do not rush and keep checking the emerging shape regularly so you can ensure it takes the correct form. Once you are happy with the overall shape, a process which will take about five to ten minutes, then you can move onto shaping with the very coarse sandpaper. This can be done with a sanding block to start with, but after a few minutes you can make a cone shape with the paper and sand the emerging float in a twisting circular movement. This part can be very satisfying as suddenly, your would-be float starts to look more like a float and less like a pinecone out of the wood.

Increasingly more circular sanding movements give the float even better symmetry and once you are happy with the general shape you can change to fine sanding to give an even finer finish. The next stage is to insert a four centimetre peg up into the float body from the lower point of the cork. Just leave about twelve millimetres protruding. To this peg whip on a short piece of 28lb plastic coated wire leaving a four-millimetre aperture at the base of the float (See photo). Take great care when inserting the peg through the float. No glue is needed, but it helps to sharpen one end of the peg to allow it pierce and enter the cork body. I also add several 'barbs' to the peg by cutting tiny upward grooves to secure each peg. Once the peg is in a firm position it will never come out, unless you use pliers and a lot of force. If for some reason your peg is slightly off centre this does not matter at all, in fact I have noticed that in fast water the off-centre peg helps to make the float ride the flow better giving the float a definite advantage for fishing in these conditions. The 'off centre peg' may look odd, but like the Lancaster bombers of World War two, these floats are built for function rather than form and there is nothing else to match them in the job they do. In short, they are simply a vital part of the tool kit.

The next step is optional, but if you want to give your float a glass smooth finish then just mix a little talcum powder with yacht varnish and paint it on all over the float in a thin layer. Next, hang the float upside down to dry for about two weeks. Once the varnish has dried completely then sand down with very fine sandpaper. A face mask should be used during all sanding stages to prevent dust inhalation. This smooth varnish/talc mixture not only smells good but also gives the float a very high-quality smooth finish, all ready for the most exciting part, the painting.

One of my favourite colours for pike floats is a white top for good visibility with a dark green lower half. This is the classic Victorian pikers colour combination and takes a lot of beating. Another favourite is a red top combined to a simple clear varnish covering of the actual cork on the lower body of the float. This idea came directly from the pages of Francis Walbrans Victorian book on fishing where he recommends this combination for his home-made grayling floats used on the Yorkshire rivers. I must admit to being very impressed with this combination, it has a classy look about it and the natural cork colours are ideal for any pike float. Another wonderful combination is an orange top with deep brown lower body. Again, an inexplicably lovely colour combination and so it goes on.

I find the painting part of the float making process the most satisfying and once painted I hang the floats up suspended on a fishing line to dry out in the float shed. The final stage after painting is to give one last final coat of clear yacht varnish to finally fix and protect the paint from the often years of work ahead. To make the entire process more worthwhile I have always made my floats in batches of three, each float is slightly different perhaps in shape or in colour chosen. However, they are all very special and far too valuable to lose, they are built with care and the pleasure of catching pike on them is a very satisfying part of the sport. One of the most underrated secrets of catching big river pike is to just keep on going, to do this you really need to enjoy what you are doing and after well over fifty years pike fishing, I still enjoy the sport a great deal. Certainly, making my own floats and tackle is a big part of that enjoyment. I hope this section will help you enjoy your fishing more too. If you just keep going you will certainly catch that much longed for Big Pike.

A range of 'Old Favourites' Top layer 'Snag Friendly' versions in varied sizes for fishing deep water. Bottom row are weedless floats used for shallow water under six feet deep. Top three on left made from Champagne Corks, the others from wine bottle corks. All biodegradable and environmentally friendly.

Hooks, Rigs and Methods for River Pike

The traditional Jardine style snap tackle is good, but for river fishing the single hook snap tackle is better. However, when fishing small natural baits under six inches long the single hook rig is best. This summarises what we have found in our never-ending search for the perfect rig for river piking.

The subject of wire traces and hooking rigs for pike fishing has been one of the most popular subjects in the history of pike fishing literature. It includes contributions from early authors like Henry Cholmondeley Pennell, Alfred Jardine and many others going back over one hundred and fifty years. Why then should we write another chapter on this seemingly well covered subject? Firstly, the answer is that pike fishing rigs which may be fine for say the Norfolk Broads or the southern reservoirs do not necessarily translate well on the fast-running northern rivers. Secondly, most pike fishermen are very inventive and make up their own rigs to suit their own parochial needs. The rigs we describe here are exactly that, rigs specially designed to fish fast flowing conditions. What we recommend here are rigs and methods we have found to work. It is one thing to read all the books and become generally well informed. It is quite another to learn from actual bankside experiences on real Northern Rivers. The latter is of course what we provide in this book. As a result of that experience, we can share with the reader a methodology of river piking which has proved very effective over a long period of time. We would not be so bold to claim we know all the answers but can guarantee that the approach given here will improve the newcomers' prospects two or threefold when tackling these northern waters.

The further you go back in time, the bigger and more crude were the tackles used. Very early on in the history of our sport large multi hook rigs called gorge tackles were placed on set lines where the pike were deliberately encouraged to pouch the bait in its stomach. These cruel baited rigs were left overnight and checked each day and consisted of little more than a long line tied to a willow branch. As the fisherman approached the set line they could tell if a fish was on by the frantic tugging on the branch. On such crude methods, which are now outlawed of course, the hooks were often baited with old bits of unwanted food like chicken heads or fish tails, anything edible could be used and every pike caught was killed for the pot. Regrettably, these barbaric methods have recently made a comeback in parts of East Yorkshire and the Cambridgeshire Fens by a subculture of feral gangs and fish thieves who have no respect for our fishing traditions or the law of the land. Thankfully, new vigorous patrols have been installed to bring these criminals to book.

As far back as the Victorian times Alfred Jardine invented the now famous 'Jardine Snap Tackle' which to this day many pike anglers still use with great success. This rig consists of two treble hooks arranged on a wire trace. The lower hook is fixed to the trace, whilst the upper Ryder hook slides so that it can be adjusted to fit baits of different sizes. In modern times the same basic rig is still often used with dead bait offerings and is certainly used more often now than when Jardine was alive. The great advantage of the snap tackle is that it can effectively be used as an instant strike rig. As soon as the float goes under your bait is in the pike's mouth, an instant strike provides a good chance of a hook hold. Though if you delay the strike hoping to give the fish more time to get the bait in its mouth you could find the pike has ejected the bait, especially if it has felt the metallic sensation of the trebles and has decided to eject the bait and hooking rig with it.

As we have seen from our biography of Tom Sturdy, most pike were killed for food back in Edwardian England, so the unlucky pike never got a second chance to learn. In contrast, modern enlightened pike anglers now return their catches giving pike multiple chances to learn. On hard fished waters today the effect of this is often shown by having lots of dropped runs as modern-day pike know how to avoid our latest ironmongery! Therefore, if you are an advocate of Alfred Jardine and his legendary snap tackle rig, we would recommend an early strike when using them, especially on popular waters where pike have learned to eject a bait if it feels metal on its sensitive dentures. It is interesting to note that Alfred Jardine's continued fame is no doubt linked to the excellent rig named after him. However, his own favourite rig was the humble single hook rig which he employed with great skill in catching his most spectacular big pike.

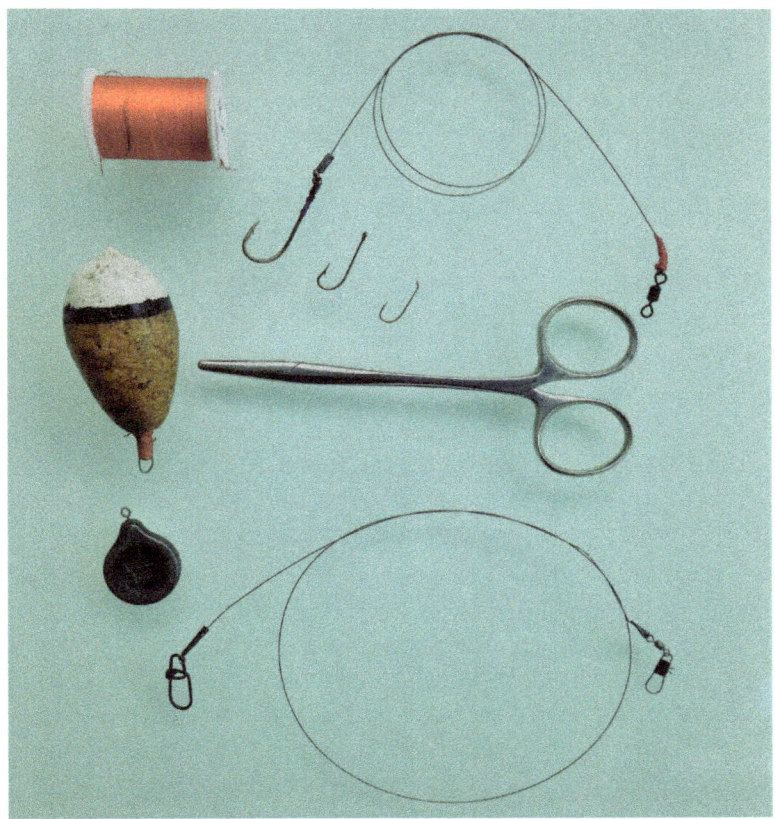

Single hook rig using size one single attached to an 18-inch wire trace. Ideal for small six-inch sardines. Next to it a size six hook ideal for sprats and finally a small size ten hook for small four-inch minnow baits. For fishing small natural baits under six inches long the single hook rig has proved to be the most successful arrangement of all. Forceps' always useful when tying up traces. Large float and ledger illustrate tackle needed to fish water around twenty feet deep. Finally, the rig should be attached to an uptrace to minimise chance of pike's teeth meeting reel line. The uptrace shown here can be attached to the trace using snap link illustrated. The reel line is attached to the Egg Snap link which is perfect for preventing float or ledger running down the trace.

About thirty-five years ago the late Colin Dyson who was editor of the 'Coarse Fishing' magazine invited me to write an article on single hook pike fishing. I was a very keen exponent of single hook piking using small baits and my belief in the single hook arrangement was reinforced after catching two twenty-pound pike and several doubles in one day. Now, many years later at the age of sixty-six I would not change a word in the early article but would like to add to it an improved version of Jardine's snap tackle designed for fishing bigger baits on rivers. Single size two or slightly larger hooks are still unbeatable when using smallish baits like sprats or small five-inch natural bait. With larger baits though like sardines or larger nine-inch baits we now prefer the instant strike qualities of the multi hook rig, like the Jardine rig, only slightly modified to meet the special conditions faced when river fishing. (See diagram which illustrates our custom built 'River rig' and its adjustable components.)

Over the past thirty-seven years in the role of Regional Organiser for the Pike Angler's Club I have lost count of the number of people who have approached me for advice with their pike fishing problems. The most common malady is as follows. "Bill, after over twenty years pike fishing, I have never caught a twenty-pound fish of a lifetime, what am I doing wrong"? These are often very sincere cries for help, especially with some members of a certain age they are worried their time is running out! Such sincere cries for help deserve special attention and we often invite them along to fish with us. This gives us the chance to help with the aim of putting it right. In many cases these anglers have become lifelong friends and supporters of the Pike Anglers Club. Without being too intrusive we can quickly discover areas for improvement. We usually find they have used conventional Jardine snap style rigs with huge hooks. It is also noticeable they have all placed one of the treble hooks halfway along the bait. The rationale for doing this has been that this hook position almost guarantees at least one treble is in the pike's mouth just prior to striking home the hooks. There is good logic to this too, but only if your quarry is prepared to hold a bait with a giant rank treble in its mouth and swallow! In the Victorian period pike were possibly more likely to swallow an exposed treble hook, but not now. On many occasions I have seen pike in clear water inhale baits and instantly reject them within the blink of an eye and without moving the float. For me this suggests that modern day pike, which have most probably been caught and released at an earlier stage, can sense check each bait carefully before deciding if it is safe. I also believe that a pike's toothy maw is a very sensitive part of the pike's anatomy and fully capable of sensing when something is wrong or out of order. When my companion Nigel Winter first started to fish with me, he asked why I was out fishing him by about four to one, he questioned our catch rate imbalance. We were both fishing the same waters and using identical baits. The only thing which was different was the fact I was using my modified single hook snap tackle whilst he was still using the traditional style snap tackle with two sets of very large treble hooks. To help Nigel improve his catch rate I just gave him one of my home-made rigs to see what would happen. Once he made this simple change his catch rate immediately began to improve, so much so that now after over thirty years we catch on equal terms. No good deed goes unpunished! Only joking.

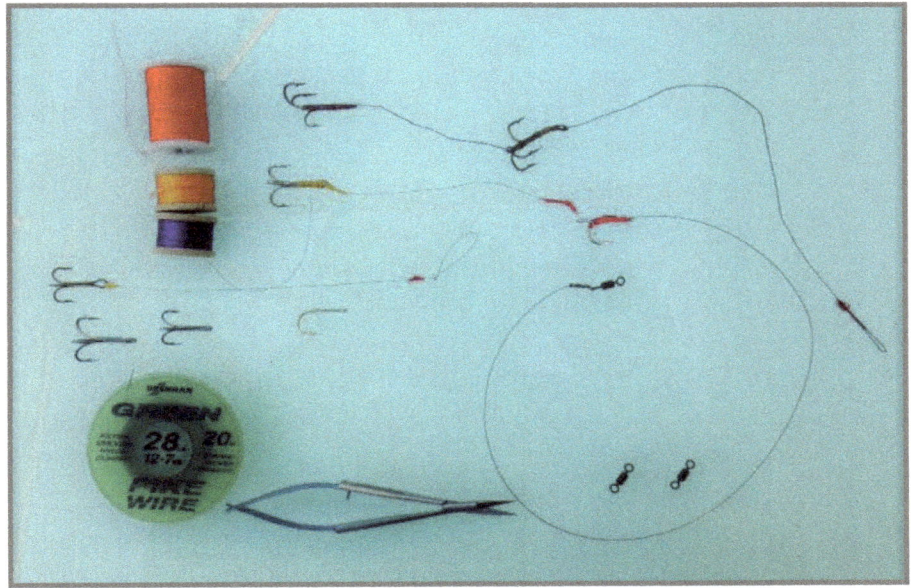

At the top of the image is the famous 'Jardine Snap Tackle'. Over 100 years old and still popular. Next down can be seen the single hook snap tackle we call the 'River Rig' de coupled to illustrate the separate components. All swivels and treble hooks size eight. Also, various colours of silk and cotton for whipping hooks to trace. Clippers used to trim cotton as required. Finally, a spool of green plastic-coated trace wire 28lb B.S. Not everyone likes plastic coated wire, but it is our favourite.

The special 'River rig' which we have found to be more successful than the conventional rigs design can be easily made up as follows.

1. Take an eighteen-inch length of 20lb to 28lb wire preferably plastic coated.
2. Whip a size two micro barbed single hook with point upwards, seven inches above the end of trace. Before whipping on a single

hook with cotton put three turns of wire round the shank of the single so the wire acquires a 'grip' on the single hook, then whip down the cotton thread tightly to fix the single hook firmly on the trace. Cover most of the shank with tight turns of cotton or silk thread. This is important to prevent the pikes very sensitive teeth contacting the wire hook. The reason I prefer a nylon coated trace wire is for the same reason, to prevent sensitive teeth contacting wire.

3. Now fix a size eight treble hook to the end of the trace in a normal way using a crimp or whipping for tidy finish. This treble hook is best attached to the dead bait as far as possible from the head, in fact right in the root tail. Not halfway along the body as almost everyone we have seen do it.

4. Finally, fix a size eight swivel at the top of the trace and whip or crimp on again for a tidy finish.

5. The whole trace should be a minimum of eighteen inches long allowing a safe margin for even the largest pike.

6. A further 20-inch up trace can be used for additional protection especially useful when using the paternoster link for live or dead baits. It is helpful to use a snap link on the bottom of the uptrace so you can quickly remove the uptrace when you have a freshly caught pike in the net.

As can be seen from the illustration of the river rig, the normal top Ryder treble hook on the Jardine snap has been replaced with one large strong single hook. When making up these custom-built river rigs the large single hook (size one or two) has been whipped onto the trace with cotton thread. In the context of river fishing, this rig has the following desirable advantages over the standard Snap Tackle rig.

[1] The tightly wrapped cotton holds the single hook firmly to the trace allowing the strong hook to take the force of a full-blooded cast without slippage.

[2] As the shank of the hook is covered by the bound thread it feels soft in the pike's mouth and feels more natural than a naked protruding treble hook. This makes it less likely to spook a wary pike when it senses checks the bait and

less likely to eject the bait as soon as it feels metal on its sensitive dentures.

[3] I do not varnish the cotton as the cotton itself absorbs fish extract scents which can be applied when still dry to get maximum absorption. I have always found smelt extract to be a useful attractant and can be purchased in small bottles from most tackle shops.

[4] The wire gape of the size two single is quite wide and makes a firm support for long range casting soft baits like sardine. If the single is inserted at the front of the eye, and emerges at the front of the opposite eye, you have a very firm hold of the bait which can be cast with as much force as required to make a long cast if needed. With sardines the body of the bait will begin to break up after about five casts, but the integrity of the single hook hold always remains fully intact.

[5] As the bait lays ledgered on the riverbed the single hook is flush with the sardine and the bait is positioned swimming upstream as is natural. This gives the bait good symmetry a quality which is particularly important when ledgering in running or fast water.

[6] The small loop whipped onto to back of the single hook allows one to change either the hook length or hook size of the treble hook attachment. For example, if you need to change bait size from say a seven-inch sardine to a ten-inch rainbow trout you just add a new link three inches longer without having to break down your tackle to re tie knots in the mainline. I always have a few spare hook lengths ready in advance of differing sizes to fit any bait size needed. I make up these terminal rig attachments on the bank side, often when waiting for some action I find this a valuable way to keep busy whilst waiting for those longed-for runs. The disadvantage of this rig is that it does take quite a lot of time making up these special custom-built traces, but when you consider they really will more than double your catch rate it makes all the detailed work worthwhile. For me, I like nothing better than to get my two dead bait rods out

with two baits in the water. Sit down comfortably under the brolly, pour a hot cup of coffee, relax, and only then make up a few special river pike single hook links. Settling down in this way helps you to relax and fish effectively too, it prevents you banging about on the bank scaring those wary big pike away. Time and time again I have had a run after settling down with a hot coffee and my trace making equipment. I certainly enjoy trace making on the bankside and knowing too it helps fish in a more productive way. A very useful message here is that success is not always what you do, but quite often what you do not do! If you can just sit quietly, out of sight, and refrain from constantly moving your baits or walking up and down, this is a great step forward on the road to big pike encounters. Nothing helps more to settle down and fish properly and making up new trace rigs from the luxury of a comfy fishing chair!

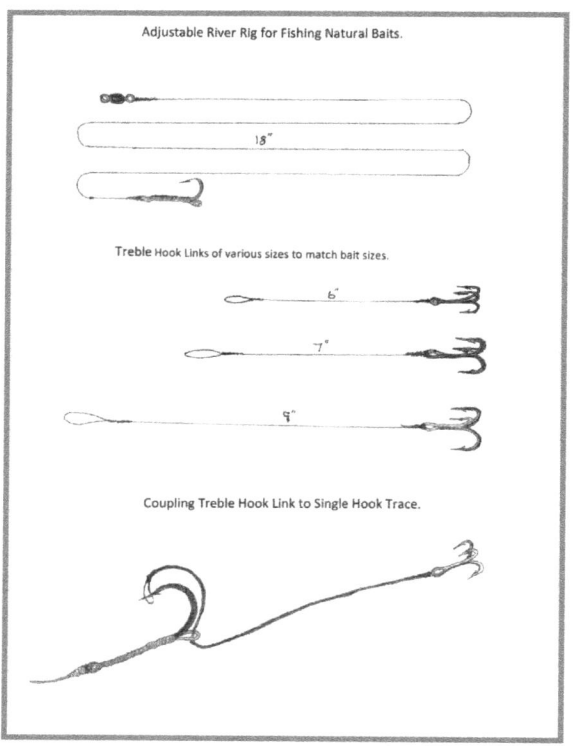

[7] There is one further useful method of fishing with the detachable treble hook link. When fishing fast water, the whole rig can be baited with one-inch sized cubes of trout or sardine. Simply cut up a whole fish into one-inch chunks. Then skewer each piece onto a baiting needle. Once needle is full of one-inch chunks, attach the hook of the needle onto the loop of the treble link. Pull tight so that the fish cubes can be threaded across onto the treble link. Once the link is full the loop can be attached to the small loop on the back of the single. In this way you can present a string of fish chunks in line instead of just a whole fish. The beauty of this method is that it releases more oily fish scent in the water than any other rig. Helpful in flowing coloured water for attracting scent hunting pike upstream. I prefer to fish this rig close into the bank where big pike are often hunting along the margins. It is a rig which is messy and smelly, but that is exactly why the pike love it!

[8] Plastic coated wire is our preferred wire choice, not just because it feels more natural in the pike's mouth. It also is less harmful to the pike's upper maxillary. Rank wire can be like cheese wire and will 'Saw' deep grooves in the pike's upper jaw, especially on fast waters where the pike are wild and ferocious. The plastic-coated wire is much more forgiving and kinder to the pike on these special waters.

[9] Some anglers are very keen on the use of barbless hooks for pike fishing. There is no doubt that barbless hooks are great for quickly removing hooks from the pike's mouth, and even better for removing them from the mesh of the landing net. Despite these genuine advantages we still prefer barbed or semi barbed hooks for two main reasons. Firstly, barbless hooks are not quite as effective when the pike makes those repeated 'Head Shakes' both above and below water level. Secondly, large barbless hooks tend to penetrate too deeply and risk entering the pike's vital organs.

A seven-inch sardine set up on the 'River Rig' providing the ultimate presentation for catching big pike.

Sliced bait presentation, ideal for floodwater conditions. Fish chunks easily assembled using baiting needle.

AN EARLY LESSON IN SINGLE HOOK PIKE FISHING.

My pike fishing career got off to a good start at the age of eleven thanks to my association with Norris Sturdy of West Tanfield. Norris had already introduced me to the sport of pike fishing when my dad took me for an evening social in the Sturdy family home in West Tanfield. In the same house where three generations of the Sturdy family had lived. Norris was sixty-five and just about to retire, he told us he was buying a brand-new Austin 1100 motor car with his retirement fund. I already knew one or two good places to fish for pike on the River Ure, so we arranged to meet up for a day's fishing as soon as Norris secured his new car. The agreement was that I would provide the baits and help carrying his tackle, in return Norris would provide the transport and expert tuition into the secrets of catching river pike. It was a perfect arrangement.

As promised, six months later Norris arrived in his brand-new car. Off we went to the River Ure famous for big trout, grayling, and Pike. After buying our day tickets at the Old Horn Inn we unloaded the rods plus a glass minnow bottle. I rushed off to a streamy section of the river which I knew (from my earlier bicycle trips) was full of minnows, dace and chub. The glass bottle had a cone shaped punt in the bottom which I had previously tapped with a hammer carefully to knock a half inch hole in the centre of the cone shaped punt at the bottom of the bottle. A seven-foot string was already tied to each end of the bottle so after baiting the bottle with half a slice of white bread the bottle was lowered into the streamy run, pointed end upstream.

Close up photo of a four-inch minnow. These little fellows provide a great meal for jack pike and doubles too.

Before releasing the bottle in the water, I had to remove the cork to allow all the trapped air out. Only then did the bottle settle on the riverbed. The weight of the glass held it in place perfectly. From about twenty feet, I watched as minnows entered the downstream cone and then became trapped inside the bottle, they did not seem to mind though as I could see them inside the bottle having a feeding frenzy on the bread. As they flashed around in excitement even more minnows were attracted to the bottle until after only ten minutes it contained several dozen minnows and dace ranging from just one inch to almost five inches long. I lifted out the bottle, pulled out the cork and just poured them all into a white plastic live bait bucket. Norris and I then walked upstream for about a quarter of a mile where there was an ox bow lake. This was a tennis court sized offshoot of the river connected to the main river by a deep channel at its lower end creating a sheltered riverside pool. It was an ideal nursery for spawning pike and the fringes were lined with weeds and was six feet deep in the middle and very sheltered compared to fast flowing river just thirty feet over a raised spit of dry gravel and boulders.

Norris was well impressed with my choice of venue and began to tackle up his fishing gear. His fishing rod was an eight-foot Milbro Spinwell model. Made from a solid green fibre glass blank. Norris had purchased this rod specially for a pike fishing trip to Lough Erne in Ireland. It was Made in Scotland for the purpose of pike or salmon spinning. To this rod he attached a very posh black sleek Mitchell 300 spinning reel which he kept wrapped in an oily rag and in its original box for protection. The spool was loaded with twelve-pound monofilament line. Next, Norris took out a spool of fine braided trace wire 12lb breaking strain and cut off an eighteen-inch length and attached a size ten single hook to one end and a small swivel at the other. Just under the swivel he placed one swan shot on the actual wire trace. Finally, the terminal gear was completed with a very small home-made float, and just large enough to support the trace, swan shot and an energetic free roving four-inch minnow.

In the meantime, I was busy keeping the live bait fresh. I snapped on the perforated lid of the live bait bucket and emersed it in the water to keep the minnows well oxygenated. Norris was now ready to start fishing, and he asked me to pass him the largest minnow in the bucket. There were about ten big ones, some almost five inches long. Norris said these were perfect pike baits and he carefully lip hooked the biggest so as not to harm the fish. "Now sit down quietly", Norris said as he cast the rig into the centre of the pool, the float was set at about four feet from the bait. Very quietly the small red float cocked as the swan shot found its depth. Then after a minute or so the float began to nod gently around the pool as if searching out for a place to hide. The tackle was so fine the minnow could move about freely just as Norris had intended. The bait was moving away from our position, so we had to pay out more line. Then after only five minutes the float vanished beneath a vortex of swirling water. Norris picked up the rod and wasted no time in connecting to it with a firm sideways pull. The rod bent double as a mystery fish tore line off the slipping clutch. Wow, we had only been fishing for less than ten minutes and we were already in! After a good fight lasting no more than five minutes, we landed a lovely pike weighing six pounds. That was the biggest pike I had ever seen at that early stage. Norris had been a water bailiff on the prestigious West Tanfield Trout Fishing Club and his job involved controlling pike, so I was surprised when he told me to release this freshly caught pike back into the main river to avoid spooking the remaining pike left in our sheltered pool. The precaution worked well as we continued catch a further three pike up to a top weight of twelve pounds.

This early introduction to single hook piking was a set piece template of good practice I have carried with me to this day. Norris told me the twelve pounder we caught was probably the largest one in residence in the pool that day. He assured me if a twenty pounder had been there, we would have almost certainly taken it. Indeed, in the shallow clear water the sight of that small live bait was just irresistible to any pike regardless of size.

My local tackle shop in Bedale did not stock the very fine wire Norris was using so I had to send off by post to Andrews Tackle shop in Scunthorpe to get the correct trace wire. It was expensive, but very worthwhile. I was so lucky to have spent a proper day fishing with a genuine top expert pike angler. I did not quite realise at the time, but I was fishing with probably the most experienced pike angler living in Northern England at that time. From his performance that day I could see why he was. Indeed, he did not say much when he was fishing, but you could see from his expressions he was deep in thought all the time, every action he took was considered and you could see his concentration never let up.

Once Norris had put me on the right path for single hook pike fishing, I purchased the tackle I needed, made up some proper home-made pike floats and set forth on my own journey. I returned to the River Ure often and caught pike and perch in the main river using the single hook method he taught me. Whenever I return to this river I always reflect on those happy distant days with huge nostalgia. When Norris died in 1987 at the grand old age of eighty-two, he kindly left me his Green solid glass Milbro spinning rod and the Mitchell 300 fishing reel. These are now among the most treasured items in my collection of fishing tackle. However, it is the knowledge he gave me which I value most, and now at the age of sixty-six I am more than glad to hand on, in turn, those skills which are so central to our northern pike fishing culture and which were so generously passed on to me from Norris, truly one of the best in the business.

It is interesting to consider that in modern times the humble minnow sized baits are very seldom considered as a viable option. Yet their availability in Northern rivers makes them a very workable choice. As a boy I discovered that to catch the bigger sized minnows, up to and around five inches in length, it was better to use a size sixteen or eighteen hook baited with a fragment of worm. When cast into a shoal of minnows you get about twenty minnows all fighting to get to the bait first and in this situation the biggest fish are the only ones to fit the worm into their mouths. This is a very selective way of catching big minnows or dace which make perfect live baits. Wine bottles are also very effective, the trick is to punch a small three-quarter inch hole in the glass punt at the bottom of the wine bottle. One interesting fact is that if you run out of clear wine bottles dark green ones also work, this suggests the minnows are guided into the cone of the bottle by smell as the dark green bottles are not transparent. Clear plastic bottles can also be used, if you get a second bottle the neck cone shape of one bottle can be cut off and stapled into the lower section of the first making a perfect cone. The only snag here is you need to insert small stones into the bottle to make it stable in the flowing water. Failing that, a heavy plate of metal can easily be attached at the base to keep the bottle stable in flowing water.

When using minnow as bait a size ten single hook is a good compromise between strength and sensitivity, but with larger sized baits like sprats or sardines we prefer a size one or two hook, not just for the additional strength, but because they are better for securing a hook hold for casting and on the strike.

Good friend Lee Maloney cradles a 24lb upland river pike taken on a size two single hook on the River Ure.

One fine example of a big pike taken on a size two single hook is illustrated above when fishing with my good friend Lee Maloney.

On this special day I was fishing on the River Ure for pike and grayling with my good friend Lee from York. On one rod I was fishing a swim feeder on four-pound line in the centre of the river right in front of where I was sitting in my fishing chair. I had been feeding the swim with maggots for two hours and catching the occasional grayling mid river, mostly small fish, but with the occasional fish over one pound. On my second rod I fished five yards downstream, again in mid river in about ten feet of water with a five-inch deadbait anchored and suspended on paternoster under a good-sized pike float. The trout was lip hooked with a size two single hook, so it moved slightly in the current with its head facing the correct way, upstream. The river was very cold and crystal clear and moving steadily at approximately four miles per hour, hence the need for a good-sized float. I could have used the ledger technique, but as so often on these northern rivers the river bottom was festooned with ugly snags. The only clear part of the riverbed was occupied by my faithful swim feeder.

The main strategy of the day was to create and hold a shoal of grayling or any other fish to have some fun on the deadly swim feeder, but at the same time possibly attract a few pike into the area by creating a grazing shoal of hungry feeding fish. After five hours I had caught half a dozen grayling nicely spaced out over the period, I had also had half a dozen missed bites, so it had been quite a pleasant visit and I always like to spend a bit of time with our beautiful grayling, aptly called the lady of the stream. I was just beginning to lose hope of catching any pike when I saw my dead bait float move very slowly slightly up stream and towards me. The float never actually went under, it just continued to move towards the side and slightly upstream in a smooth motion. That was it, I picked up the pike rod and wound down hard making strong contact with our long-awaited pike. I instinctively lifted my rod to try to bully the unseen force upwards out of the snags which I knew from bitter experience were there. I knew right away it was a big fish and shouted to Lee my friend to help net the fish as the bank was slippery and treacherous. Thankfully, I did manage to get the fish into the mid part of the water column, but it was so heavy I really had no proper control to start with. At last Lee came with his net and wound in my swim feeder to clear the decks. I was glad of Lees company, at least he could witness how the fish was tearing line off the spool and the frightening bend on the rod, all necessary though to keep its head out of the snags. Eventually we caught sight of her as we made our first attempt to net this powerful beast. She did not like the look of Lees net though and she put us through several more gruelling minutes before she finally slid over the net. We placed our prize in our capacious keep carp sack to give both the pike and us time to recover our equilibrium. Fortunately, the hook fell out into the net so there was no need to place it onto the unhooking mat. We carefully weighed her and took a few quick photos. What a beautiful fish, she weighed just over twenty-four pounds, was scale perfect, had very distinct primrose flecks and she looked as though she had never been caught before. We quickly returned her back to the company of the trout and grayling to hopefully fight another day. With this fish we made contact within about fifteen seconds of seeing the run developing, though it was a very gentle take which is typical of very big fish. In the strong flow, the size two single hook proved to be perfect with this small lip hooked bait, but in certain conditions bigger single hooks can be used. In fact, in the diagram showing three hook options the size ten and two are only used for baits under about five inches, whilst a bigger size one hook can be employed for suspended baits up to about eight inches long.

During winter droughts when the river is very low the whole river course can resemble canal conditions with barely any flow at all. Under these conditions I recently fished a nine-inch-long sardine suspended mid river on a large size one hook with a gape of 15 mm. The middle of the river was twelve feet deep, so I set the float to fish at a depth of ten feet and let the bait just drift very slowly down stream. After about fifteen minutes it grounded about twenty yards downstream only about ten feet from the bank. After approximately half an hour the float started to bob and disappeared. An instant strike met with a very solid fish which headed out into mid river. It then shook its head with a very slow frequency which can only mean one thing...Big Pike! On this occasion I was fishing with my friend Nigel Winter who kindly netted the fish, all twenty-two pounds of her.

All these fish have been taken on single hook rigs using hooks varying in size from the tiny size ten used for minnow or sprat sized baits running up to bigger baits around the six-inch size taken on size two singles and finally the huge size one hook which is great for drifting large nine-inch dead baits horizontally on suspended rigs using an appropriately sized float to hold up the bait. When using these large hooks in low flow conditions there is no need to use a weight as the weight of the hook is sufficient to hold the bait down when conditions are calm. As always though any indication of a bite needs to be attended to with a firm strike and do not worry if the hook pulls out as if this happens the fish will almost certainly come back for a second helping if you make a further attempt.

A 22lb pike taken in crystal clear water on a suspended deadbait using a single hook in water over ten feet deep. In this case a nine-inch sardine was fished 'Horizontal' with a size one hook in its middle.

As mentioned earlier we like to make up our pike traces on the bank as it helps keep one busy when waiting for those electrifying runs. Made up traces can be stored on commercial rig holders which are very good but very expensive and bulky to carry. I have always used a simple homemade rig card which is made from two rectangular cards stapled together for rigidity. At opposite ends half inch slits can be cut to hold the wire traces. The important thing with this system is to avoid attaching the wire too tight otherwise it may cause a kink in the wire, but if you attach it gently it will keep the wire straight and the whole card can be stored in a compact flat tin for protection. It is obviously very important to keep the trace card full of ready to go traces, nothing could be worse than running out of traces when the pike suddenly come on the feed!

Although very effective we hardly ever use livebaits anymore. The problems encountered transporting big live baits are just too much hassle, and when moving from one water to another they become illegal. For bigger natural dead baits upwards of six to ten inches long we use our river 'Single hook snap tackle' rigs already described. Baits like sardine, rainbow trout, mackerel, have been the mainstay of our big pike fishing ventures. Such baits are easy to purchase, cast very well and do not swim into nasty snags on purpose! Also, for the past few years we find that live baiting has become an unpleasant method to use. I ask myself, "Is it really necessary to use such an unpleasant method to catch pike?" The answer is always no, it makes one feel very uneasy for a variety of reasons. Plus, the amount of high maintenance care it requires prevents one from getting to grips with big pike. It is also generally recognised that the bigger fish fall to dead baits anyway so why bother with all the messing about. The thing I really dislike about live baits is that they seem to attract every three-pound jack pike in the area before you finally get to the big pike. Far better we think to use dead baits and go directly to the bigger fish, yes it may take a little longer, but at least the extra time allows one to relax which for us is one of the main aims of going fishing in the first place!

Live baiting has already been banned in Scotland and I have noticed that several of the big city clubs in Northern England have also banned its use. I can see this method being banned nationally in the not-too-distant future for the reasons just discussed. No need to worry though, the dead baiting methods just described here are much better by far. In fact I would now say the sheer hassle of collecting and maintaining live fish actually prevents you from getting through to the bigger fish making it counterproductive in many ways.

DEADBAIT SPINNING. A NATURAL ALTERNATIVE TO LIVEBAIT

If live baiting is ever banned there is no need to worry because there are plenty of alternative baits which are not only just as good, but more importantly are a lot more convenient to use. One good alternative is of course the time-honoured dead bait spinning method. Small baits like sprats or minnows can be used on light tackle in a very enticing manner to fish out deep stretches of river. Our favourite rig is to use a size two single hook which can be attached in the frontal eye sockets of the sprat with a size ten treble link attached to the root tail. This set up can be cast out dozens of times before it begins to break up or is more than likely torn to bits by the attentions of a good river pike. We suggest an eighteen-inch trace with just one swan shot attached to the upper part of the trace. If such an arrangement is cast next to willow bushes on the opposite side of the river in say fifteen feet of water, the bait will sink very slowly in a most enticing way. Just before it reaches the riverbed a few sudden twitches will put life into the bait and this is often when the pike will attack. Then the bait can be slowly fished back but with occasional pauses to keep the bait in the river for as long as possible. This method is like a halfway house between live baiting and dead baiting, it really is one of the best pike fishing methods of all.

If you are fishing a stretch of river which you know is ten feet deep with lots of snags, then the same rig can be used only this time with a float set at a depth of seven feet so once you cast out the float will fish the bait just a few feet above the snags. If the bait is cast to the far bank and slightly up stream then the float can be twitched every thirty seconds or so as the bait is fished most effectively on its way down stream. This is a most effective method of searching out the swim and the light swan shot as weight gives the bait a lot of freedom to move slowly through the water column. Yes, even dead baits can be fished in a very lifelike manner and the occasional light pressure to the float creates that extra movement which pike find so irresistible. On each river there are dozens of unique opportunities each one of which can be explored using this simple dead bait wobbling method. The key is to fish the bait with as lighter a lead as possible. Once again here we have yet another example of how 'Less is More'. Big weights, just like big treble hooks are to be avoided. Just as very complicated rigs should be avoided too. The more complicated the rig, the more there is to go wrong. The single hook river rig just described for float ledgering is ideal for dead bait spinning only the half ounce lead need to be replaced with one swan shot of course.

DEADBAIT SPINNING AS A LAST RESORT

Imagine the situation, it is just starting to snow, the sky is dark grey and the river is beginning to freeze over in the margins. Worst of all you ate the last of the pre-Christmas mince pies two hours earlier and the flask is empty! After patiently willing your floats to move for seven hours nothing has happened at all. You have pre baited up the swim carefully so you know the riverbed is well seeded with delicious pike attractors in the form of fresh one-inch chunks of oily mackerel and trout, fresh ones too, the best money can buy. Years of experience give you an instinctive certainty there are one or two really big pike down there just waiting to make their move, and yet they still hold back.

Finally, as a last resort one of the static baits is brought in and the float and ledger is replaced with a fresh seven-inch sardine attached to a river rig, size two single through eye socket and size eight treble on its tail. A single swan shot positioned just an inch from the mainline below the swivel on the trace completes the rig. This deadbait spinning rig is cast beyond the baited-up area and allowed ten seconds to sink in the water column. Then slowly and carefully the bait is retrieved in an intermittent motion back through the baited area. First cast nothing. Second cast nothing, but just after the bait was taken from the river there was a great upheaval of inky black water. Yes! there is one there and its hungry. The hands begin to tremble a little from a mixture of cold and raw excitement. Out goes the bait, this time only twenty feet, the bait is once again allowed to sink slowly into the black depths, it is almost dark now, then bang, something heavy hits the bait with force and the fish is on. This wonderful pike plumbs the depths of the river ripping line off the centrepin with impressive force. It is still snowing slightly; the landing net is frozen solid but melts as soon as it enters the relatively warm river. It takes a further several long minutes before we even catch a glimpse of our well-earned winter prize. Finally she reluctantly enters the net and is thankfully secured following a dogged tussle.

The marvellous event described above and recorded in the adjacent photograph was yet another 'Last Resort' success secured by using the deadbait spinning method as a final last-ditch attempt to save the day. This exact sequence of events has now happened so many times I have come to think of this method as the ultimate final solution when all else has failed. I have tried it earlier on with limited success, but when used at the days end just before darkness it really seems to come into its own. This explains why this photograph is a little on the dark side, but the atmosphere is absolutely true to the event and the frozen bank captures the stark reality of sub-zero fishing. This was another late December event, just a few days before Christmas.

After a long day in the cold with no success a change of tactics to spun deadbait finally brought action in the form of this beautifully conditioned twenty-pound pike. The practice of using this method as a last-ditch solution has proved good so many times I now consider it as the ultimate last resort game changer at the end of the day.

WEIGHTS USED FOR RIVER PIKE

Once again when choosing which weights to use for river piking the old maxim 'Less is more' comes into play. Of course, there are special circumstances where a heavy four or five-ounce lead may be needed to hold bottom in deep fast river sections, but these are the exception rather than the general rule. For most situations, a simple half to one ounce lead is all that is required. In recent years we have seen public broadcasters recommending abandoning ledger weights when static dead baiting. In effect to fish, one's bait freeline. This is a big mistake! A freelined natural bait can be picked up by a pike which may lift the bait and move towards the rod tip. If this happened there would be no resistance in the line to register a run leaving the poor pike vulnerable to swallowing the bait. The good thing about using the ledger is that when the pike moves away in any direction the slight tension of the line created by the ledger weight instantly registers on the rod tip and alerts the angler to the run. Even a tiny half ounce ledger will serve this purpose, but there are no two ways about it, for static dead baiting the ledger weight must be used.

Ledger weights come in an amazing range of shapes colours and sizes. Some round bullet leads, some pear shaped, others even square with rounded edges! These rounded versions are best for trundling baits along the riverbed, in effect they can roll along giving a steady movement downstream and, on our spate rivers, often straight into a snag! For northern rivers, our first preference is therefore the flat leads which have a very low profile in the water. These flat leads make very good 'anchors' for the float, they will prevent the bait running into the snags all day. Also, they come in a good range of sizes and even the half ounce smaller versions grip the riverbed surprisingly tightly. Coffin leads are similar and serve the same function. Due to the snaggy nature of our rivers, we obviously prefer the latter flat leads which will hold the rig in a fixed position to avoid losing fish and tackle. They are just as effective too for anchoring a paternoster rig in flowing water. In both these arrangements the low centre of gravity of the weight helps greatly to hold its position in flowing water. The general rule to choosing which size to use is regulated by water depth and speed of flow. So, for example, in twenty feet of water flowing gently at three to four miles per hour a two- or three-ounce lead would be sufficient to anchor the bait in mid river. At the other extreme, if the water in your swim is only eight feet deep and is almost stationery, then a weight if only half an ounce would be sufficient to hold the bait in position. In both these scenarios we would recommend the flat profile design.

One of my favourite methods is to present dead baits suspended about one foot above the riverbed under a float with stop knot set to required depth. In this situation a simple drilled bullet of half an ounce will suffice in most situations. The weight needs to just be sufficient to cock the float so it can be seen clearly as it trots its way slowly downstream. When it reaches its limit, it can then be retrieved, in stages, back upstream along the riverbank. In this way a lot of the river can be searched without changing position. If the river is clear and shallow just a couple of swan shot would be sufficient. On the other hand, in deeper water then a half ounce bullet would be more suitable. This would hold the bait deep in the water and allow a good forty-yard trot downstream. Barrel leads are also good for fishing suspended baits, especially those in the small half ounce size.

When the river has a strong flow during high water conditions a float fished in mid river needs to suspend the line directly from rod tip to float. If the line is floating on the river surface it will collect debris which will build up and wash the whole rig off downstream under its weight. In this situation a large two-ounce flat lead will hold the float with sufficient force to allow the float to support the line safely above the water surface. Eventually, the float itself will accumulate debris too, but not for a good hour or so depending on the amount of flotsam in the flow. When it does a quick 'tidy up' of the line must be done so fishing can recommence. If one is fishing deep water close in, then the float could be removed allowing one to fish a straight through ledger rig. Again, the line could be fished at a steep angle thus minimising exposure to floating debris.

These are just a few of the possible scenarios which face the river piker and different swims will need a range of slight adjustments in tackles to meet the special circumstances on the day. With experience one begins to know exactly which rigs will fit the conditions on the day. By knowing your river and finding what is good on the day soon becomes second nature. Yet one can never be complacent, no matter how well you know your river it will always surprise. Sometimes the surprise will be one of disappointment in what you consider ideal circumstances. Then there are the other surprises when having given up all hope you catch an unexpected big pike. The mark of a good river piker is someone who, after several blank days still enjoys each day and despite the blanks feels fully confident in the face of what may at times seem a hopeless cause.

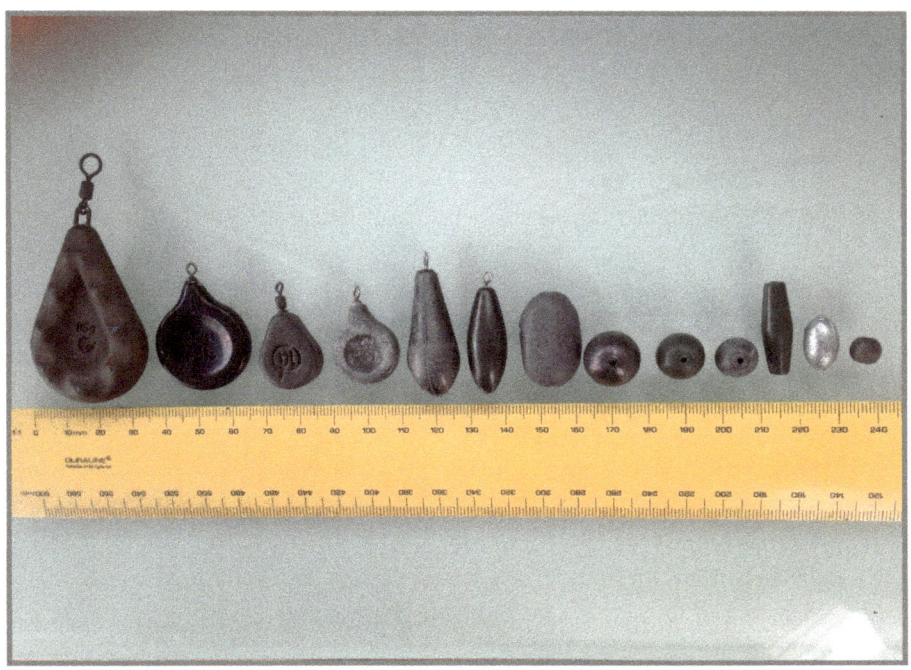

A range of non-toxic Ledgers from flat weights on the left to pear shaped weights and bullet leads on the right for suspended baits in deep water conditions.

Bill Winship

Static Deadbaiting and River Hotspots for Pike

As we have already seen from our biography of Tom Sturdy deadbaiting as a method for catching pike was well known about and practiced in Edwardian Yorkshire. However there is no doubt that for many anglers, including the Sturdy's, live baiting was the preferred method for catching pike which is why they borrowed some live trout from the fish hatchery to finally lure their biggest pike. However, using live fish for bait is only good if you can transport them legally, carry them for miles effectively and have the spare time to catch them. Now in England it is generally illegal to move fish around the country without special permission from the authorities making it just too much trouble to be viable. Yes, we have used live bait very successfully in the past, but the sheer hassle it involves has turned us away from the practice so in the last decade or so we have focused on other more user-friendly methods.

Thankfully, on the northern rivers there is no need at all to use live baits when perfectly good sea baits can be purchased from the fishmongers at very reasonable cost. During the pike season in October onwards, the top supermarkets sell a range of baits including trout, salmon, sprats, sardines and mackerel, all ideal for pike fishing and very accessible. For example sardines, our favourite pike baits, only cost thirty pence each. Rainbow trout too are available amongst a range of top-quality options. My favourite fishmongers are the independent ones like the retailers set up in the Victorian market in Leeds city centre. In this market they have a very wide range of fish to match any purveyor in the whole of the UK. By purchasing from these professional fishmongers you can fill your freezer up for the winter ahead with a clear conscience and fish in perfect peace without the need to worry about catching baits. There are also various online pike bait suppliers who can supply a good range of frozen baits, these are advertised in the angling press and more recently online. Peace of mind is an important aspect of fishing. To simply relax behind your rods after a busy week at work is a joy. Live baits always deliberately run into the nearest snags and worst of all continually attract a series of small jack pike. In contrast, deadbaits never make for the nearest snags and they selectively attract a bigger stamp of pike which makes deadbaits our first choice every time. My favourite deadbaits are the fresh sardines or trout from the giant supermarket chains. Fresh fish are fish which have not been frozen, in this super fresh condition they look and smell so much better than after they have been frozen. My fishing partner Nigel and I have noticed time and time again how much better fresh fish are when they are available. Why are fresh deadbaits better than frozen? The answer is very simple, they just taste a lot better! We travel to Whitby by the sea to enjoy fresh fish and chips. The taste is just so much better than our local restaurant where frozen fish are used. Don't get me wrong, frozen deadbaits are fine and they do work, but if you can get hold of fresh its worth paying the premium because river pike love them.

After using dead baits exclusively on the northern rivers for the past decade or more we now have great faith in them, in fact we have become so specialised in dead bait fishing we now believe that when done properly they out score live baits in their overall effectiveness. This is especially so in very cold weather. When water temperatures are hovering around freezing point pike seldom chase after fast moving baits, but they will pick up a static dead fish positioned near their holding areas. At these very low temperatures, which are common on the cold northern rivers, pike become very slow and comatose and literally hug the riverbed to the extent they often collect a ring of leeches on their abdomen. This is a phenomenon we normally witness in late January when their metabolic rate is at the lowest ebb of the year. Very few anglers witness this, because few ventures out in such cold weather and not without good reason, not only is it uncomfortable, but also pike become very hard to catch owing to their semi dormant state. We continue though because quite often, after several blanks, some very good fish do turn up, often the biggest fish of the year too which make it worthwhile. This was a lesson I learned at the age of fourteen when after a freezing cold day we caught a 19lb pike as the shore was freezing up before our eyes. We had been shivering for hours on end in the cold, but suddenly, thanks to that fish we were as warm as toast for the rest of the day! That fish also warmed my attitude to cold weather piking right up to the time of writing, some fifty-three years later!

Fishing in very cold weather is much more tolerable when fishing with good friends, and when the temperatures plummet you really do find out who your real friends are! In these condition static dead baiting methods are generally the best to employ. The success of the day is often dependant on the place you choose to fish the night before you go. It is in making these choices long experience really does come into play in choosing the best viable option. On one river we regularly fish our preferred cold weather pitch is situated on a straight north/south axis along the river which is generally about ten feet deep. From the surface the whole half mile straight looks perfectly uniform. Yet in one short section the river plunges invisibly down to a depth of twenty-two feet and runs at this depth for about one hundred yards. It is in fact what could be described as a true Pike hotspot. There is just sufficient room for my friend Nigel and I to fish without crowding each other. The hotspot is positioned along the eastern bank which is thick with willows which grow horizontally from the steep bankside, this eastern side the bank shelves down to the full twenty-two-foot-deep trough which is only about six feet from the willow strewn bank. Over the years Nigel and I have together caught over twenty-three fish over a weight of twenty pounds in this venue. The far bank is owned by a farmer who does not allow access to anyone. Furthermore, we have never ever seen anyone else pike fishing our secret venue. Although it is a hotspot, it is not always easy fishing. Indeed, on some years the whole area seems to be devoid of fish. Then, perhaps a couple of years later its back in good form producing fish after fish with the different twenties showing up with amazing regularity.

Working through the blanks can be a bit dispiriting of course, but with a good friend even blank days can be great fun. In very cold weather we like to take along the Kerry kettle which is a bankside wood stove which is fuelled by any small twigs and dry grass on the riverside. It can heat up a litre of water to boiling point within about five minutes, free of charge. The smell of wood smoke is very evocative too and immediately transports one back to childhood days by the campfire. We always have fun getting it going and once it boils, we have more hot water than we can cope with. Flasks are fine up to a point, but on a really long cold day it is good to have piping hot water for soups and coffee, it is a much-valued morale booster on those days when sport is slow.

Our primary method of fishing this deep-water hotspot is to set the stop knot at a depth of twenty-five feet and cast the bait to within six inches of the overhanging willows on the far side. Once the flat lead hits the bottom the float cocks indicating all is well. In the very gentle flow the snag friendly float holds its position faithfully. Once the rod is in the rest, we tighten up carefully to the float and keep the rod tip as high as possible to prevent the line from picking up debris floating down the river. A run is normally registered by a gentle nod of the float, with a simultaneous movement of the rod tip. We have noticed that quite often some of the largest pike give the gentlest of takes on the float, another example of less is more. At this stage we wind down the tackle and pull firmly into the pike, we do not strike, but rather just allow the hooks to find their own safe hold in the pike's jaw and then keep a firm constant pressure so they do not come out. If they do, no harm done, just recast and the same pike will most likely retake the bait again anyway. This has happened many times in the past so we just tighten up as soon as the float moves.

Electronic bite alarms are very useful when static deadbaiting. In this case two are in use, one mounted on the rod rest, the second one is built into the Mitchel 'Electronic' reel. Its difficult to watch the floats all the time so audio bite alarms are a great backup tool and help prevent deep hooking pike when deadbaiting.

When using frozen soft baits like sardines they hold together better when still frozen and hence are better for casting. Once in the water the gradual thawing process allows the fish oils to be released gradually as the bait defrosts and thus prolonging the dispersal process. Our ground bait consists of chopped up fish in one inch diameter chunks. It is very important to de frost these the night before, if they are used when still frozen, they will simply float off downstream and end up about half a mile from your swim! When fishing a swim which is twenty feet deep it is important to calculate where the ground bait need to be positioned so it lands near your bait. If the defrosted ground bait is dropped around the float by the time it reaches the riverbed it will possibly be about twenty meters downstream from the bait. To avoid this, we use a catapult to send out the fish chunks, one by one to land about five to ten yards above the position of the float. In this way the ground bait will settle nicely under the float where it should be within sight of the main bait.

Freshly chopped up sardine ready to be catapulted out to the fishing area one by one. When positioned around the bait they make perfect ground bait in exactly the right place and at the right time. Pike attractors like the smelt extract also help too. We believe pike will travel upstream for a mile or more to check out the scent trails flowing downstream in the current.

By using these methods carefully we now believe dead baiting is better than live baiting on the rivers. A well-positioned dead bait surrounded by chopped up ground bait will attract pike from possibly a mile or more downstream. If the river is flowing at a gentle one mile per hour, then a seven-o clock start will mean that by ten o clock every pike within a mile or so downstream will be aware of your offerings. Live baiting on its own does not offer this kind of reach in the river environment. It is interesting too that the first runs of the day usually come around ten o clock onwards, as if those pike from downstream are homing in on the scent trails.

On the subject of Pike hotspots we have already described in detail our deep river hotspot which we often occupy during very cold weather. There are many other hotspots with differing morphologies though. One of the most enduring and prolific pike hotspots we have ever known is situated in only four feet of water. This is again positioned alongside a long row of dense willow bushes on the far bank. Within the river course it is set about three hundred yards below a long shallow streamy river glide no more than two feet deep. A rocky riverbed noted for its trout and grayling. Then, about four hundred yards below the river it again becomes fast and shallow with challenging rapids much enjoyed by the local canoe clubs.

The Authors son Jonathan aged eight next to a haul of six pike between eight and twelve pounds in weight. This is just one third of the total haul taken from the shallow water pike hotspot alluded to in the text.

Therefore, between these fast shallows we have a three-hundred-yard section of slow water around three feet deep affording sanctuary to a sizeable pike colony. As in the deep-water example, the pike love to haunt the overhanging willows which provide complete protection from the far bank side. Once again, the static dead bait, float ledgered and anchored hard against the willows provides the perfect controllable solution. In one afternoon we caught sixteen pike from this hotspot, just one after the other. As soon as the bait hit the water it was taken straight away, time and time again, yet most of these willing pike were under ten pounds. We returned several times and again had great results, but after over twenty-five years of trying still no twenties and yet still a great pike hotspot. Clearly, there is something about this shallow water hotspot the twenty-pound class do not like. My own pet theory on this is that pike over twenty pounds in weight generally prefer much deeper water, or at least they do here. No matter, it is still a fantastic place to fish. Having said that, we have caught plenty of twenty-pound class pike in only two or three feet of water, but with hindsight, these latter shallow water catches were only a few yards away from deep water over twenty feet deep. These observations have led us to believe that if you are selectively fishing for twenty pound plus pike make sure there is a deep-water sanctuary nearby for the big girls to retire to.

Another favourite pike hotspot for us lies below a large weir on one of our larger northern rivers shown on the map. On this river the water falls a good seven feet over the sill of the weir providing a constant pounding noise below the weir as the force of the water descends into the plunge pool below the weir. This creates a great deal of froth which collects in the marginal shallows where the water settles out from the frantic main flow. The froth in this case helps to locate the pike which love to hide beneath its wide veil. The conditions we describe here are present on all the sixteen rivers covered in the rivers section. Most, if not all the weirs in the lower river sections provide great pike hotspots where well oxygenated water and prolific weed growth combine to produce ideal territory for pike of all sizes. These are the exact conditions which produced Norris Sturdy's 56lb mammoth pike from the river Ure. In this case it was a pike which took full advantage of countless number of salmon detained by low water below the weir on their migration runs to the Ure headwaters to spawn. When one considers that this big pike had the opportunity to snack regularly on five pound plus salmon it was hardly surprizing it and many other pike in the UK grew to such huge sizes. That was of course at a time when our salmon rivers were full of fish freshly run from the rich feeding grounds of the Greenland shelf.

Another peculiar version of a river pike hot spot we favour is situated in deep water behind a large bend in the river. At times of high water the river forms an eddy which is only about the size of a squash court but provides a nice tranquil shelter out of the main force of the river. Time and time again we have scored good catches in this hotspot and is the opposite to the shallow hotspot mentioned earlier in that this this deep-water eddy only produces pike over twenty pounds. The swim in question is about fourteen feet deep. For some strange reason we never ever catch pike under twenty pounds in this hotspot. If the float moves, we know it is going to be big! We sometimes blank on this venue, but we can cope with this, indeed, my friend Nigel had his personal best here with a pike of twenty-eight pounds! Now that was worth a blank or two!

Nigel with his personal best river pike weighing over 28lb. This pike came from a deep-water eddy about fourteen feet deep but close to the bank. This hotspot only ever produces pike over the twenty-pound mark, never any smaller. This sounds very unusual and yet after over thirty years fishing together this has so far proved to be the case!

We know of about thirty pike hotspots on the northern rivers, they are all very special to us and after catching several big pike from them they become like Holy ground, that is, places we just love to be and fish from. The kind of place you know from experience that at any time something very special can happen, and with a bit of effort it always does.

In this section we have described the different conditions which can create a pike hotspot. This will hopefully give the reader some pointers on what features to look out for, not just on the northern rivers of England, but equally and on a larger scale for our friends in Canada, Russia, the U.S.A. and all of mainland Europe. We believe instinctively that our northern pike are pretty much the same the world over. For example I would wager that whilst I have never fished for German Pike I am fairly certain those big German pike will prefer fresh to frozen baits every time. Also, that their pike live in hotspots just as our northern pike do. I also know their pike will collect in the shallows to spawn in springtime. In this way we are fairly certain that the guidelines given in this book on river pike will be perfectly transferable on a global scale. I do hope so and I hope our experiences of pike behaviour help you the reader to catch pike more regularly wherever you fish.

Spinning for Northern River Pike – The Most Rewarding Method of all

Have you ever hooked a twenty-pound northern river pike on a spinner? If you have, you will know what it is like to be locked into quite a nerve-racking struggle. Sometimes it starts off with you thinking you have snagged a sunken log, but then the log begins to swim upstream! At other times you can feel a low frequency head shake deep down on the riverbed. Then it starts to move away, slowly and cautiously at first, then as you increase tension it realises its mistake and powers off wrenching line from a screaming reel. In either instance all you can do is pretend you are in some sort of control! You can check the tension control is set correctly, you can coax and steer to a certain extent with your rod, but in the early stages of play the pike is in full control. Gradually though, with patient cajoling your heavyweight prey inches towards the net. Then for the first time you see those huge jaws and then equally exciting, as the pike sees the net it triggers another long thrusting run giving you a fatalistic sick feeling in the pit of your stomach. Eventually, after much begging and praying to God your fish does finally succumb to the awaiting net. At this point all anxiety evaporates and as you lift your net up and instinctively realise it is over the magical twenty-pound mark. You also know then that you are a member of a very small club of anglers who have landed a twenty-pound pike on a spinner from one of the northern rivers.

In our experience we have had a lot bigger pike on natural baits than artificial, so we rate naturals as the better option for selectively catching big pike on the northern rivers. Yet in the past authors like R.D.C. Barder have argued strongly to the contrary that spinning is the most successful method of catching pike. On some waters it is certainly true too. He backs it up too with sound reasoning in his excellent book, "Spinning for Pike" published by David and Charles. We would concede that on the great lakes of Sweden and Holland modern lure anglers catch huge pike up to over forty pounds on artificial lures where lures provide the most viable way of covering these huge waters and so a lot depends on the size and quality of water's you fish. On our more intimate northern rivers, we have certainly found natural baits are better by far. Despite this we still believe that the sheer joy of spinning is irreplaceable and just too good to miss out on. Thinking back to when Norris Sturdy hooked his biggest ever pike on a Colorado spoon then lost it when it broke free. It is interesting to reflect that upon his return to catch this great pike, despite several visits he could not tempt his pike again on a spinner. Yet when he returned with a can of natural baits, they were able to re catch it within a couple of hours. We believe the lesson here is that pike do 'wise up' to artificial baits very quickly. On today's intimate northern rivers pike have possibly already fallen to spinners at a young age and soon learn to avoid them. Therefore, catching a twenty pounder on the northern rivers is a particularly special event to be savoured. Over ninety five percent of our river twenties have fallen to natural baits, many of these I cannot even remember the details of capture without referring to the diaries. However, the twenties taken on artificial lures are still seared into the memory as the experience was so vivid and so much more memorable. Therefore, as far as we are concerned spinning for pike is just too good to miss as a method, even though we have found it is a less effective for twenty pound plus sized pike on our waters.

Back in the 1960s the fishing tackle manufacturers A.B.U. Sweden distributed an annual catalogue in the post to customers who simply asked to be included on their mailing list. This catalogue showed the full range of their lures and rods in full colour. The selection of lures was very extensive and interesting. Ever since then I have been an avid collector of all kinds of spinners, spoons and plugs and like the float collection mentioned earlier it has become a lifelong hobby within a hobby. The catalogue also had photos of giant pike taken on ABU Lures, there was even a photo of the Swedish royal family endorsing these fine products!

Never to be outdone the Shakespeare company, founded in the USA in 1897 also had its own fishing catalogue too. In the mid-1960s Shakespeare merged with three English tackle firms Allcocks, Youngs and Lees. The new combined catalogue called the 'Allcocks and Norris Shakespeare Anglers Guide' was a wonderful annual publication featuring not only a wide range of tackle but also useful articles on various topics including spinning for pike. Just like the ABU catalogue there were lots of artificial lures to choose from, many of which are now collectors' items and sell for a great deal of money. Also memorable were the very inspiring photos of huge pike caught to fully endorse the effectiveness of their tackle.

Now, with online shopping the range of choice is much more extensive making it even more interesting to study the various ranges available. When leading pike spinning expert John Milford came to Harrogate to give us a talk on modern lure fishing, he made it clear that its best to buy quality known brands like Rapala, Shakespeare and ABU. John emphasised that the "Christmas Cracker" type lures may be cheaper, but these imitations of the real brands can just fall to pieces at the worst time possible, so his advice was to buy the best-known brands to avoid disappointment. John also emphasised that one should carry a good range of lures to meet the various conditions likely to be encountered each day.

Top Lure. The authors favourite spoon for selectively catching big pike, The 40g A.B.U. 'Pike' spoon. Below, Barrie Rickards favourite the 'Lucky Strike' Lure, ideal for fishing shallow or deep waters at slow speeds. Both these lures have accounted for countless big pike on the Northern Rivers.

Another top lure angler Barrie Rickards and author of an advanced book on pike spinning called 'Modern Lure Fishing' by Crowood Press. Barrie also recommended carrying a good range of lures to meet all eventualities. During one conversation I had with Barrie, he told me his all-time favourite lure was the Lucky Strike Lizard Lure in a hammered copper and silver finish. I purchased a few of these lures and found they are very effective indeed on the Yorkshire rivers. Their main winning quality is their ability to be fished very slowly and yet still emit a broad silver flash which is very lifelike indeed. They are most effective on the deep slow sections of the river Ouse when the water is low, and flow is minimal. If there is a stronger current, they tend to be carried with the flow too much as they are a little on the light side. Far better though on his local Fenland drains when conditions are settled.

"If you want to catch a big pike you need to use a big lure" this was the classic advice I got from my boyhood mentor Norris Sturdy. He knew all about the Yorkshire River pike and had himself a very handsome collection of plugs and spoons. Before meeting Norris, I was using very small bar spoons Devon's minnows and plugs, mostly seen in my local tackle shop, Wrights of Bedale. I greatly enjoyed catching lots of small pike and perch on these especially in the River Swale which was full of jacks in the early 1970s. Not long after meeting and fishing with Norris I upgraded my collection with some big ABU Hi-Lo Plugs and some Big S plugs by Shakespeare. Now at last I started catching pike of a much bigger size category.

THUNDERSTORMS, WATERDOGS, THUNDERBUGS AND FLOODWATER PIKE

As a relative youngster of twenty-two in the mid-seventies I had a summer job which topped up my student grant nicely. If I had to live my life by just one single guiding maxim it would be 'Labor omnia vincit' which is pure Latin for 'Work Conquers all'. This is so true as without my summer job there would be no car, no fishing tackle and minimal access to the Northern Rivers. My Austin 1100 was a very important piece of fishing tackle as it gave instant access to all the Northern Rivers. In those happy days I had the energy to work a full ten hours, come home for my tea (thanks Mum) and still go fishing on those long balmy summer evenings on the local river Ure. On one of these evening sessions and unbeknown to me there had been a thunderstorm high up in Wensleydale causing the river to rise five feet above the normal level. There had not been a drop of rain in Ripon for days, so I was surprised to see the river in flood.

River Pike in Northern England

A good selection of pike spoons and plugs. The plugs are best for shallow water conditions whilst the spoons are better for fishing deep water up to twenty feet or more. When casting out the spoon on a new stretch of deep water, start counting from the moment the spoon hits the surface. Keep counting until it reaches the bottom. This gives a good idea of water depth. If you count to twenty at one second intervals the water will be about twenty feet deep. On successive casts start winding back when the spoon is at the count of sixteen. In this way one can fish just above the riverbed.

Not wishing to waste my petrol and effort I fished on in the dubious brown peat-stained water. My new Shakespeare Big S lure had a good loud rattle inside its plastic trout scale body. It also fought well as I retrieved it upstream through the coloured water. The rod was juddering to hold the Big S in place within the flow. As soon as I stopped winding in the plug popped up to the surface providing a good level of control for avoiding the deep snags which I knew were protruding up from the riverbed. After only ten minutes I cast the Big S into a moderate flow of about five miles per hour. This was in deepish water of ten feet next to a half-submerged willow bush which flexed and rocked backwards then forwards in the flow. As I played my energetic plug through the current, I was ultra-careful not to allow it to get snagged. Being very young and new to pike fishing with only ten years' experience my expectations were rock bottom. Therefore, I was shocked when my vibrating plug was hit by a pike with tremendous ferocity. It was such a violent strike it came as a shock; I was quite stunned. This was a July pike; the water temperature was fifty-five-degrees Fahrenheit and I swear that pike fought harder than many a twenty pounder I have caught. It was in fact only fourteen pounds but so very strong. Just a few months previously I had been spinning from a boat on Norfolk's famous River Bure. The pike on the Bure were noticeably fatter than my local Yorkshire Pike, very beautiful fish, more numerous and generally heavier. Yet despite these desirable qualities I found them no way near as ferocious or hard fighting. Without doubt the Ure pike, though smaller in size and numbers, possess a steely tenacity which was absent in the Norfolk River pike. A bit like comparing a well-fed Labrador dog (Bure Pike) with a lean hungry wild wolf (Ure Pike). I am not suggesting one is better than the other, but the differences were immediately apparent to me and very interesting to observe. In over fifty years of pike fishing on a wide variety of waters, the only pike I have caught which have been almost as strong as fast Yorkshire River pike are the Loch Lomond pike which are similarly thin firm fish like the fast Yorkshire River pike.

Catching that fourteen-pound pike in coloured flooded water taught me a very important lesson. Namely that coloured floodwater conditions can be good for catching pike, even in a good flow of high water. This is something I had never seen recommended in any pike books or articles on the subject. Of course, the great thing about spinning is that you can cast about in all various parts of the river very quickly, testing different pools and slacks to search out the fish. A few weeks later I returned to another area of the River Ure in Wensleydale where the river stands at a height of three hundred- and twenty-feet above sea level. This area is better known for its top-quality trout and grayling than its pike, but I knew there were a few good quality pike in residence so gave it a try. On this visit the weather was again very thundery. The air was close, it was early August and the farmers were busy gathering in their straw bales from the fields after harvest. I knew thunder was in the air, the river was again in flood with peat-stained water. It was time to do some thunderstorm plugging. This time I used my ABU Spinning rod with a multiplier and a combination of Big S plugs and of course my ABU Hi- Lo plug selections. Again, after a long day at work I rushed up to the river and found the river very high indeed, about seven feet above normal. The sky was full of 'Waterdogs' which are dark, almost black cumulous clouds reaching high into the upper atmosphere and fresh in from the

Atlantic Ocean. The sky between the clouds was a beautiful bright azure blue which reflected across the river surface and made a very pleasing contrast with the threatening dark cumulous (Waterdog) clouds.

I only carried one rod and quickly set up, this time, after my earlier floodwater induction I was quite happy with the coloured water conditions and began to fish with higher expectations. The only slight annoyance were the clouds of tiny black flies called thunder bugs, which, like midges, required constant swatting to keep at bay. Using my favourite Big S lure, I started to fish some quiet water on a large bend in the river but had no success. At this point there was a huge downpour, the heavens opened, and I sheltered as best I could under the wide bough of a large beech tree. Then the thunderstorm stopped as suddenly as it started. I then walked two hundred yards downstream onto a straight section of river. On this section the river was really bowling silently down the centre at a fast pace, possibly as fast as fifteen miles per hour in the centre, but along the sides the flow was almost stationery and rafts of flotsam were accumulating along the edges. By selecting a seven-inch ABU Hi- Lo plug I cast towards the middle and allowed the giant plug to float downstream. A little tension made the plug spring to life and it began to dive downwards and further into the sheltered margins.

The plug fished perfectly along the margins in a slow enticing manner, as good as any live bait in the coloured flooded waters and a hundred times more mobile. After just a few casts the giant plug was seized in no uncertain terms about twelve feet from the riverbank in about six feet of quiet water. The large treble hooks on the Hi-Lo plug held very firm as the unseen fish powered off into the fast central flow of the river. Holding my rod high I kept my left thumb over the spool of the multiplier reel to maintain some control, but the force of the fish really ripped line from the spool at a frightening pace. Despite the line being wet I still received line burn on my thumb, but it was a happy price to pay for doing battle with such a magnificent pike. It took about fifteen minutes to bring this energetic fish safely to the net, then finally there she was, a beautiful pike, metallic green hues sparkling in the late evening sunshine. She weighed in at fifteen pounds and measured thirty-six inches long. The thunder bugs were still biting my arms and neck, but somehow it did not matter anymore!

We have only covered about half a dozen different types of artificial lures in this section on spinning, but there are hundreds of different types. Many of these diverse patterns are I am sure aimed at catching anglers rather than fish. Perhaps I should apologise here because I only use spinners to catch pike and not anglers, there is a big difference! I know for example there are some wonderful rubber or soft baits available now and I do use them, they are so realistic in their action that it beggar's belief and the pike certainly like them. I have seen some very large rubber baits used in Holland by young boat anglers who troll the immense lakes they have near Amsterdam. Some of the plugs they use are over two feet long and yes, they do work. I have seen young Dutch anglers catching pike over the magical fifty-pound mark on them. No that is not a typo, and I do not blame you for thinking it is. I would never have believed it possible, but I have seen it happen without any shadow of doubt. It makes me want to book a fortnight in Amsterdam right away, boats are available to hire there, so it is something for the bucket list. Having said that we have already had fifty-pound pike in the northern rivers and as the salmon numbers begin to increase again, they could already be there just waiting to be caught. We will deal more specifically with this opportunity later in the book.

One annoying thing about some lure manufacturers is that they bring out a good bait which works well and then discontinue it after about five years. For this reason, if I really like a certain spoon or plug, I buy several in case they are discontinued. I must say that ABU Garcia are not guilty of discontinuing winning lures in fact they are very good at retaining old favourites. For example, one of my favourite spoon baits is the ABU Atom lure. It casts like a bullet and has a wonderful wobbling action which big pike find irresistible. One of the top Swedish angling experts Evelina Henriksen has recently recommended them and has caught pike up to 110 centimetres long on them, over twenty pounds in weight! I can remember seeing the Atom lures advertised in my nineteen sixties catalogues, so they have been on sale for well over fifty years. Well, if it is not broken why fix it? For this reason, I will always carry large Atom lures ready in my lure box.

In the discussion so far, we have only dealt with spinning in coloured or high-water level conditions. Obviously, big pike can also be caught in clear conditions too, but not quite so easily in our experience. I do have one very fond memory though of catching a big pike when the river was running low and clear. The event took place in mid-September. I had been working in Newcastle all day and arranged to have an evening's fishing on my way home on the River Ure in North Yorkshire. The good thing about September is that the sun goes down reasonably early allowing a couple of hours fishing after work and crucially for a working man who must be up for work at 6.30am each morning, you can fish the twilight period without staying out until midnight. On this evening I parked the car at the Old Horn Inn, a very fine public house within easy walking distance of the River Ure. There are about four miles of bank space along this section held by three of the big city club waters. Since I was a full member of all three of these clubs, I could roam freely and enjoy uninterrupted access to about four miles of this lovely mixed fishery in the heart of Wensleydale.

On this evening I walked up stream passing by several mouth-watering swims and eventually settled to fish on a large sand bank on a massive inside bend of the river. I could tell by the undisturbed sand that no one had touched it for weeks on end, the only footprints were those left by various waterfowl. The water was only about one foot deep in the edge but sloped gradually towards the middle where it was about twelve feet deep. Then, further out the water became even deeper running at eighteen feet very close to the outside bend of the river. I started off by plug fishing the weedy inside bend, casting short distances to selectively cover the weedy shallows. Hundreds of minnows and tiny dace sprayed the surface as my floating plug neared the surface. Many of the larger plucky minnows chased after the lure too, even though they were fifty times smaller than their quarry! After about ten minutes of careful fishing the shallows I changed my lure to a deep running spoon, this time an eighteen-gram silver spoon which was ideal for fishing the deeper water. In a crafty way I was pleased I had not taken any small Jacks in the shallow weeds, instinct told me there was probably a very good reason the Jacks were not there! On the far side of the river the whole outside bend was lined with dense banks of willow bushes which had been planted by the farmers to prevent the bank from being eroded. This made the river completely unfishable on the opposite bank, perfect shelter for big trout, chub, grayling, or pike which may take advantage of this remote sanctuary. It was a long cast though, fifty or even sixty yards.

The rod I was using was my trusty Milbro Spinwell rod make from strong solid green fibreglass. It was easily strong enough for the job in hand and I cast the spoon first to the top end of the swim and on each successive cast working downstream I cast further out. On about the fourth cast the spoonbait my casting range was spot on. The bait landed about one foot from the willow bushes trailing in the water. As soon as I saw it hit the water surface, I started to count down the estimated feet as it sank, the bait did not even reach the bottom as it was taken on the count of ten in the clear water. A firm strike and I felt a deep low frequency head shake which can only mean one thing…Pike on! I tightened the line-up firmly and held my rod as high as possible to keep the pike from running too deep. It did run deep though, as fast as it could downstream hugging the bottom. Thankfully though it found no snags and following a long fight it eventually succumbed to the safety of the net. It was a wonderful scale perfect pike with the length of a twenty pounder and the weight in fact just over eighteen pounds. The sun was setting in the West and Penn Hill was silhouetted jet black below a bright yellow, red and blue sunset. What an amazingly colourful close to a wonderful evening. I released the pike safely back into the river which was ablaze in the reflected colours of the skyline. Once back at the car I changed into my driving shoes and drove away steadily down the narrow roads leading a winding course through lower Wensleydale and back home. I did not put the radio on as all I wanted to do was to live in the moment and savour what had just taken place.

    I had the very good fortune to spin for pike in the Yorkshire Rivers with Barrie on at least half a dozen occasions unfortunately whilst spinning we caught virtually no pike above about six pounds. Fishing mainly in clear waters in daytime even Barrie could not catch. He used a wide range of spoons including his famous Barrie's Buzzers on which he caught some fine chub, perch and very large brown trout. If we had fished late evening, I am sure we would have done better. Barrie told me he had never caught a Yorkshire River twenty and I promised him we would soon put that right. But sadly, he died before we accomplished that, so I never managed to fulfil my promise to him. Barrie did not care though; he had caught almost 2,000 doubles from all over the United Kingdom. He also caught over two hundred and forty-three twenty-pound pike, again mainly from the Fenlands but also from other parts of the United

Kingdom. Barrie was not just a great angler though, he also contributed more to pike conservation than any other angler alive. He also left a huge legacy within the numerous books he wrote on pike including his first book 'Fishing for Big Pike'. His best book, in my opinion was 'Success with Pike', which he wrote a good eighteen years later. The additional years of front-line experience really made a notable difference, I thought.

Before finishing off this section dealing with spinning for pike in the Northern Rivers, I would just like to point out that in Yorkshire and the north there are numerous smaller tributaries to the rivers shown on the map. Several of these smaller rivers have good stocks of smaller pike running up to about five or ten pounds in weight. Yes, they do have the occasional twenty-pound pike too, especially where they join the main rivers. However, further upstream beyond the first waterfalls which prevent upwards movement of pike, the size of the pike become much smaller owing to the constraints of their surroundings. In these waters pike numbers can be quite prolific and great fun can be had catching these smaller pike on light spinning tackle. By using a light spinning rod and smaller lures these pike can really show their mettle and often fight harder size for size than their larger relatives further downstream. They are also suitable places for youngsters to fish where pike are more numerous and occupy streams which are much safer to fish. In summer pike can easily be spotted in the shallow water and nothing is more exciting than spotting your prey then devising a way of catching them. These feeder streams are often full of minnows too giving the opportunity to catch bait in minnow bottles for live or dead baiting. Lower down at the point where these tributaries meet the main river is often a good place to catch big pike late on in the season too. Quite often the tributaries are more sheltered than the main rivers and provide valuable spawning sites for pike to congregate in any time from February until June. On the upper tributaries of the River Derwent, it is not just the salmon who head upstream to spawn, but also big pike too. There are instances of big pike up to twenty-four pounds in weight being caught in tiny rivers barely seven feet wide and only a couple of feet deep. By fishing light spinning tackle and using the mobile approach such waters can be fished very effectively and provide some unexpected surprises!

MODERN SOFTBAITS THE ARTIFICIAL LIVEBAITS

There are now a wide variety of soft baits in all sizes which are replica lures made from very soft material which both looks and feels like a live fish. I make no apologies for the paradoxical title because these modern lures really do swim like real fish, so much so there is now even less reason to ever use live baits again! Soft baits are not new though, the Victorians used Wagtail Baits made from leather and later rubber. These original soft baits were no way near as realistic as the modern versions. The two baits illustrated here are made by Savage and are the best on the market. The brown trout version shown is ideal for the northern rivers which are of course well stocked with wild brown trout. The yellow bait next to it is an eel imitation and swims just like the real thing. Although these baits are very expensive, they are worth every penny. We quite often use them as a change bait to connect with those wily fish which follow in the bait when spinning but fail to take at the last minute. By changing to these very realistic baits the pike very often succumb to their irresistible movements. If there is a reasonable flow in the swim these baits can be just held back in the current until a predator comes along and attacks. In almost every case if a pike is in the swim, they will normally succumb to the lifelike movements of these baits making them the most realistic baits of all.

Modern Soft baits are the most lifelike artificial baits of all. It is very difficult to justify the use of live baits when there are imitations as good as these!

DEVON MINNOWS

Few modern Pike anglers rate the Devon minnow baits as a good spinner for pike fishing these days and yet in our experience, they are very effective indeed for catching pike, especially on fast rivers like the Nidd, Ure and Swale. They have also accounted for more than a few big pike by salmon anglers fishing on the River Wear, Tyne and Tweed.

A selection of Devon minnows. There is no doubt pike love Devon Minnow baits and they are particularly useful on the fast Northern Rivers where they can hold their own in strong currents. A great many big pike have fallen to these lures in the past, especially by salmon anglers fishing the River Tyne and Tweed. For these reasons I always carry a few Devon Minnows in the lure bag.

Pike charge at the Devon minnows with mouths open to scoop up as many minnows as possible. Hundreds of minnows can be seen spraying out of the water surface in panic, often followed by an upward moving pike which bursts out of the water fuelling its reputation as the water wolf. Memorable and regular scenes like these have made us 'Real believers' in the in the value of this often-neglected bait. We are not the first, indeed, Tom Grey the author of 'Pike Fishing' in 1923 was a lifelong Pike fishing expert on the southern rivers. In Toms book he states out of all the lures available his most favourite was the silver Devon minnow. Not surprisingly either since he caught pike up to thirty pounds on his trusty Devon minnows. Toms' sobriquet in his local angling circle was thus the 'Silver Devon'! What a lovely name and one of many reasons we just had to reserve a very special place in this book on river pike for the deadly and effective Devon minnow baits.

As touched on earlier we have noticed that pike assault the Devon Minnows with amusing force and speed. I suspect this is because they target the lure not as an individual fish but rather as a shoal. In this way they power into the bait target as fast as possible with the intent of engulfing as many minnows as possible before they can escape. For these reasons we rate the bait as simply indispensable and just too much fun to miss out on.

The one limitation of the Devon minnow is that it tends to cause line twist. This problem manifests itself by line repeatedly becoming twisted round the top ring of the rod. Even with the use of several swivels and anti-kink vanes it still seems to occur after an hour or twos spinning. To correct this, remove the bait and wire trace from the line leaving the line free. Next, go to the top of the riverbank and put the rod on the ground with bale arm open on the reel, then draw off fifty yards by walking along the bank, then, walk back to the rod and wind back the line slowly to allow the line to straighten itself back to normal. In this way the line can be seen to unravel and comb out its twists in a very satisfying controlled way. A second repeat process may be needed in bad cases, but even that only takes a few minutes and provides a cathartic break!

BAR SPOONS

Bar spoons are another artificial lure we have found to be very effective for river fishing too. These often-overlooked lures have the great advantage of sending out high frequency vibrations which are ideal in coloured cloudy water. They also reflect the light very well in clear conditions and like the Devon minnow is probably seen by predators as a flashing shoal of fish. We have done well with the humble bar spoons in various rivers across the north. Our most memorable catch was a twenty-one-pound pike taken in shallow water in spring. For some reason on that day, we chose the Ondex size six (See the gnarled lure itself in the illustration). A lovely large lure with a red tag attached to the treble hook. On about the third cast we saw a bow wave heading towards our lure in about five feet of water. This pike soon came into view in the crystal-clear water. It was obviously a big pike and we expected it to grab the lure at any moment and yet it didn't. Instead, it just followed the bait in with its snout only about one inch behind the spinning bait! As it came forever closer, we could see what a big pike it was and at the same time it saw us and shot off without taking the lure. We knew the pike had been spooked so rather than re cast straight away we walked about two hundred yards along the bank to deliberately avoid stressing this lovely fish any further. Once in our new pitch we caught a smaller pike which took the bait instantly without hesitation. Out of all the spinners we have discussed so far, we have found the bar spoon to have the most impressive hooking rate with a ratio of about 99%. Other more modern lures have very poor hooking to catching ratios of about 60%. or even worse. After returning our small pike to the water we quietly returned to our indecisive big pike in the hope that it may have forgotten our earlier encounter. Out went the Ondex lure for another try and after just a few turns of the reel handle our big pike obliged us by taking the bar spoon with a hearty tug, the fight was on and what an interesting tussle we had in the shallow crystal-clear water. This was a pre spawn pike, as fat as a pig and in wonderful condition. For us, that pike finally proved the notion that bar spoons are a serious lure for big pike. If you are still not convinced then also don't forget that on the 9th of March 1990, famous rugby player Gareth Edwards caught the new official British record rod caught pike on a size five Mepps spinner, the same spinner lent to him by his fishing friend Fred Buller! Gareth's pike weighed in at an amazing 45lb 6oz! ……Enough said!

Last but by no means least a sparkling shoal of bar spoons! These lures are probably the most underrated lures of all. Not only are they good at attracting pike (Including the British record). They are also the most successful lures for hooking pike on the strike. In our experience these baits have the highest strike to hooking ratio out of all the artificial lures on the market today.

River Pike in Northern England

Transporting Equipment

There is no doubt that one of the most important pieces of equipment for transporting fishing tackle is the car. As a youngster the only access to the rivers was either on foot or on bicycle or public transport. Then, when I finally owned an actual car a whole new world of pike fishing opened. Suddenly all the northern rivers became available with so much good fishing it was difficult to know where to start! Once parked up there may still be a mile or so walk to the best venue. There is of course a natural tendency to just settle down in the nearest swim from the car park, this is usually a mistake though as these are the very areas which get overfished and so fish tend to avoid car park pegs like the plague. For this reason, we believe generally it is worth the effort to fish as far from the car park as possible. In doing this one is tempted to travel very light but again this can be a mistake because if you want to fish purposefully on a cold winters day you then need all the kit to keep warm and comfortable. This includes the brolly, the chair and lots of hot food to keep you warm and motivated on a full-blooded fishing day out. Without these basic comforts it is difficult to fish properly but how do you carry it all? A modern Rucksack with padded straps is ideal as it swallows tackle in its voluminous hold, and it leaves the hands free to carry rods. It is also good for climbing over fences, stiles, or very rough ground.

On a frosty winter session our average payload of essential equipment is about forty to fifty pounds in weight. If there is a mile walk ahead then we are looking at quite a formidable trek and this alone generally cuts out about ninety percent of anglers. With a little bit of forward planning, it really is not that difficult though. First, on the walk to the venue, it helps to just remove coats and only wear a shirt to prevent getting over heated. No matter how cold the weather is one soon warms up when 'man hauling' all the gear. Even in sub-zero temperatures the cold is no problem even when steam can be seen visibly rising from one's shoulders when you arrive. This is good as it shows you are burning off calorie's and have already benefited from the day out. Make sure you are dry though before donning the thermal suit, there is nothing worse than sitting in the cold in soaking fishing gear. For many anglers all this is too much like arduous work, and yet millions of people think nothing of paying a small fortune to work out in gyms and there is nothing wrong with that, but when you go fishing the exercise and fresh air is free! Fitness experts do say that vigorous exercise is addictive, and I must confess that one of the most enjoyable parts of the fishing day is just settling down in the fishing chair behind two rods and enjoying the endorphins 'high' as they rush through the body following a healthy walk to the venue. The longer distance from the car, the better one feels and the bigger the pike because big pike do prefer to live in more remote, seldom fished places.

Transporting rods is another aspect which deserves consideration too. My own favourite method is to use a six by five-foot green canvas roll up holdall. The roll up bag is useful because it completely protects the rods, reels, lines, and hooks within the wrap. In this simple system rods and tackles can be ready made up so once at the bankside you can just bait up the rods and start fishing in under about three minutes. If you must tackle up at the swim it may take as long as ten minutes per rod, which, with two rods is twenty minutes lost fishing time! Do not forget to set up the landing net first though, this is important as it is not uncommon to get a run as soon as the bait hits the water, even when the bait is still frozen solid! Another system is to use the quiver roll up, which is a lighter 'Robin Hood' shoulder strap version of the full roll up model with the rods protruding like arrows from an archer's quiver. Both designs can be used for carrying rod rests, brolly and landing nets to good effect too. Finally, there are a complete range of modern 'zip up' rod holdall systems now available including designs to cope with carrying three rods, all at very reasonable prices. My own roll up version mentioned above is a green canvas one made to my own design with pockets to hold rods and bank sticks separately. It was made up by a local saddler who used industrial stitching methods to produce a very fine product at about a third of the cost of propriety versions. I still have a lighter model of a green cloth roll up version made up by my wife Liz before we got married. It still works well and is ideal for carrying light spinning rods for holiday trips in Scotland and Ireland.

Many of the lowland river sections are protected by Levees and flood barriers which run parallel to the rivers on both banks. These features provide very smooth walking conditions on the top of the bank and are ideal for using the fishing tackle barrow. The mechanical advantage provided by the wheelbarrow is quite amazing. Even weights of up to 120 pounds can be lifted effortlessly. Yes, it is a bit more hassle loading the barrow into the car, and yes, it is awkward getting over stiles, but apart from those two minor drawbacks the humble barrow is a godsend making it possible to carry all the gear needed to fish those distant hotspots. Match anglers use them all the time and they are good for pike fishing too. As I become older and not so athletic the mechanical advantages of the wheelbarrow have become increasingly attractive!

There are however many good pike fishing rivers where the terrain is far too rough to use the barrow. In these uneven often wooded areas, the backpack S.A.S. style comes into its own and is the most popular method of carrying fishing tackle today. Modern soldiers often use very large backpacks called Bergen's. These are big enough to carry everything you need and are particularly valuable on overnight stays when brolly camps and sleeping bags are required.

I also have a fishing box which I purchased in 1968 from an Army and Navy shop in Ilkley. It is in fact a very strong wooden box lined with khaki felt. Its original use was to carry high explosive detonator caps for the British Army, hence the protective felt lining. The same felt is now used to protect my camera and fishing tackle. It is also very strong and has served well as a fishing seat too.

To sum up, this small section dealing with transporting fishing tackle may not be the most exciting part of this book, it may even seem peripheral. Yet in truth getting this part right is every bit as important as any other aspect. The logistics of getting all one's equipment to where the pike are is critical, often you must go the extra mile to find the best areas and that is why a lot of thought needs to be put in on how to get there. Pike fishing on the Northern Rivers is not for the faint-hearted. Those long marches carrying fifty pounds in weight to remote willow lined banks are often hard work, but when you get there, relax back in the chair, then watch your floats set up and ready, you know it is all been worthwhile!

RED LETTER DAYS - PROOF OF THE PUDDING

Red Letter Day One

TWO TWENTY POUND PIKE IN ONE DAY

My good friend James was not a fisherman, but he was keen to give it a try so after several months putting the day off for various reasons I finally phoned him and invited him for a day on the River Ure. "I will pick you up at 7.00am on Saturday James". My old friend was keen to go and promised to be ready. When I called round to pick him up it was pouring down with rain, the weather forecast was light wind with occasional showers, so it was not too bad. Fortunately, after a forty-minute drive we arrived at the river and the road was bone dry, there had not been a drop of rain and the river was clear and in good trim. We started off by catching pike baits on single maggots. We had brought a large plastic bucket to keep the bait fresh and after an hour or so we had a good selection of live baits including large minnows, gudgeon, dace, and a tiny jack pike. James was more than happy to keep the bucket topped up with water which he did very effectively. He really enjoyed catching these smaller fish too and continued catching them as I put together the pike fishing tackle. Although I was a fully paid-up club member for the year, James was not, so I bought him a day ticket in advance. That way we could fish two rods and greatly increase our chances with a clear conscience.

The rig I had chosen to use was a single size two hook fastened to an eighteen-inch wire trace supported by one of my home-made, specially designed weedless floats, to fish the shallow weedy parts of the river. There was no weight on the line. No need really, as the water was crystal clear and only three to four feet deep. It was in fact a spawning area for coarse fish which was occupied by pike of various sizes all summer. I selected one of the live baits from the bucket and carefully lip hooked it and gently positioned it about fifteen feet out in the river with a slow underarm cast. At this point James announced he wanted a smoke but had left his matches at home so had to return to the pub in the village to get a new box of Swan matches. "No problem, James" I said, so off he went. Just as he disappeared over the brow of the river embankment my live bait became very excited and started to run back towards the weedy margins.

Then, whoosh, it was taken by an unseen force. The float remained still for a moment, then went marching off into the centre of the river slowly disappearing as it was taken into deeper water. Coils of line were being peeled off my reel spool, it was time to make contact! A firm pull set the hook easily and off it went pulling down hard on the rod and ripping line from the reel. Then I felt a grating sensation from the line, it was still being pulled slowly from the reel, but was obviously chafing against an underwater boulder. The line then parted, and the float came to the top, but it had been pulled forcefully about ten feet above where it was originally set. The trace was gone though, I was devastated! I checked my line by pulling it carefully between my fingers, the line was strong, fifteen pounds breaking strain, but the lower ten feet were seriously chaffed, so I removed the damaged line and set up a fresh rig the same as before. Out went a fresh bait in the same place just beyond the marginal weeds. After only about three minutes the second bait was taken by an unseen force, this time though I stood up as I tightened up and bullied the unseen force upwards and hopefully away from the boulder out in the river. As I was playing the fish James came back in the nick of time and did a great job of landing a very energetic but controllable seven pounder. Yes, we had our first pike and James was amazed at how big it was. "Not half the size of the one we just lost though". My comments went straight over his head, but I did not clarify as we were too busy with our seven pounder. Our first fish of the day was quickly unhooked and out went our baits again. "Keep catching those baits James, we may need them". James was more than happy to oblige and was very absorbed catching small silver fish for his growing collection. The weed bed we fished was about twenty yards long and extended about five yards into the river, beyond these dimensions the river dropped into deeper water of eight to twenty feet deep. We were effectively fishing a ledge of sheltered warm and well oxygenated water which crucially afforded good cover for the pike and everything which lived there. It even had its own small stream at the top end which was facing the sun affording its own unique microclimate. It was and still is a Pike hotspot and owing to its unique geology and aspect has most probably remained one for thousands of years.

    As I carefully watched my float as it nodded its way slowly upstream, I saw a large double figure salmon leap bodily out of the river in mid-stream. It was instantly recognisable with its metallic silver flash, a joy to behold.

We speculated about its motive for leaping in flat water, was it being pursued by a big pike perhaps? As a fish moving upriver it was channelled into the deep bottleneck, possibly this forms an ideal ambush point for very big pike, no one will ever know for certain, but just a minute later the live bait was quietly taken. The float started to judder as it transmitted those tell-tale jaw snapping movements of a pike. Straight away I stood up and pulled the single hook into a very solid fish. Off she went heading straight for the sunken boulder in mid river. This time though the rod was held high to steer the pike away and prevent it getting its head down. The ploy worked and the big unseen force went kiting off upstream in a completely unstoppable run. When it finally broke surface, James was amazed at the size of it. Eventually, after a fight lasting at least fifteen minutes she came into the safety of the net. "Wow its blooming enormous" James said. It was, and we were both ecstatic. Best of all though, it was the same fish we had lost earlier, and the proof of that was it still had the previous trace in its jaws, so we were able to remove both traces which gave us two reasons to celebrate. We weighed her in at over twenty-two pounds, deduct two pounds for the net, yes, just over the twenty-pound mark. After one or two photos, back she went with a big whack of the tail as she moved her way into the deeper water.

Bill (without the beard) holds his twenty plus pounder. What a tremendous fight it gave. Oh yes there are certainly big pike on the northern rivers, but they are not easy to catch by any means.

After all that we were ready for a break and enjoyed some sandwiches and coffee from the flask. It was still a dull and hazy day; it was now about quarter to two and the sun had not broken out at all, the atmosphere was close and very warm. We carefully considered our next move, should we stay here or go to another good pike hotspot over a mile downstream? After being fully recharged with food and drink we chose the latter and quickly packed up our tackle and moved downstream. We judged that we had probably fully farmed out the first peg for today and would do better going onto fresh pastures. In the close heat of the afternoon, the long walk weighed down by about sixty pounds of gear, made the journey purgatory. However, we realised the pike were for some reason, really feeding well so we pressed on heading to the new venue over a mile downstream. On our long walk we were chased very closely by a herd of about twenty young bullocks who must have thought we had come to feed them. They jumped about very excitedly and completely surrounded us. This would have been a terrifying experience for ordinary townsfolk, but James and I were both born and bred countrymen and we realised the young stirks were only playing with us. To us it was not the beast themselves which were a nuisance but rather the clouds of blowflies accompanying them which were the real annoyance. By the time we reached our goal, another weedy hotspot very similar to the first, we were soaking wet with perspiration and immediately sat down for a few minutes on the meadow grass to recover our energy. "It's your turn to catch a big pike now" I said to James trying to revive his spirits. The poor fellow was not a motivated angler and he had just carried the baits all the way." There is no way I could have carried all that gear myself" I said, and I thanked him for making it possible and suggested he should now use the last of the live baits as reward for his efforts. Sure, enough James then went on to catch several good pike into double figures and finally a four pounder, all of which I gladly netted. The river here was over sixty yards wide and we were fishing the outside bend of the river which had a similar weed bank to the morning venue though somehow on a much bigger scale. The weeds were full of roach, dace and minnows, but we had run out of maggots and down to one dead bait which had already been mauled by a pike and was almost good enough to fish with. We had no choice anyway as it was our last bait.

By this time, we were both tired and we still had the daunting prospect of walking all the way back to the car laden down with our heavy gear. James had now had enough and wanted to head back, he did not say as much but I could tell by his body language. "I will just have a couple of last casts" I said to James who was sat down waiting to go.

This time I hooked my small dead bait under its dorsal fin and trotted it downstream through the thinly spaced pikey dark green reeds. About halfway down the reed bed my float stopped. I knew it was a pike by those tell-tale snapping movements betrayed by my float, but instead of moving off it just stayed in the same position. This was quite unusual, but I decided to tighten up hard anyway rather than risk any deep hooking. In the shallow clear water, the whole weed bed seemed to rock as something big shot out into deeper water. The line was connected to the pike, but so was the weed bed. I rushed downstream and lifted the line clear of the weeds and then thankfully I was in direct contact with a very big fish which for the first ten minutes ran alternatively up, then downstream in its efforts to be free. Following a good fifteen minutes and at least two surface eruptions she finally came to the net. "Well done, James" we have done it" By this time my arms were not just aching but were in pain with such a struggle. We left our prize in the water for a few minutes to rest and then got everything ready for a weigh in. The scales went down to 24lb, we deducted two for the net which made her 22lb. We were both on cloud nine by this point. Back she went into the river, as strong as ever, long, lean and exceptionally fit. What an absolute beauty.

We took our time walking back so it was not so difficult. Also, the flask was empty and so was the bucket, so the payload was about thirty pounds lighter. It took about half an hour to get back to the car and I promised James a pint of the best at one of the numerous coaching Inns which peppered our return journey. We found one next to the river in West Tanfield. It was still warm and hazy, the sun never broke through once and yet it was so humid, eighteen degrees centigrade. We sat on a wooded seat and table right next to the River Ure and after five minutes a young lady brought us two freshly drawn pints of Yorkshire Bitter on a tray. Wow, did they taste good! Almost certainly the best pint I have ever had, on probably the best days pike fishing ever too. What more could any pike angler wish for... Oh yes life is good!

My good friend James with his big pike. His smile says it all!

    It had been a very full and interesting session. There were two main things which we discovered on this amazing day. Firstly, the advantages of fishing with the single hook method. Not only had it provided us with arguably the ultimate in bait presentation, but also the fact that having been lost, the single hook did not prevent the first twenty pounder from feeding again within sixty minutes or so. If that had been a treble hook left in the pikes jaws it would more than likely have been unwilling to feed again so quickly. I was so impressed that I wrote up a full account in my angling diary, recording the exact details of the day.

    Secondly, and most importantly, it taught us the value and importance of fishing with a friend. Not just because of the companionship aspect which is a reward in itself. Also though, the teamwork which made it all possible. It would have been very difficult for one to have single handedly carried those baits and tackle so far on such a warm and humid day. The photos too were only possible thanks to having a spare pair of hands which also assisted with the crucial job of landing all those fish. Had we been alone we would have stayed put at the first venue and probably ended up with just the one twenty. Finally, it would have been sad indeed to have to drink alone after such an epic day, no one else could have properly understood what had just happened. Yes, I think it is safe to say that fishing, like a lot of other great sporting activities is best done in good company!

Red Letter Days Two

SPINNING ON THE RIVER OUSE IN SUMMER

The Yorkshire River Ouse is naturally a wide river compared to its smaller tributaries and covers a vast area of water. The section which runs from its source near Ouseburn and down to York covers an area of over three hundred acres alone, and this is just part of it. It is both wide and deep and every inch of it is haunted by big river pike. The scale of the river makes one feel small and on any day, you can only fish a tiny portion of what is available.

The task of getting to grips with the pike in such a large area is a compelling one and a hugely fascinating aspect of the sport. Firstly, what about access? and secondly, how do we approach this vast acreage of water and find those big pike? The first question is very easy to answer. The fishing rights on the bulk of this section are owned and leased by three main city clubs. York, Leeds and Bradford. If you join all three clubs, as we would strongly recommend, you gain access to almost the whole length of this prime section of the River Ouse. Secondly, what is the best approach to get the best from this vast waterscape? The answer to this is in two parts. In summer, when the river is running in trim, we prefer to spin for pike using artificial lures. In wintertime after October dead baits are fine to use as the pike's metabolism has slowed down sufficiently to make them safe. For that reason, we recommend the use of static dead bait methods in winter supported by spinning in carefully selected areas. Both these options provide exciting opportunities to catch those huge river pike which hunt along the entire length.

A GLORIOUS EVENING ON THE RIVER OUSE UPSTREAM OF YORK

It was the 29th of June and a lovely warm day. As usual I arrived home from work at about 6.00pm and felt worn out by the day's exacting duties. After having tea though I found my second wind as the weather was just too nice to stay in, so I decided to go for an evening's pike fishing on the River Ouse. I arrived at the fishing club car park next to the river at 7.30pm and parked on a smooth grassy area bordered by red flowering clover plants. As soon as I opened the car door my senses were filled with the riverside atmosphere. It was just like entering a perfumery and temperatures were just beginning to cool off from the heat of the day. The river was in trim and moving along in a lazy liquid silence. Only the sand martins disturbed the black velvet water as they flicked low over the surface collecting juicy insects for a well-earned supper. Thankfully, the match anglers had fished the previous weekend and cut through the six to seven feet tall jungle of red flowering willowherb and giant cow parsley. Although I stand well over six feet two in my wellies I was dwarfed by the tall vegetation, I felt like a young boy again standing on the loose sandy soil it was impossible to see over the dense vegetation, so I just followed the green passage down to the waterside clearing.

On this spontaneous evening out, I was travelling light with just a shoulder bag of artificial lures, one spinning rod and a large net for the pike which I knew frequented the whole river course. As I prepared the first cast of the evening, I was just bursting with excitement at the prospect of getting to grips with some of these ferocious demons. There was no size target on this trip, it was just a joy and privilege to be here, alone in such a peaceful atmosphere. I carefully attached a small floating plug to the trace link and cast it to the left to fish along the edge of a long weed bed. The plug fished close to the surface and as it came in hundreds of tiny fish fry sprayed away from it, they thought it was a pike! On the second cast a pike hit the plug at high speed, it was not much bigger than the plug itself and was only about ten inches long, an ideal live bait, but no, I had no intention of harming anything on such a wonderful evening like this. I then moved downstream to the next peg which was about twenty yards away. I cast the plug into the middle of the river and felt a bump, then nothing, but saw a white broad flash as something big turned away from the bait at the last minute. I decided to come back here later to pick up this cautious fish, it would be less careful towards the sunset period with lower light levels. No point now as it was understandably spooked by our brief encounter. Then onto the third peg. Here a four-pound pike took the bait on first cast. How good it was to get a good bend in the rod, then back she went to grow bigger.

After fishing a further four pegs five additional pike came to the net, the biggest six pounds and all very welcome. For the last ten minutes or so I was subconsciously aware of an intermittent whooshing sound which

I then consciously realised seemed to be getting closer. When I realised this, I looked up and there above was a giant red air balloon suspended at a height of about five hundred feet. It was a wonderful sight silhouetted against the yellow and orange evening sunset. I felt glad it was not me who was suspended in that fickle wicker basket, especially with all the high voltage power lines running across the country and with darkness fast approaching too! Hope they had a happy landing!

Up to now there had been a pike in every peg, the next peg downstream was over a stile and into a grass field which made a change after being in the jungle field. I climbed down the steep river levee onto a sandbar right next to the river and cast into deep water using a large silver spoon bait. When the bait hit the water, I counted down the bait to fifteen feet, quite deep, and then began to work it back slowly just above the riverbed. At about the halfway mark the bait was grabbed by a powerful fish which plunged deeply towards the riverbed for a good ten minutes, then came reluctantly to the net. It was not a twenty, but still a good fish and weighed in at fourteen pounds. It was now sun set, I looked onto the horizon and could see the Sun only just above the distant Pennines, but only about twenty minutes away from sinking out of sight behind Penn Hill.

The late evening mood of summer Pike fishing is captured in this shot. As lighting levels fade the pike begin to feed better than in the bright daytime conditions experienced earlier in the day.

I rushed back to the earlier peg where a big pike was too spooked to commit. It took a good ten minutes to get back and now it was really getting dark, so I quickly recast the silver spoon out to hopefully coax the elusive fish to take. First cast nothing, all seemed very quiet, second cast nothing, then third cast, and I had almost given up hope when about twenty feet from the bank I was shocked by a powerful take, yes, it was the missing fish, and it felt very heavy indeed! It took a good ten minutes to get it safely in the net and I weighed it in at eighteen pounds. It was a very slim summer fish, and I thought, come February it would go to over twenty-two pounds, even more. No matter, I was absolutely delighted, back she went and that fulfilled the evenings' theme of a pike in every peg. In the whole intensely golden evening, despite my careful efforts I had only covered one quarter of a mile if that and there was still about twelve miles down to York! Just imagine how many thousands of pike of all sizes in all that space, all three hundred or more acres of it with even more to go at below York. Yes, it is safe to say the River Ouse is something of a sleeping giant. To sum up though on this evening's events, it was not just the pike fishing, which was so very rewarding, but also the opportunity to fish in flower scented wild and peaceful setting, the golden sun setting in the west over such a clean and pure river. Thanks, are again due to John Eastwood and the thousands of anglers who have fought hard to preserve the purity of our rivers and have donated millions of pounds to support the rights of anglers for seventy-three years at the time of writing. To think there are growing numbers of people around today who would deprive us of all this if given half a chance.

Pike after Sunset. This big Pike refused to succumb to spinners in broad daylight but did not hesitate once it became dark. This photo was taken about twenty minutes after the sun went down.

In recent years there has been some controversy about the safety of catching pike in summer owing to overheating problems and pike dying from heat stress. The good thing about our northern river pike is that their waters flow from springs high up in the Pennine hills, many over 1,000 feet and some above 2,000 feet high. This colossal network of springs and rivulets have a great regulatory effect on the water temperatures of our rivers keeping them often warm in winter, but crucially, cool in summer. Even in the mid to low river courses with altitudes of just 150 feet or even lower the Yorkshire gravel bed geology still provides underground springs which keep replenishing fresh water even in the worst of drought conditions. As a result of this we know it is usually perfectly safe to continue the tradition of summer piking in our Northern spate rivers. There may be rivers and artificial lakes which are known to produce bigger pike in other parts of Britain, but very few can provide continuity of sport throughout the year like our Northern Rivers. To miss a little summer pike fishing would be a big loss indeed.

A WINTER TONIC ON THE YORKSHIRE RIVER OUSE

The months of January and February can be depressing as many perfectly healthy people become afflicted with seasonally affected disorder or S.A.D. as it is now commonly known. This condition is caused by a of lack of sunlight and vitamin D. We have countered this by arranging strategic winter long weekend mini breaks. Every February and March I reserve at least four of my annual leave days and take four separate Friday holidays resulting in a series of those long, glorious weekends. This just happens to coincide with the end of the season when pike fishing is at its very best, so it has a dual function! The following account provides conclusive proof that long weekend therapy really does work in lifting the spirits during our often-gloomy British winters.

It was Friday 19th February, 'Pike Friday' to be more exact. The alarm clock went off at 6.30 am and I set off twenty minutes later. Before driving off though I had to de frost the windscreen on the car, the ice was like concrete, so care was needed to avoid shattering the glass. The sky was a beautiful light blue with very high wispy ice clouds in the upper altostratus. I would have preferred a warm winter heatwave but as a worker one must just deal with whatever mother nature throws at us on our chosen days off, but over the years we have learned to just go with the flow and make the best of whatever conditions mother nature gives us. On this day I chose to fish on the lower River Ouse just upstream from where the river silently blends into the tidal section. The swim I chose to fish had a shallow weedy shelf but was adjacent to deep water. If the pike were congregating on the springtime shallows they should be there, if not the deeper water was only a cast away beyond the drop off point. By the time I reached the river the car was lovely and warm inside and a pity having to get out! No matter, the barrow was loaded up ready to carry the winter gear a full mile to the secret swim on the river. The mud track too was frozen solid like concrete which made it easy to push the barrow, so it only took about fifteen minutes to reach the chosen venue. Despite the very cold temperatures I removed my coat and jacket before the trek and pushed the load wearing only my tee shirt, it was hot work and within five minutes I was as warm as toast, even though the air temperature was well below zero. On this long-range venue I often pack a spare dry tee shirt. Once at the riverside the wet tee shirt can be replaced by the dry one. Only then do I put on the dry shirt and jumper;

the thermal outer garments can finally be donned to keep out even the coldest winds. In addition, If the wind is strong, it helps a great deal to sit with the wind behind you. The chair itself acts as a great wind break.

On this particular day I arrived at the venue and the float ledgered dead baits were positioned out on the shallows, with rods placed firmly on their rests. The freezing air quickly cooled me down after the long trek, thankfully though, I was comfortably dry and after the vigorous exercise the pheromones were doing an excellent job. It just felt great to relax in the chair with both rods out in position, this is what it is all about, perfect peace, perfect comfort and the landing net at the ready should a big pike come along. Oh yes life is good! Using the catapult, I placed half a dozen cubes of chopped sardines next to the two floats. All was now ready for the action.

Following three hours without any sign of a pike the initial optimism was beginning to waver, to make it worse I had seen cormorants flying up and down the river like the harbingers of doom. I suspected they wanted to fish my weedy bay, but too late the position was already occupied! Still nothing had moved, I decided to do something about it by passing a spinner through the swim to wake the pike up if nothing else. Wound in one of the static baits and removed the sardine and float tackle and mounted a large blue and silver ABU Pike spoon bait. This large spoon bait looks for all the world like a young salmon working through the water. I did not expect to catch on the lure today, the main aim was to just draw the fish from across the river towards my baited up shallow bay. First cast was about sixty yards over to the far bank to try coax any fish over from that area. On about the tenth cast I felt a bump on the lure as if something had grabbed the spoon and immediately dropped it. I then cast the bait beyond the action point and once again drew the bait through the same area. Nothing happened again, but then just as I was about to lift the spoon out of the water it was snatched from the surface at the very last millisecond by a sizable pike. The spoon bait was no more than a foot from the bankside, and I saw the lure being engulfed in a flash. The actual attack only lasted half a second or so, but I witnessed those huge jaws fully open then close over the blue spoon. The pike pulled down hard and shot out into mid river in under about four seconds. There was no time at all to set the drag mechanism of the reel, I was just glad it was set correctly in the first place ready to give out line.

Knew of course it was at least a double figure fish, my first conservative guess was about ten pounds. Then after about five minutes battle, with little success of getting it anywhere near the net I increased my estimate to about fifteen pounds, it was just so strong. Then thankfully, after a good ten minutes she finally came to the net. Saw her from above and thought yes, about eighteen pounds, I did not want fate to think I was being greedy! Then when it came to lifting her out of the water, I could just feel a dead weight, it was then I realised she was well over twenty pounds. Wow, I was really pleased and astonished to get such a beauty whilst just trying to wake the pike up with a spoon bait. Then, as I laid her out on the unhooking mat, I saw her impressive girth, scale perfect and her primrose marking reflecting perfectly in the weak winter sunshine. What a wonderful fish indeed. Catching a twenty-pound pike from a northern river on an artificial bait is something which certainly does not happen every day to put it mildly, although not my first, I knew I was the proud member of a very small club of pike anglers who had taken a northern river twenty on an artificial lure.

For a good two weeks after catching that pike I was buzzing with pleasure, I would for example, be just sat watching television with my better half and start smiling as I recalled this amazing event. "What are you smiling about"? asked my wife. I explained I was just thinking about the big pike I caught last week. This is I believe conclusive proof that Pike fishing really does, not just get through the dark days of winter but look forwards to it. In effect the perfect antidote to S.A.D...... Happy days.

River Pike in Northern England

Bills 22lb Ouse Pike. Air Temp. -4C Fish like this are the perfect antidote to the wintertime blues!

Although this fish was taken on the artificial spoon bait, I suspect it was attracted to the area by the loose ground bait. How ironic that I only fished the spoon bait to attract the pike towards the dead baits. Then ended up catching the big pike on the spoon! It just goes to show how it pays to be flexible in one's approach.

Red Letter Day Three

A BRACE OF TWENTY FOURS

It was 13th March 2016 just a few days before the end of the coarse fishing season. For my fishing partner Nigel and I it was effectively our last chance to fish because of work commitments. In view of this we decided to make an early start and to save petrol we met at my house at 6.00 am and travelled together in my car. It was a very foggy morning with visibility of only about thirty yards, so we kept our speed at careful thirty miles per hour. When we got to West Tanfield we stopped next to the road bridge and looked at the river to check if it was fishable or not. The river looked perfect and very picturesque set below St Nicholas's Church, the morning mists giving the whole scene an ethereal quality. As a boy of five my Father was a bell ringer at this Church and every Sunday morning my brother Dennis and I sat and watched the bells being rung in the freezing cold church tower. Whenever I hear bells ringing on a Sunday, I am immediately transported back to those happy days in the 1950s. On this misty morning it was still only about 7.00 am and most people in the village were still in bed and missing the best part of the day. The river looked so good, yes it was about one foot higher than normal and slightly tainted but very much to our liking, past experience had taught us that a little colour and extra height in the river did no harm at all. The omens were looking good!

We set off on the final leg to our chosen venue. We had in fact about twenty miles of fishable riverbank to choose from but since it was almost mid-March, we judged the pike would be entering the shallows with a view to spawning amongst the marginal weeds or, if not actually on the shallows, they would be close by in readiness to perform their annual duties. We therefore chose a very shallow part of the river which was between one and four feet deep. This part of the river was only about two hundred yards long where the river straddled a rocky geological fault. Below the fault the water became much deeper and was our regular haunt in winter. This shallow section was very weedy and flanked by Willow Herb, Sedges and Reed Mace which, when combined to the Willow and Alder trees gave the venue a cosy pikey atmosphere. We knew from previous years that nothing was guaranteed, even with the benefit of local knowledge our choice of swim was still a gamble, but we did know with absolute certainty that in March this area has had good form in the past! Similar conditions were available up and down the whole river course which also had good form but for some reason, let's just call it instinct, we chose this one.

As soon as we arrived, we set up the landing nets and introduced some ground bait which was step one in our mission to get the pike interested in feeding. The water was about three feet deep and flowing at a fast-running pace in the centre of the river but was almost stationery in the side. It was here in the margins that we positioned our floats and continued to feed chopped up sardines about once every half hour. The colour in the water made it impossible to see any pike, but neither could they see us, especially as we sat motionless and well hidden amongst the reedmace. We know to our cost that pike are very easily spooked so we kept out of sight and equally important, were very careful when walking. A careless stumble on the bank can scare pike off feeding for a long time. This is particularly important when one is fishing close to the bank. I suspect a pike lying close to the side can probably feel the vibrations of one's heartbeat pumping through the bed chair legs and down through the bank. Very often a run can take place just after you have quietly left your chair to attend to some minor detail five yards or so along the bank! This has happened so many times it is far more than pure coincidence. Yes, even when you are quiet and out of sight, I am sure they still know you are there, their whole senses are so very finely tuned.

From about one mile away we could hear the church bells pealing and calling in the faithful. The resonance was softened and improved as it passed through the mist and over the lush, sweet meadows, different in tone to the pure rich almost deafening clanging sounds I experienced in the bell tower as a boy, but that rich sound has stayed with me for over half a century and counting. The last time the Church bells stopped ringing was in 1939, fifteen years before I was born when a chap called Adolf was threatening to overrun our land and very nearly did. Just upstream from me was Nigel with his two baits out in good order, we were both fishing dead baits. My own were set in three feet of water only about ten feet out on the edge of the current. I really enjoy the company of my pal Nigel, not just because of the humour and the mutual Angling knowledge we share, but also in practical things like helping each other land our pike or take photos. Also though, as we both contribute to feeding the same swim with ground bait it doubles the effect increasing our chances twofold at least. Once the floats were positioned, we could just sit back and do what we had come for, to simply relax and enjoy the surroundings with a real chance of meeting up with some good pike.

After about five hours we had not seen a single fish, nor had we had any dropped runs or follow ins to at least confirm the pike were there, we had as a result almost given up all hope of catching anything at all. No matter, we had seen some lovely wildlife, including several blue flash kingfishers and a large formation of about thirty swans flying together as they were just returning from the frozen north. When we first set off the air temperature was minus one degree centigrade, but now at lunch it was nine degrees centigrade and the sun had burned off the morning mists. "Should we try somewhere else Bill"? Nigel was clearly losing faith in the area chosen and wanted to move to deeper water. Very understandable considering our lack of success, Nigel could see a big blank heading our way. In all fairness my heart felt the same, things were not very encouraging and yet my gut feeling told me everything was fine. Despite the lack of any kind of action I told Nigel that he could find a new spot if he wanted, but that I was staying put! Together we had laid out a considerable bed of ground bait and at some considerable cost, so I was not going to move an inch. In a friendly way I told Nigel to move on if he wanted and we could meet later at the car at a given time so no hard feelings. This was the downside of having a fishing pal, we both had divergent opinions on what to do next, although I was not at all offended by Nigel's loss of faith, it was a bit of a strain knowing my Pal felt down hearted. Despite all this there was no way I was going to move just as we had fully primed this part of the river. Indeed, if we moved, we would be starting a new spot from zero and the risk of missing out on the pike we had tried to attract. In the end Nigel stayed put, though I would not have blamed him if he had moved.

After about one further hour I too had lost all hope but still refused to move as there was still a chance, perhaps a big pike may at this very moment be following scent trails to my bait. It may be coming from two, three or even four hundred yards downstream. Finally, it happened, at last my white topped float disappeared and it began moving off, I was shocked and my pulse started to race. A firm strike and it was fish on, I held the rod high, but the fish ran straight towards me and under a snag, probably a tree root as it certainly moved in the general direction of the willow bushes. I felt carefully for the pike with a taught line and found it was well and truly snagged. I was utterly sickened. All was not lost yet though; it was still connected to the line, so I just put the rod back on the rest to leave it for a few minutes. Thankfully, after about four minutes the line started to peel off the reel again. The pike had freed itself and was now swimming off towards the centre of the river. Carefully, I re connected and it felt great to be back in direct contact with the fish again! "Thank you, God, for giving me a second chance!" Then I shouted for my friend to help with the net. Nigel was as pleased as punch and stood in readiness for the fish to come into view. The water was still coloured, so we did not see the fish for a good few minutes, but eventually she came into the net. "Wow, it's definitely a twenty Bill". Nigel exclaimed in a high-pitched voice. We nursed her carefully onto the unhooking mat where we quickly removed the hooks and returned her to the water to rest whilst we got the weighing scales and camera ready. She weighed in at just over 27lb, but deducted two pounds for the net, so we estimated she was a solid twenty-four and a half pounds, possibly a twenty-five, it did not matter really, she looked more like a thirty.

When first hooked she ran straight into a snag. I thought the game was over, but after giving her a little time she swam back out of the snag on her own accord and I made direct contact with her once more. After returning her safely I was exhausted so packed up my gear. It was 'Lucky 13th March'...Happy days and a real 'red letter day'!

Over the last twenty minutes I had experienced a mixture of horror, relief and finally pure delight, but now my appetite for pike was fully satisfied so I decided to pack up my fishing gear slowly, allowing Nigel to fish for the last half hour or so in my place which at last seemed to be producing the goods. Nigel brought over his rod and placed a fresh sardine on his special single hook snap tackle. "Where do you suggest we try?" Nigel asked. "Just cast straight out to the line where the slacks meet the current" I said. As soon as Nigel cast in his float disappeared into the current. At first, we both thought his bait had been sucked under by a small vortex of water, but no, Nigel bent straight into a very big pike which ran off into the fast water. Nigel, fishing with the finest pike rod money could buy soon had the fish under control, but we both knew it was another big fish and finally, after several long searing runs, she succumbed to the net. The weighing scales were still out so we weighed her quickly and she was the same weight as mine. At first, we thought it was the same fish as they were the same size and looked identical. No matter, even if it were the same fish, it would still count. Back she went again to join her courtiers who were no doubt waiting for her return on the weedy shallows. At that point Nigel and I were both bursting with excitement, we did a 'high five' followed by spontaneous bear hug! We were both quite stunned by disbelief. Within half an hour we had gone from pure boredom to the heights of excitement, it was almost too much to take in and we both feared it was just a dream and we may wake up any moment. I had already packed up my gear, so while I waited for Nigel to de tackle, I checked my digital images of both pike. Thankfully, we had good photos of both fish facing west, so it was possible to check the markings accurately.

River Pike in Northern England

Nigel poses with his twenty-four pounder. We had fished for the whole day without a touch, Nigel wanted to move to another swim. Thankfully, our patience was rewarded by the sudden appearance of these two beauties, both caught within about five minutes of each other. Both fish looked as though they had never been caught before, they were scale perfect, dark green with lovely primrose flecks. Who could ask for more!

It is well known that all pike have their own unique markings, just as we have our own unique fingerprints. This enabled me to quickly check out if they were both the same fish. To do this I like to check the markings near their tail or on their head. In this way it only took me about three minutes to confirm to Nigel the good news that they were 100% certainly different pike, very possibly sisters from the same year class. Both Nigel and I were on cloud nine.

Although both of us have caught bigger river pike in the past, I can honestly say that these fish and the way it all happened were the most memorable and satisfying we have ever had. We really did fish hard to catch those pike, which were the result of a lot of work and above all local knowledge built up over the years. At the end of the day though there was inevitably the element of good luck involved to make it happen. It was March the 13th of course so it was another case of the old charm 'Lucky 13' once more coming into effect.

There were several learnings to be taken from this catch, firstly, not to move after feeding the swim. Had we moved on we would have almost certainly missed our opportunity. Secondly, and most importantly, if a big pike forces its way into a snagged area never try to force it out, just leave the tackle loose and give the pike time to swim out of the tree roots under its own steam. Finally, when you catch a big pike get another bait into the water as quickly as possible. Big pike often have big friends around, especially when they are congregating before spawning. It therefore can often pay to try again even after catching the best pike of the season. It's worth a try anyway.

Both these fish were in pristine condition as you can see from the photos. They were also caught after the cormorant onslaught of our Northern Rivers, and yet somehow, they have managed to thrive despite the cormorants and otters. Yes, they are far fewer in number than before, and yet that somehow makes them even more special. They were also caught from a Club water available to everyone and yet in over fifty years I have never witnessed another pike angler on its lovely grassy banks. All these factors combined to give a very strong sense of 'Place' to the Northern Rivers which can only be described in an angling sense as 'Holy ground' and for me at least the finest pike fishing on earth. To cap it all when the local parish church bells chime and send their message of faith across the serene valley, we instinctively know all is well. Oh yes, life is good!

River Pike in Northern England

Red Letter Day Four - Fishing With Pike Royalty

AN INVITATION TO CAMBRIDGE AND PIKE AT MIDNIGHT

During one's life, you can meet certain people who have a considerable influence on the way you think. For example, as a boy of ten, meeting Norris Sturdy launched me on a lifelong interest in freshwater fishing. Then later at the age of thirty-six I met Barrie Rickards who I had only previously known as a reader and admirer of his various books. I had written to Barrie about pike fishing several times and I told him I was working on a new book called 'Pike Waters' and asked what he thought about my project. Barrie had already read several of my articles in the commercial press and hence knew a lot about my scientific pro pike interests. From the very start Barrie was keen to help and invited me down to Cambridge to discuss the new book project and take me for a good day's pike fishing on the Cambridgeshire fenlands.

On the 9th of March 1990 I motored south in my car to meet Barrie for the first time. We met at a Pizza restaurant in Cambridge at about 7.00pm and discussed my new book. After fully laying out the plans Barrie confirmed he would help and gave some valuable guidance on getting the book published. It was a done deal. Now came the most enjoyable part of the weekend, fishing on the Fens with the man whose name was synonymous with the Fenland Pike...Barrie Rickards. Before that though Barrie found me an overnight billet within the grounds of Cambridge University. Barrie was of course a professor there and spent a huge amount of time lecturing the students in Geology. Barrie kindly put me up for the night in the Geology Department premises and promised to return for me at 4.00 am so we could get onto the river by 5.00am, just before dawn. It seemed quite odd sleeping in the geology department with an enormous collection of fossils. I slept well but was woken up at 2.00 am by a lot of screaming and shouting outside. I got out of bed and went to the window; outside I could see a bunch of young undergraduates falling around completely intoxicated with drink. Before I knew it, the alarm went off at 4.00am so I got ready for the exciting day ahead. Barrie came bang on time and after collecting the live baits from the biology pond we set off down a network of narrow roads leading deep into the legendary Fenlands. When we arrived at the venue at 4.45am Martin Gay was already there fishing. Then later Colin Brett came to join us too. We all spread out along the river, which was more like a canal, there were miles and miles of bank space. In fact, there was so much space I decided to start off by spinning to try get ahead of the illustrious company! Barrie settled in behind two rods, one dead bait and the other live bait, the sun was just coming up over the horizon and all was well. I walked up the bank for about five hundred yards carefully spinning with a large silver spoon. Suddenly my lure was taken by a very sizable pike, it looked every ounce a twenty but somehow threw the hook. After a further fifteen minutes I worked my way back to Barrie and described to him what had happened. When I told Barrie it was almost certainly a twenty, he suggested we swap rods for half an hour, I agreed and settled into Barrie's comfortable chair whilst he went hastily up the bank with my rod to pursue the lost fish. Ten minutes later I could see Barrie in the far distance spinning for my lost pike, at that very moment my, or should I say Barrie's float shot out of sight and line was running fast from the spool. I looked towards Barrie, but he was a good seven hundred yards away, so I wound down and struck into my first Fenland pike. It weighed in at just over twenty pounds. I felt very embarrassed and apologised to Barrie, but he just laughed it off and assured me I had done the right thing.

Bill with his Twenty-pound Fenland River pike caught on Barrie's rod!

From that point on I thought it best to keep a low profile, so I found a place of my own and put out two rods to fish static dead baits for the rest of the day. As the day progressed, I had the opportunity to have a long talk with Martin Gay, himself a great pioneer of Pike Conservation with several books to his credit. What a lovely man he was, such a gentleman. Similarly, I had an enjoyable chat with Colin too. Now, as I look back over the years meeting 'Pike Royalty' and great characters like Martin, Barrie and Colin stand out as treasured nostalgic highlights of one's fishing career, each one of these characters having something incredibly special and unique about them. Yes, there is no doubt in my mind that fishing is every bit as much about the people you fish with as the fish you catch, though of course both are important. The realisation of this fact enabled me to celebrate this aspect of our sport when I became President of the Pike Anglers Club of Great Britain. It was a great honour to hold this position for three years. During that time, I set in motion a series of articles to be based on Fishing friendships to run over the three-year period written by twelve guest writers. Each guest contributed a full article on 'Great Angling Companions'. This series celebrated the great 'Fellowship' which angling as a sport can foster. Yes, of course it is great to catch big pike, but it is the way it is done, in cooperation with good friends which makes it so much more meaningful and satisfying. To sum up, we believe life is more about people than things. That at least is our firm belief which is why we have structured this book as much on people as big pike within a northern river context. My pike fishing mission to the Cambridgeshire Fens finished at about 3.00pm, as I had a long journey back home, I said my goodbyes and thanked my companions for inviting me to their favourite venue which I promised to keep secret. That was easy as in the dark approach, along a maze of narrow roads I hadn't a clue where I was anyway! It had been a very memorable day though, Barrie had caught two twenties, I had caught one twenty and a fourteen pounder. Colin had caught two twenties and Martin had three upper doubles. Together then we had caught four different twenty pounders and it had been a truly red-letter day if ever I saw one. I did notice very clearly these Fenland Pike were very much fatter than our Yorkshire spate river pike. Short for their weight and had a chunky appearance. It was also obvious they were all a bit tatty with lumps, sore patches and fins missing. Yorkshire river pike are generally not so big, but they all tend to present a more pristine scale perfect appearance. I suspect this is because there are a lot fewer pike anglers in the north. To go to this river for the first time and catch a twenty straight off made it clear these Fenland waters are very much richer than the northern rivers and are probably five to ten times more productive as pike fisheries. On the way back I began to nod off at the wheel as the tiredness was catching up with me, so I pulled over and had a thirty-minute cat nap. This proved very refreshing and I completed the journey feeling fine. One week later I sent a letter to Barrie to thank him for his kind invitation and invited him back to fish the northern rivers to return his kind gesture.

Owing to the closed season Barrie could not make it up to Yorkshire until the 19^{th of} June, but it was not Pike he wanted to fish for, it was barbel. Martin Gay had made a new ground bait for coarse fishing which was apparently second to none, it was a secret recipe of course and good for pike fishing too. June was a long way off, so I had plenty of time to find the best spot in Yorkshire. After our successful day on the Fens, I had to produce something good. Thankfully, I managed to secure a day's fishing on a good barbel stretch a few miles just downstream from West Tanfield on a very private piece of water. Before we knew it June was upon us, we invited Barrie round to our house in Harrogate and my wife Elizabeth cooked all kinds of treats in preparation. After tea at about 7.00 pm we left home and went to our River Ure venue to do an overnight session on a deep stretch of the river known to hold double figure barbel. Once at the water I gave my guest a quick look round pointing out the deep areas and some of the local history. The river was full of grayling, trout, barbel and exceptionally large chub. Also, some noticeably big pike too. After this mini tour Barrie chose his own favourite spot, he seemed keen to concentrate on the deepest part of the river which was twenty-two feet deep which he promptly started to feed up with a covering of the new secret ground bait. I watched what Barrie did to prepare his swim and I followed suit only about two hundred yards downstream. My chosen spot was much shallower, about twelve feet deep but quickly shelved up to just twelve-inch rapids only one hundred yards below my chosen swim. Barrie kindly gave me some of the secret bait and boilies which I put on one of my rods. However, unknown to Barrie I put a jack sprat attached to snap tackle on the second rod and fished it tight up to the bank in about seven feet of water. It was only about twenty feet away from my bed chair.

Just before dark I checked Barrie was settled in and we agreed to help each other if help was needed to land any big fish. We were just within ear shot.

I then returned to my peg and put out the baits again, set up the bite alarms ready for the darkness which would soon envelop us. I just put a big coat on and relaxed back in the bed chair and felt extremely comfortable. Both our pegs were in the middle of a wood and once darkness fell there were all kinds of strange movements in the undergrowth. Thankfully, it was a full moon so despite being in the wood there was still some light and it was very pleasant to observe the stars across the infinite universe above. It was impossible to sleep though with the constant rustling in the bushes behind us. Then I heard heavy breathing which seemed to be getting closer. Now I was really getting spooked and resorted to grabbing my torch to see exactly what it was. At the same time, I was worried what I might see! A quick look around confirmed my fears were groundless, there was nothing to be seen, it must have just been a rat or a rabbit harmlessly moving in the night. I then drifted off into a kind of half sleep, but at least felt more relaxed. At about 11.50 pm the buzzer on my left rod screamed into life. My god I have a run on the Jack sprat. Line was really shooting out of the spool, so I tightened up into a powerful fish in the dark. My landing net was at the ready, but I could not see a thing. Then I remembered to switch the landing net torch on which I had previously strapped to the handle with strong tape. My rod was bent double and the only control I had was with the slipping clutch which I could regulate easily in the dark. This really was a massive fish though and so I shouted for Barrie's help. Thankfully, Barrie came to the rescue and took control of the net. At this stage Barrie thought it was a barbel so when he netted it and went to lift it out, he thought we had a record barbel in the net! Then once on the bank he saw it was a pike, a really big pike too over forty-four inches long and weighed in at twenty-two pounds. It came to the net at midnight making a great start to the night. Back she went and we fished on with renewed enthusiasm. Then it was Barrie's turn, about an hour later I netted a large Chub of over five pounds for him and a big eight-pound barbel, so we had both done well. I later had a two-pound brown trout, then that was it. What a tremendous night though for both of us. Barrie had successfully field tested his new ground bait and caught some of the best fish the river could offer. We took some great photos and all our fish went back unharmed. Later, Barrie told me he had seen a massive sow in the middle of the night, it had been harmlessly digging up pig nuts on the forest floor. It was a massive beast, a good twelve feet long and potentially weighing a quarter of a ton! So that was what I heard shuffling around in the night, it must have escaped from one of the many local pig farms. It was harmless though, so we never reported it. We then returned to our house where we had a much-needed shower, breakfast and well-earned rest.

Barrie was a born and bred Yorkshireman, although he lived near Cambridge and was famous for his fenland pike fishing exploits, I could sense he had a special liking for the Northern Rivers. I always made sure he was well catered for and we shared many great days fishing together in both summer and winter. These are treasured memories for me and it was an honour to have fished alongside the best in the pike business. This is what fishing is all about, great friends, great fish and great memories. Its priceless!

22lb Pike at midnight – 44 inches fork length. Happy Days!

Red Letter Day Five

PIKE FRIDAY ON THE FLOODED RIVER WITH STORM DENNIS

It is of course a great privilege to have a full-time job which you enjoy doing and equally good having an enjoyable sport like angling to help keep the work/play balance right. For me though it has always been family and work which come first in the order of life's priorities. What spare time left is very precious and devoted to the fine art of angling. When booking holidays from work I have developed a very agreeable system of booking off a series of Fridays towards the end of the coarse fishing season. This is of course the best time of all to catch pike when they are in their peak of condition before spawning. The only trouble is that the holiday dates must be booked six months in advance so you never know what the weather will be like so far ahead. Therefore, when I booked Friday the 21st of February 2020, I had no idea that Storm Dennis was set to coincide with this very date! Weekdays off work are like gold dust, so if it is snowing, I go, if it is raining, I go and even if there are storm force gales with rain, I still go. This is exactly what happened on this incredibly special Pike Friday which ironically resulted in the best catch of the year.

On the morning of 21st February weather conditions were a little borderline to put it mildly, especially so when at the age of sixty-five I was no longer in the prime of life! The motivation was as strong as ever though and there were never any real thoughts of missing a valuable day's fishing. I took the precaution of parking the car a safe distance from any trees as the high boughs were really groaning and struggling to stand firm in the gale. Target area for the day was over a mile along a public footpath which ran along the riverside. On this stretch I normally see several dog walkers but not today, they were all safely battened down in the safety of their homes. This made me feel a little uneasy, perhaps I was pushing my luck a bit? As I reached the river, I could see it was about six feet above the normal level, but I could tell it was on its way back down. The banks were silty and very slippery in the receding floods and close to where I was fishing the earlier flood had deposited a huge beech log which was about twenty-five feet long and four feet wide. At a guess it must have weighed about four tons yet was left stranded like a mere twig at the high-water mark which was recorded accurately along the whole riverside by a long tide mark of leaves and sticks and all kinds of floating debris. Best of all though I could see from the riverbank that no one else had been on the bank for ages, there were no footprints, it was all fresh and untouched.

There was a nice piece of slack water in the main river close to the edge, it was about twenty-five feet in diameter and an ideal sanctuary for all kinds of fish. So, this was the chosen venue for the day. The bankside mud was so soft I had to scout round to find two pieces of wooden railing to prevent the chair legs sinking deep into the mud. The rails provided the perfect support for the chair legs. Next, the chopped sardines were fed along the slack water and the landing net set up. Then two rods baited with float legered sardines were placed in the slack water only about twelve feet from the edge. Whilst doing all this the wind and rain were battering my small fishing camp continuously and threatening to trash my rods and brolly. Thankfully, the gripper rod rests held firm in the gale as I minimised the effect of the storm force winds by aligning the rod butts exactly in line with the wind direction. In this way the wind had no traction on the rods which helped maintain stability. The brolly too was set up behind the chair as a wind break, suitably held firm by seven-foot-long guy ropes to hold fast in the winds. Finally, I climbed into the chair very carefully to avoid knocking it off its wooden perch. This really was a high maintenance fishing day but once sat in the shelter it felt great. The gale did not let up though and the heavy rain was horizontal at times. The rods were still getting quite a battering in the wind but the rod rests proved well up to the job. Ok they were expensive but so worth it today! Despite the heavy rain the water level peg indicated the river level was still going down which was a good sign. Yes, we have often caught pike on a rising river but it is usually better when the river is on the fall.

At about ten o clock it was time for a coffee. It felt very cosy sat safely in the fishing shelter drinking coffee and eating chocolate. The river was about eighty yards wide at this point and it was fascinating to watch trees and branches floating downstream in the mid current. There were no cormorants or otters to be seen today but our old friends the rooks and crows were still present and could be seen occasionally battling the wind. I observed that they were paying particular attention to the shallow pools on the meadow. There were about a dozen of these hardy villains hungrily scavenging stranded minnows and dace trapped on land after the flood. So, cosily tucked away under the brolly I thought I hope I do not get a bite until I have finished this coffee. About two minutes later the right-hand float gave a nod, then another two nods and was held an inch or so below the surface. Then the float began to nod in a very erratic way. This was signalling the jaw snapping mouthing of the bait. It was time to make contact. A firm pull and something about twelve feet below the surface moved and slowly headed out towards mid river. Oh yes, this was a good fish and I pulled firmly and relentlessly away. It took a good five minutes or so to get this beauty to surface near the net. Good, I could see the pike was securely hooked in the front of the top lip but the upper single was flying free. The bank side was very slippery and sloped down into ten feet of water. Therefore, I had to stand well back for safety. Thankfully, the landing net handle had a good extension and it was possible to land this beauty at a safe distance from the slippery slope and truly angry river.

After a couple of attempts the big pike was hauled gently onto the muddy bank. Wow, not only was it a very long fish, it was also broad across the shoulders too. This wonderful pike was quickly weighed in at twenty-five and a half pounds. It was too windy to take a time delay photo, so I just lay my prize on the unhooking mat and took some quick photos to record the event. Then back she went to her flooded watery home. It was still only about eleven thirty and maybe I should have stayed on longer. However, I had caught a superb pike and safely put her back and I felt glad that I had had enough so I made an early retreat to the car. I just did not want to push my luck any further in the dangerous weather conditions.

A careful look through my angling diaries reaching back over fifty years reveals that about half of my big twenty pound plus pike have been secured in floodwater conditions. The only trouble with these circumstances is that they are extremely dangerous. Just after the floods have abated the riverbanks are as slippery as could be. This is caused by a fine layer of silt which acts as a lubricant on the surface of the bankside. Also, the banks themselves are super saturated with water making them very unstable at the edges. A vertical three-foot drop into the freezing river would mean certain death. There simply is nothing to pull yourself up the bank on. Even if you drifted down to a willow bush it might be possible to hang on for a while but it would be almost impossible to have the strength to climb up the bankside in a soaking wet thermal suit. In summer when the water temperatures hover around sixty degrees Fahrenheit one could survive two hours or so in the water. In winter though, in freezing temperatures, hyperthermia will kill anyone in under half an hour. A life jacket would of course keep you above water but the cold would still drain the life out of even the youngest or fittest person.

For these reasons try to avoid fishing from vertical drops into the river. There are often places where the riverbank slopes gently into the water. In such places it is much safer and easier to crawl out of the river if the worst happens. Also, ensure you have a good extendable handle to the landing net which makes it possible to stand a yard or so behind that deadly water's edge. As good as floodwater conditions can be absolutely no pike is big enough to risk your life for. When considering the extreme options, it is far better to be a live blanker than a dead hero! Never forget that for the 'Live Blanker' there is always tomorrow! Always a second chance if you are careful. For the 'Dead Hero' it is just game over!

A big pike caught in 'Storm Dennis' conditions were a little borderline so after catching this twenty-five-pound beauty I made a safe exit whilst the going was good. The gale was so strong it was impossible to use the camera self-timer but this photo records the event perfectly. It was my best river pike for the 2020 season.

Red Letter Days Six
A CHRISTMAS CRACKER

For many working people Christmas is the busiest and most hectic time of year. How we look forwards to a few days off to recover from all the excitement that the festive period brings. The main priority of course is to spend Christmas day with family and friends. Open our Christmas presents which often include some novel items of fishing tackle and of course eat and drink heartily to celebrate our ancient and much-loved Christmas traditions to the full.

During Christmas 1988 we had a great family get together, the only sad thing was that my brother-in-law Michael could not attend. Michael was a trainee medical doctor at Manchester University and important things were expected from him. In fact, he had been on duty at the accident and emergency for five days nonstop. By the time he came to stay with us he was utterly exhausted. After a good night's sleep and plenty of Turkey and mince pies we soon had him back to normal. We had planned to go fishing together on boxing day, but this had to be postponed to the 29th of December. No matter, we took the bed chair so our guest could really take it easy and enjoy the fresh air. By good fortune Christmas 1988 was the warmest Christmas for sixty years. On our chosen day, the air temperature was 48 degrees Fahrenheit, it was just like a summer's day, only without the flies. Jonathan my son was only eight, and he came too to spend a day's pike fishing with his dad and Uncle.

This was a very leisurely day out together and we arrived at the river at 10.30am. I quickly set up our special guest in a comfortable bed chair and told him to take it easy whilst we set up three rods with all the necessary equipment. The river was about one foot above trim level and my indicator peg placed on the waterline showed the water was still falling steadily. The water temperature was an amazing 45 degrees Fahrenheit, an elevated temperature for December.

To keep things as simple as possible we just had one rod each and we spread out along a one hundred yards straight run and fished our small trout baits about ten feet out from the riverbank in about six feet of water. We used half ounce paternoster weights to fish the baits about six inches from the riverbed. The water was in fact still coloured with visibility of about eighteen inches. I know all this because the details have been faithfully recorded in the trusty angler's diary.

After only twenty minutes Jonathan had a run on his reel, he struck into his butting rod right away and carefully played a good-sized fish which we netted soon after, it weighed in at eight pounds, a great start to the day, we quickly unhooked the pike, and she swam off strongly moving upstream into the current. Twenty minutes later Michael had a run and was extremely excited to play a very strong pike which set off across the river ripping line from the spool, after a good five minutes we finally netted his pike which weighed in at fourteen pounds. "Yes, they are really on the feed" Michael said. "I am so pleased I came; I had forgotten how good it is to be out in the country" After we returned Michael's pike we paused for a break. Poured out some coffee and we sat in the winter sunshine. The local village church tolled the bell twelve times, it was mid-day, and all was well. During our leisurely break Michael brought us up to date with his recent duties in the accident and emergency department in central Manchester. He was on twenty-four-hour call which meant he could only catch some sleep between busy times. The problem was that at Christmas, with so much alcohol flowing, there was no quiet period, so he had to just keep on going. A lot of his work included very detailed work like stitching up face and body parts and even removing broken glass from deep wounds. This was difficult enough when you are fresh and clear headed, but after not sleeping for thirty-six hours it was much more testing. It made us realise just what doctors must achieve to qualify, and it was good for both Jonathan and me to hear these front-line accounts of very frightening incidents.

Following our interesting lunch break I noticed my float had disappeared. At the same time the line was tightening up as it ran into the water. Without wasting a second, I tightened up and connected with a massive fish which was moving out into mid river in a determined manner. It was a heavy fish indeed, and I concentrated on trying to keep its head up out of any snags on the riverbed. Under a lot of pressure, the line made a high pitched 'singing' sound as it was tensioned through the rod rings of my old ABU Svangsta made spinning rod. Jonathan and Michael watched on in fascination as the fish moved first upstream and then back downstream, it did whatever it wanted, it was just too strong to control at this early stage. Michael and Jonathan realised that something very special was happening before our eyes and waded out into the river with the net to be ready. I walked back up onto the bank behind me and walked forward when the pike surged, and then walked gently back to bring it closer to the net. I had seen Salmon anglers using this technique on the River Tweed, I had not planned to do it, it just seemed the right thing to do at the time. At last, the pike came within netting range of Michael, it was just over the net but made a last-minute tail walk and jumped away in a dramatic fashion! Off she went again, causing me to walk forwards, then ripped more line off the spool. Back I walked, again bringing the net close to our guest. Again, she did not like the look of the net and powered off on another long run. By this time, my arms were aching like mad. No matter, we again drew her towards the net and we finally had her safely in the fine folds of our net. Huge anxiety was instantly replaced by jubilation as we all looked at the size of our prize. We quickly lay her on the unhooking mat, the winter sunshine highlighting her beautiful primrose flecks. Absolutely scale perfect, and a fork length of forty-two inches long with a girth of nineteen and a half inches. Her condition scale registered 0.46 on the 'Fatness' scale. A very portly pike indeed for a spate river pike.

A 25lb real Christmas Cracker caught during the warmest Christmas for forty years.

This fantastic day was thirty-two years ago and was certainly one of the top angling days in a long pike fishing career. Not just because of the great pike we caught, but also the circumstances in which we did it. It was a Christmas family day out, no early morning start, no great journey, just a lovely day's fishing in the company of loved ones. Now, many years later we relive the memory every Christmas. It has in fact become part of what Christmas means to us. If I had done the same day alone it would have been nowhere near as special. Yes, for us Pike Fishing is best done together, no shadow of a doubt.

Michael's challenging work at university paid dividends, he qualified as a doctor and has risen to become a Professor of Neurology at Queens Square, London and travels the world giving lectures on his research. We still see him at Christmas and whenever we mention the words 'Christmas Crackers' we are instantly transported back to that happy fishing trip when we shared the best festive season we have ever had. When Michael retires, we plan to spend a lot more time on the riverbank! Jonathan also did well at university and is now a fully qualified dentist. We suspect it was was unhooking pike which gave him a professional interest in teeth! It is a skill which has served our daughter Charlotte too. Charlotte also became a dentist and later joined the British Army, again showing how the challenge of unhooking pike from an early age can lead to wonderful things!

To this day we have never recorded such warm temperatures as we did over that 1988 Christmas period. Once again, the angler's diary has proved to be a crucial resource for looking at factors affecting pike behaviour over the years. On this fishing trip we were only fishing for about four hours and the river was producing pike one after the other. It is therefore interesting to just highlight what the trigger factors were which culminated in such an enjoyable day. Firstly, and most importantly, we recorded high pressure over central Europe which produced the famous 'Bartlet high' effect where for weeks on end warm southwest air masses come barrelling into the U.K. from the Atlantic. In late December 1988, these warm air masses were coming up from the Canaries bringing with them very moist warm air. These warm air masses condensed very readily over our northern hills causing sudden floods and triggering a sharp rise in water temperatures. The results of all this atmospheric activity culminated in triggering some highly active feeding behaviour amongst the pike and other fish too. These weather combinations are almost always associated with flood water conditions which make them our top favourite and by far the most productive conditions to enjoy in the north, especially when they arrive during the Christmas festive break!

Brother-in-Law and son Jonathan admire the handsome proportions of our 'Christmas Cracker' before its safe return to the water.

Bill Winship

Red Letter Day Seven

TWO FROM THE LUNE

By guest writer David Holden

Bill asked me to contribute a chapter describing a day's pike fishing on the River Lune in the northwest of England. The River Lune is of course mostly famous as a trout and salmon river but there have always been quality pike fishing opportunities for those in the know. The event I am about to describe is set in the mid-1970s and describes in words and photographs a nostalgic event which, in effect, is a priceless snapshot of my early pike fishing career. It was a time when the new specimen hunting movement was beginning to take hold amongst serious anglers. Those who were part of this enigmatic sect were identifiable by their floppy hats, waxed green jackets and scruffy beards and often spoke about 'rod hours' in their quest for big fish. A number of notable anglers were starting to amass impressive tallies of 20lb plus pike from the drains and fens of Lincolnshire and Cambridgeshire. The Pike Society was beginning to show signs of contraction and it would be two more years before Barrie Rickards was persuaded to relaunch it under the new name of 'The Pike Anglers Club of Great Britain.'

In my local Lancashire area things were not as buoyant. There were too many factory chimneys which still stood over those dark satanic mills sending out large volumes of soot, carbon dioxide and a whole host of other deadly pollutants. Pike that managed to survive and put on a few pounds were quickly given a traditional 'headache' by the general angling community who were unable to come to terms with the pike's place in our waters. In Lancashire, a 7lb pike was seen as a good fish. A 'double' meant that the first round of drinks at the local bar were on you. 'twenties' were almost unheard of and would immediately propel the captor to stardom.

I was coming to the end of my first season as a would be 'serious' pike angler and despite the odds I had managed to put my net under two fish from the Lancaster Canal and Glasson Dock (near the point where the canal meets the sea). 10.03 and 10.00 lbs, respectively. It was at Glasson that I met and formed a long relationship with Jim Lee from

Lytham. (R.I.P. – A better friend one could never wish for). Shortly after our first meeting, Jim told me of a backwater on the River Lune which he knew had produced pike to 19.08 and 23.00lb to a local angler. There were also tales of bigger fish coming out but were unsubstantiated. Wow, it got even better, Jim had access to the venue and was allowed to take a guest. Did I fancy a day on there? Pass me a pin so I can prick myself to make sure I am not dreaming! He did warn me though that it was a hard water and that it was an event to get a take and even then, it was most likely to be a small fish, there being an apparent absence of medium sized fish. Furthermore, even in those days it was a 'deadbaits - only' water.

David weighs a solid twelve pounder from the River Lune backwater. All made possible by his good friend Jim who shared his expert local knowledge and created a lifelong memory to be cherished forever.

On our first visit together, we arrived at the water just after dawn. Ever dressed in the guise of Richard Walker and Chris Yates, Jim took me to a suitable swim and advised me to tackle up far away from the riverbank, then creep down slowly and position the baits with an underhand lob just beyond a large marginal weed bed. Out of the bag came a rainbow trout and I set up a float ledger rig. A light swing and it was in place, the float sitting proudly on the ripple-free surface. I crept back to my base and began to set up my second rod. As I looked back, I thought I saw a few rings emanating from my float. Yes, I did, I beckoned Jim to say that my float was away. He lightly walked up to my swim by which time I had just struck into feeling that satisfying thump at the other end of the line. Straight away the pike shot skywards out of the water trying to lose its breakfast, thankfully without success as my hooks had held the pike well. It was a most impressive sight and in my limited experience I was convinced it was a good twenty pounder! This is what a sudden shock does and accounts for so many of those famous 'the ones which got away' tall stories. After a good fight Jim had the net under fish which he expertly landed in his large frame specimen hunter's net. We then unhooked our prize and weighed her. She pulled the scales down to 12lb exactly - a new personal best for me at the time and such a beautiful fish. Better still, I just could not believe my luck catching it within just a few minutes of casting out the bait. I had not even set up the second rod! Unfortunately, there was no further activity that day for either of us, but the drive home was filled with exciting thoughts of what to do next.

River Pike in Northern England

Another immaculate double figure pike from the River Lune. Just look at those well-defined markings. Since this photo was taken in 1975 there has been a huge revolution in attitudes to the pike. Now at last these fish can grow up to twenty pounders and even thirty-pound pike are now a possibility in the River Lune. All thanks to the Pike Anglers Club of Gt. Britain.

We did not have long to wait; the next weekend saw us back on the water and I still had a trout bait left from our first visit. I had kept it safe in the freezer compartment of our domestic fridge, no dedicated freezer in the garage in those days. When we returned, I decided to fish the same swim using the same successful method of float ledgering. The float ledger was positioned just beyond the marginal weed and I then crept back to base to set up the second rod. "Did I see things or did that float move? Jim, do dead trout swim?" Jim replied, "The last time you said that you caught a twelve pounder" I promptly struck and tightened up to another massive fish. "This feels nice Jim" I replied, by which time he was once again walking lightly towards me with the net and verifying to me the capture of a different twelve pounder.

Before the season ended and again with the involvement of Jim introducing me to John 'Watto' Watson my personal best went up to 14.08 then to 17.04 in a few short weeks when I joined John on his Fenland weekends in early 1976.

Lancashire is now thankfully a different place. All but gone are the factory chimneys and the pike killing practices of old. Local waters, including the River Lune have produced pike in the twenty-pound bracket. I have been lucky enough to manage two over the thirty-pound mark in Lancashire, both witnessed by my other long standing fishing companion since 1964, Dave Pimley. I have not fished the backwash which was the scene of my early triumphs since 1975 but I did meet one of the old gang at Jim's untimely funeral in 2008 who commented that it was inevitably silting up and that half of it was now unfishable.

When I close my eyes at night, I see those motionless floats start giving off rings. Every day I go fishing I can't help but think of Jim and wish he were still here to share in each other's experiences. It isn't about catching fish or how big they are, but the people one meets on the way who leave long lasting memories that never fade. Thanks for everything Jim, this is for you.

Red Letter Day Eight

HALYCON DAYS IN A NORTHERN DEER PARK
By Nigel Winter

I first met Bill Winship at work in Asda in 1986. Bill worked for Hillsdown Holdings and needed a lift into the storage racking to do a stock audit. This process took a good half an hour and, in that time, we discovered we were both keen anglers. Bill then invited me to one of his angling slide shows at his Ripon branch of the Pike Anglers Club of Great Britain. Up to this time I had been more interested in chub and barbel, but the P.A.C. slide shows made me realise a new interest. Over the next year or so I attended several fund-raising events in aid of the Anglers Cooperative Association. Although Bill was the regional organiser for Ripon P.A.C. he was also an evangelical supporter of The A.C.A. and the great work they have done in fighting river pollution.

Within about eighteen months I started to fish regularly with Bill, mostly on the Yorkshire rivers like the Derwent, Ouse, Nidd, Wharfe, Swale and Ure, but with occasional trips to Hornsea Mere and a few other waters in the northwest when Bill organised pike fishing days out for the club. It was very enjoyable, and I was impressed with the number and size of the big pike we caught. Annoyingly though Bill was catching at least three times more pike than me and I could not understand why. "What am I doing wrong" I asked, I was at that time using standard leger rigs size eight snap tackles as recommended in the textbooks.

For river fishing Bill was using a different hooking rig, and much smaller homemade slider floats. Bill kindly lent me a set of his special rigs and it made an immediate improvement. From that point onwards I could almost compete on equal terms. Not that there was any hint of there being any competitiveness, but I just wanted to hold my own. After a few weeks I started to make my own special river floats and made up my own rigs based on the exact size and pattern to the ones Bill had kindly lent me. I then gave Bill back the float, but not the rig as it was all chewed up by the numerous pike it had brought my way!

I went one step further with my float making by using a lathe, in this way I could shape my floats with a high degree of precision and much faster too. I have never had to buy a float since. I was also able to return the favour and give one of my own creations to Bill, an act of kindness much appreciated by his royal highness!

In summer we like to give the pike a rest and fly fish for trout. On one special day we fished a water near Bedale, locked safely in the grounds of a deer park which was full of rainbow trout and more than a few pike too. Fishing from the boat in crystal clear stream I hooked my third trout on fly and was just playing it towards the net when suddenly the trout just sprinted off at high speed to the left causing my fly reel to scream out as if in mortal pain, it then headed towards the boathouse and swam right in at high speed. Then it came back out of the boathouse at which point the tackle just locked solid as if the trout had swum round a log. Feeling puzzled I increased pressure to find out what was going on. Then, slowly, very slowly the 'log' moved off to the right. Still holding the rod high and firm I began to realize a big pike had taken my trout. In a huge swirl the pike shot off and snapped my 5lb leader like a piece of cotton.

Still aroused with a mixture of curiosity and excitement we paddled the boat towards the scene of the abduction. The water was about five feet deep and in the bright sunshine and clear water, we could see every detail of the waterscape. Moving forwards very slowly a good-sized pike came into full view, slowly starting to swallow our trout, which itself was about five pounds in weight. We deliberately stock with big trout to guard against predation from Cormorants and pike. Not this pike though, it was clearly intent on being partial to its generous sized meal. We watched in stunned fascination and awe for several minutes as the trout, all eighteen inches of it, was slowly engulfed headfirst by the big predator. Exciting as it was to visually see this big pike, it was also a melancholy experience to closely witness just why the pike has earned its reputation as the 'water wolf'. When you see them in action like this it makes you realise what fierce and merciless fish they are.

Water wolf in action

After this dramatic big pike encounter, we resolved to try to catch this impressive beast when winter returned. There was no rush as we knew we were the only anglers fishing the water for pike. The longer we waited, the bigger the pike would grow. There was no rush at all! It was a unique feeling and made the long wait for February such a happy form of anticipation. I always remember in December we always looked forwards to Christmas on the 25th, but our second big day was always the first week in February. Uniquely to us it was our second Christmas day!

This water was part of a duck shoot, so for our own safety we were not allowed to resume fishing until after 31st January which marked the end of the duck shooting season. This arrangement suited our needs perfectly as it gave the pike time to achieve their peak condition before spawning in March and April each year. It also gave us time to recover from the festive season. So, for many years, fishing this water was the highpoint of our pike fishing Calendar. Bill and I shared the water with a small handful of trout anglers who had no interest in pike, so we had the pike all to ourselves. It was an ideal arrangement and we felt very privileged to have our own secret North Yorkshire spot. A fully protected venue part of a country estate complete with an ancient Castle, a full-time gamekeeper, and deer park as the scenic backdrop. Even if Bill and I had both been multi-millionaires there is no way we could engineer a better pike fishery.

Now as all experienced anglers know the weather in early February can be the most challenging of the entire year. Storm force winds, sleet and snow, heavy rain we have seen it all. However, whatever the weather threw at us we would always be down at our secret venue on the first Sunday in February. Often it was strong south westerly wind and rain that we had to cope with, and we often joked that "no one could pay us enough to work in these conditions." Yet for pike fishing we never gave it a second thought! We anchored our umbrellas down on the south bank with the wind behind us. This meant we cast downwind often in fifty mile per hour gales which made casting amazingly easy indeed. We just cast the dead baits upwards, and the wind carried our offerings twenty, thirty or even forty yards or more if needed. Furthermore, with our protective umbrellas behind us we comfortably watched as our home made red or white pike floats rode the waves beyond. Often the floats just disappeared for a second as the large waves peaked, but then re appeared a second or so later in a regular sequence. When watching these floats holding fast in the water the one-way movement of waves gave us both a dizzy sensation when you took your eyes off the water. If for example you got up quickly to go for a walk it was impossible to walk in a straight line just as it is when you spin round several times, the action activates a temporary vertigo, but the effect only lasts a minute or so.

Back to the floats, it is when they fail to re appear you know you have a run, or a pike has picked up the bait. On one special day this is exactly what happened and as the red float vanished, so too, line began to peel off the reel causing the lightly set spool to click and signal a take……. "Bill I am away." This is what we were waiting for, with all those untouched pike around we knew anything was possible, the adrenalin really began to flow, hands shaking partly through cold but now sheer unbridled expectancy. As the tall trees behind us took the full force of the gale they groaned under the mighty weight of the wind. Now as I tightened up the line the rod took the full weight of something solid and heavy out in the open water and as the line tightened it began to make a high-pitched singing noise in perfect harmony with the groaning trees behind us. About twenty yards out we saw a large disturbance of water, then we saw a huge caudal fin reach upwards as the massive fish plunged itself into the weeds. For a minute or so the fish was completely stuck. The stream was only about four feet deep at this point with a one-foot layer of bottom weed, I decided to just slacken off the pressure and wait. After a brief time, line started to run off the reel indicating the pike had moved away from its weed bed retreat, I gave line, then across to the left we saw another boil of water. At first, I could not make direct contact as the line was still trapped in a thick clump of bottom weed. Step by step I gradually made direct contact with the pike albeit with a tennis ball sized clump of weed still stuck on the line. Bill stood on anxiously with the landing net already sunk and ready in the shallow margin. With one final pull the pike slid innocently into the folds of the forty-two-inch net with a big clump of weed still attached by the up-trace swivel. Once my prize was safely in the net, we both felt a sudden sense of relief followed by unbridled joy. Bill left the big pike in the water to give the pike chance to recover. We also needed a little time to recover our own equilibrium too. It had all been very tense. Then out she came, I of course did the honours, I could feel by its weight it was well over 20lbs. In fact, I had to use both hands lifting it to prevent damaging the net. I laid our big fish on the unhooking mat and easily removed the hooks easily. The fish was huge and looked even bigger than many of the pike featured in the Domesday book of mammoth pike, the girth alone was almost twelve inches deep, and it was scale perfect except for a few small red spots along one flank We thought this may have been caused by some stray shot from the duck shooting syndicate as shotgun spray can cover a big area from about one hundred yards and more, it must have been at range as it only caused harmless red bruising. Now the moment of true reckoning, we carefully measured a weight of just over 25lb. We were both delighted. Was this the same pike which snaffled the five-pound trout the previous Summer? We think not. This pike, though weighing over 25lb had a proportionally very small head. When we looked at its jaws neither of us could imagine it being capable of swallowing the 5lb trout we lost back in Summer.

Despite my very satisfying catch, it was good to know there was at least one bigger fish left in the water, the one which took the big trout. That's for another day, perhaps tomorrow or very soon. That is the wonder of fishing, there is always a big tomorrow when anything can happen, and we can always catch our personal best. Fishing in general the world over has a great underlying philosophy of hope and optimism. At its heart it has a deep and long-standing tradition of perseverance, clear goals, and a continuing striving for better. Most of all, if our goals remain unfulfilled there is always tomorrow, always another day to succeed, what an impressive set of values to have, not just for fishing, but for life in general.

Nigel displays his big pike which was so worth the wait. 25lb of pure Joy!

Red Letter Day Nine

THE RIVER HULL

By Guest Author Adrian Brayshaw

The River Hull is a small to medium sized river whose water source is the chalk Wolds of East Yorkshire. The River Hull has a number of feeder streams in the vicinity of its source which is near the market town of Driffield. Driffield is known as the 'Capital of the Yorkshire Wolds,' an area of natural beauty and situated twenty-three miles to the north of Kingston upon Hull. The Yorkshire Wolds extend through East Yorkshire northwards into North Yorkshire. The prime waters which feed the main River Hull are composed of small streams such as Kelk Beck, West Beck, Frodingham Beck and the Driffield Canal. The name Driffield Canal is misleading as most of the aforementioned waters are in fact chalk streams.

The calcium carbonate (chalk) geology of the tributaries is an important aspect of why the entire system is such a rich environment for fish. The high calcium content of the water aids the development of food items like water snails and freshwater shrimps providing a rich food chain with ideal growing conditions for fodder fish and pike too.

The River Hull system is mostly navigable and was once used to transport grain and various agricultural products to the Hull urban area for processing. This gives the whole area a fascinating cultural heritage which forms an interesting part of the local atmosphere.

RIVER SECTIONS

To help better understand the River Hull system I will break it down into several distinct sections. Firstly, the West Beck section which is a nationally renowned water best known for its game fish and particularly its quality grayling fishing. The majority of West Beck is privately controlled and the most northerly chalk stream in Great Britain, in fact I am sure it is the most northerly chalk stream in the whole of Europe.

In addition to West Beck, we have Frodingham Beck, Driffield Canal, Kelk Beck and Old Howe. All these tributaries have big pike in residence at certain times of the year. In fact, there is a movement of pike from West Beck into the non-tidal sections of the River Hull. The pike can be found just about anywhere, and part of the catching process is actually tracking them down. This takes time as they can be found almost anywhere depending upon weather conditions and the seasonal variations of temperatures. Old Howe is very shallow and resembles a Fenland drain.

This photo shows part of the upper River Hull system in good flow after a few days steady rain. Although a small to medium sized river the fish in the Hull system enjoy having one of the most productive food chains in the north. The evidence of this fact is shown clearly in the generous size of the fish caught in this part of East Yorkshire. (Photo courtesy of Adrian)

The non-tidal Hull includes all the upper Becks and canals. It also incorporates the important section upstream of Hempholme Lock, up to the confluence with West Beck and Frodingham Beck. This section is just over a mile long and has been artificially straightened and thus is very reminiscent in appearance to the fenland drains.

The tidal Hull in modern times is considered to start at the Hempholme weir. The river runs clear and shallow here which makes it possible to locate fish by spotting them in the river. Over the years the flood defence teams have had to raise the flood banks higher as the riverbed itself has become higher due to fluvial deposition. The higher banks protect the surrounding rich farming areas from flooding. Downstream from Hempholme weir, looking east, the river seems to run above the level of the Holderness plain. The tidal influence here is more noticeable on spring tides when the high tide arrives about two hours later than at the King George dock in Hull.

The River Hull meanders through arable land and eventually arrives at Beverley. Depending on the rainfall the river pace has now quickened but can still be sluggish during periods of low rainfall, especially in the summer months. The flow rate characteristics here can completely change from summer to winter when you can use up to a four-ounce weight to hold a pike bait in place.

On arriving at the outskirts of the city of Hull the river now narrows and its flow has markedly increased in pace. The difference in tide height here can quite easily be eight feet between high and low tide. The flooding tide can often be seen to be faster than the ebbing tide.

FISH SPECIES PRESENT

There are now regular runs of Sea Trout from the lower River Humber into the River Hull. They also grow to a very respectable size and I have heard accounts of fish into the ten pound plus range, mainly encountered by pike anglers fishing with deadbaits.

An interesting observation from past years has been the 'escaped' rainbow trout from fish farms located in the higher reaches of the River Hull. This happened on a few occasions in the 1980s and 1990s. Resulting in thousands of rainbow trout being released into the River Hull system and in some instances the offending trout farms were prosecuted. Every cloud has a silver lining though and these 'trout spills' resulted in some superlative pike fishing as these River Hull pike grew rapidly on the pellet fed trout.

The River Hull also holds good stocks of barbel and before the 2009 influx of seals, barbel sizes were on the ascendency. The River Hull record (reference the barbel fishing world website) is 12lb 8oz captured in 2006. Undoubtedly, from 2000 onwards the seals decimated the pike and barbel stocks. The signs are clear that it has taken a restocking programme and twelve years to nearly get back to where we once were. One of the very few effective initiatives from the Environment Agency has been the introduction of a barbel stocking programme at various locations along the River Hull. These Barbel have been stocked at under a pound in weight and are demonstrating good growth rates in the rich environment. I have fished for them myself in the past year and have captured good, conditioned fish to just over 6lb. They certainly give a good account of themselves in the tidal Hull on a 1.25lb test curve tench rod. There are certainly bigger fish around now and I predict that a new river record could be claimed soon. Let's just hope the seals don't return in numbers!

As for pike, well at one time the river Hull was probably the best big pike river in northern England. Which is surprising for a venue that has had little publicity over the years. The River Hull Pike record equals that of the great southern rivers such as the Hampshire Avon, Dorset Stour, River Test and the Hertfordshire Wye and still has the potential to be great again. Its demise as a pike fishery reached a climax in the spring of 2009 when the seals arrived. Prior to that the pike stocks were under pressure from prey balance problems caused by the cormorant onslaught. Also, newly arrived immigrant workers taking pike for the pot to be eaten, was also a factor plus the deaths caused by handling and unhooking mistakes. There are still the occasional good fish caught, but I struggle to see it ever being the good pike fishery it once was. Social media platforms don't help either! This may seem a highly pessimistic appraisal, but it is just the way I honestly see it.

The River Hull also contains good quality chub, roach, Ide, perch and of course grayling which have been caught to over 3lb plus. Again, these fish have all been badly affected by cormorant predation along the full length of the river.

MEMORABLE DAYS ON THE RIVER HULL

Bill has asked me to write about a couple of pike related captures whilst pike fishing on the River Hull. A 'red letter' type of day!

The first one relates to the start of some exceptional pike fishing for local pike anglers on the River Hull 'grape-vine' This was over twenty years ago! How time flies!

The second one I have chosen because it conveniently covers just the one nine-month river season. The fishing is now gone as the land is now controlled by the Yorkshire Wildlife Trust.

LANDING NETS FULL OF PIKE

To refresh my memory from over twenty years ago I have just recovered my angling diaries. They were boxed up on the top of a bedroom wardrobe gathering dust. Looking through the 1999 diary I had almost forgotten how prolific the pike fishing on the River Hull was at that time. This confirmed my opinion on how important it is for an angler to write down the events as soon as possible following a 'red letter day' It is so much easier these days to record the details with a smart phone just as it has happened with details like weather conditions, baits used and of course the results of fish caught. I use modern technology these days whilst on the bankside and then write it all up properly in a permanent paper diary. It is so important to do this and whilst reading my 1999 diary so many wonderful memories suddenly came flooding back.

It was nearing the end of the 1998 season when a chance encounter would lead to some of the most prolific pike fishing that I and others would ever experience on the River Hull. I had just passed a stick float angler as he was playing an obviously decent pike that had snatched his roach. His light tackle was no match for the pike and the fish just slowly swam around the swim unaware that it was hooked but it was attached to a small hook and light line. I stopped and watched for about ten minutes, then the inevitable happened, the line snapped and the pike parted company. Unfortunately, I did not even get a glimpse of the pike but it seemed highly likely that the pike was no small one. Very interesting I thought as I made a mental note of it and I was determined to return to this very same spot the following winter. I had fished the swim on previous occasions but only on short trial sessions and had no success. I pondered again and then decided to return for a longer session to give the place a more thorough try. In the meantime, there were other venues I was preoccupied with, so it was some time before I got round to fulfilling my resolve.

The following Autumn arrived and I was as keen as ever to start. The River Hull can be very weedy in early autumn until the winter temperatures plummet and the flood water flushes out the weed into the tidal Humber Estuary. To avoid the weed I started the season by fishing the Yorkshire Ouse and a local gravel pit known as the Tillery. The Tillery was well known in the Yorkshire area for its big carp. I had a good start by taking a fish just under 21lb from the pit. I then had a trip to Ireland and caught a pike just below 23lb from a remote Lough.

Back home again and with the River Hull now beckoning and looking in its tip top winter condition. As luck would have it there was also a rumour leaked that pike were showing up on the 'now to try' stretch. It was all word of mouth in those days. Mobile phones were the size of house bricks and there were no such things as social media platforms.

I initially started on a solo mission, mostly static bait fishing, moving about the stretch, covering water and trying to locate the fish. I also launched my boat on a few occasions to try to locate the fish using float trolling techniques. Fish were now being regularly caught, small at first, then the numbers and sizes began to increase up to a weight of 17lb. It was all getting quite interesting! One day in late February I turned up with the intention of static fishing for the session in an area where the fish had been located three days earlier. Two rods were baited and cast into the margins on a tight line to a float fished paternoster. The baits were very fresh and the day was a good one with fish of 20lb 12oz and 12lb 2oz. Then a small one of 13lb then a 21lb 10oz and to cap it all a final fish of 17lb 2 oz. Incidentally, the first fish was to grow much bigger in subsequent years to reach a size so big it would probably rank as the biggest ever caught in the River Hull.

I don't normally return to the swim after a really good day as it is generally disappointing. This day was different for some reason or other. Daren Clark and I were to have a pike fishing session together. We met up just after 8.00am on Saturday morning. Past experience had proved that the current conditions were ideal. Bright, fairly mild with a light breeze. D.C. started fishing with his rods downstream of mine. I caught a double figure fish almost straight away and was running low on bait due to the mega day on the Friday. I needed some fresh bait, so I wound in and went to purchase some from Brandesburton. When I returned DC had a fish of 12lb and a much larger fish sacked up in the margins. We took the fish out of the sack to photograph it. What a good-looking pike it was, it was a stocky 40.5-inch-long fish from snout to fork of tail and weighed a magnificent 26lb. It was a very dark coloured fish in great winter condition. I took some quick photographs on my Canon SLR.

A Beautiful 26lb pike caught by Daren Clark from East Yorkshires famous River Hull. The huge girth on this fish reflects the rich environment which pike in this water enjoy. The River Hull is one of the norths top big pike rivers. (Photo courtesy of Adrian and Daren)

Things were proving a bit slow for me after taking the photo so I moved upstream one peg to where I had been fishing the day before. I started to catch immediately and landed a fish of 17.2lb then a fish of 17.4lb another very small fish but then the icing on the cake was a final fish of 25lb exactly! The 25lb fish had a length of 39.5 inches and was amazingly fat!

Adrian displays his very well-conditioned River Hull pike weighing 25lb. This beauty was just under forty inches long which make it a very plump lady indeed! It registers about 0.7 on the pike condition scale featured in the appendix. (Photo courtesy of Adrian)

Both of the bigger pike were reminiscent of artificial trout water pike due to their bulk. For Yorkshire River pike they were exceptional and in my long experience they have never got better than these superb fish.

The following pike season I moved onto new pastures. I started fishing the Yorkshire Derwent and the local drains which I really enjoyed. I continued fishing the River Hull, although much less frequently. I reasoned that the River Hull pike could wait another couple of seasons. I was in fact looking for new challenges, in hindsight this was a mistake. Although repeat captures of larger pike on the River Hull was not an issue. Limited success was experienced with the big pike on the River Derwent, although I was hearing on the grapevine that others were doing quite well back on the River Hull. Three years later, just before the close of the season in March 2002 I returned to the River Hull with renewed enthusiasm to catch my largest pike at that time which weighed 31.15oz.

A SEASON ON THE WEST BECK

The West Beck in East Yorkshire is a nationally famous game fishing fishery. At the time of writing there are a handful of clubs and day ticket stretches at Wansford near Driffield. Probably the best known is the West Beck Preservation. This is a strictly private fishery for members only who fish mainly for grayling and trout, both of which grow to goodly proportions. I have fished it once on a guest ticket with an angling friend, and some years ago I was offered the opportunity to join as a paid-up member. Unfortunately, I had to decline the invitation for personal reasons. I know on good authority that the fishing is of a very high quality.

Downstream from the West Beck Preservation is a stretch that used to be owned by Ken Ryder. Ken started his Humberside fish dealing business from the property. He dug out a large acreage of shallow ponds adjacent to West Beck. As an interesting aside, one of Kens employees told me that a Viking sword was unearthed whilst relocating soil on the property. Water from the West Beck was used to maintain water levels in the ponds which were shallow to optimise the ideal growing temperatures for the stock fish to gain weight. These ponds were used to grow carp and other species to sell all over the country. Ken at one stage in his business life was one of only a handful of individuals that was known to be a national authority on carp breeding. Owing to this he featured in several angling media articles in the 1970s. He once told me that he had gained a lot of his knowledge from spending time with carp breeders in Croatia and some say that his early passing was due to his contact with the fish pest control, biocide. Ken also bred rainbow and brown trout for as far afield as Scotland, southern England and of course for the River Hull. If only Ken had written a book he could have passed on his unique knowledge for future generations, like Tom Sturdy and other local Yorkshire experts many of his secrets of success died along with him.

Kens stretch was about half a mile long and consisted of meandering bends, shallow riffles and deceptively deeper straights. At the lower end of Kens river there used to be a bridge and weir. The weir created deeper water immediately upstream and obviously restricted boat traffic from getting beyond the weir. I believe the current owners, the Yorkshire Wildlife Trust, have removed the weir to lower the water level. Presumably for the benefit of wading birds. I have not returned to the property since Ken sold it on to the YWT.

Prior to Ken selling the property I was lucky enough to be a member of the syndicate for the last season of his ownership. Ken initially wanted to sell to an angling concern. However, there was little interest from the local angling clubs for the price he wanted to help fund his retirement. 'Big Dave' had proposed my membership and he was the former proprietor of the Tackle Box, on the Beverley Road in Hull. I had always hankered after fishing Kens stretch but up until then an opportunity had never arisen. My primary interest was in catching the big pike which the river was reputed to hold. Prior to being accepted as a member I remember a conversation with Dave. He related about how one day he and an angling friend spotted a huge pike in the water. River pike are not always the easiest fish to spot at the best of times and Dave's friend could not focus on it at first, but when he did, they were both taken aback by its size. They agreed that this was a fish that they estimated to be in the mid-thirties. A huge fish indeed for such a small river. However, big fish of any species can be difficult to estimate when there is no yardstick with which to compare their size. More especially a really big pike. At that size they tend to be fairly solitary individuals. I took note of what Dave had to say with interest, but as time went on it faded into the back of my memory, more on this later.

I had been working away in Scotland so my first session on Kens stretch started on the last day of June in 2011 when I started fishing for Chub. The West Beck contains reasonably sized Chub although I certainly was not expecting big Chub by national standards. I started my approach by using mobile stalking tactics using floating baits to tempt the fish. This enabled me to survey the whole fishery not just for Chub, but also for any pikey looking areas. I continually checked the depths and generally spotted fish and other features to gradually build up my knowledge of the whole length. It proved to be a very interesting water and I had it all to myself not seeing any other syndicate member during my whole session there. I immediately started catching Chub up to over four pounds off the top. I also spotted the expected trout, grayling and roach and a few medium sized pike. Features of note were mentally logged for the coming winter pike pursuit. I even waded in the water at the edge as deep as I could manage. It was at its low summer level but was still deeper than six foot in places.

The stalking off the top approach was great fun and I eventually caught a species of fish I had never seen before. At first sight I was mystified as to what I had caught but then I realised it was an ide. This was also caught on floating bait and weighed over 3lb. Ken was at hand and kindly photographed it for me holding this novel fish. That first ide opened the 'floodgates' and I was to consistently catch them until I started to fish for pike later in the autumn. I caught lots in the 3lb size, a few in the 4lb size and finally one specimen exactly five pounds. Once Autumn finally arrived it was time to focus on pike fishing. I did manage to fit in some long-range visits to Chew Valley Lakes near Bristol and a few trips to the River Wye in Herefordshire. However, my important local fishing venue would be of course Kens exclusive club stretch.

I started to fish on Kens private fishery in the second half of October. In 2011 there had not been much rain so the beck was running low, clear and with a very low flow. Thankfully, the pike liked my deadbaits and I experienced good consistent sport with lots of beautiful pike up to a modest 18lb. Gurnard was the new in bait and was working very well and was a new catching experience for me. On the $14^{th\,of}$ November 2011 I fished and recaptured the 18lb pike I caught earlier and another fish of about 5lb. It was a clear cold day with winter fast approaching. I was just packing up at dusk and retrieved my dead bait. It was then that I noticed a dark shadow on the bottom about halfway across the narrow beck. It looked like a weed bed. Strange, I thought the streamer weed had died back by now. I removed my bait from the hooks and threw it into the side of the river and watched it sink to the bottom. I looked up again and had further suspicions about the 'weedbed' in front of me, I was having doubts about what it actually was. Was it a fish? It can't be its too big! I then flicked my unbaited rig over the weedbed expecting to wind back a clump of weed. Instantly, as soon as the float and lead hit the spot this huge fish bolted off upstream leaving an almighty cloud of mud and silt in its wake. In the low flow conditions, the cloud remained suspended for over a minute.

What a mistake I had just made. Was that fish in the vicinity just about to take my bait switching onto the feed at dusk? Would it still be around for my next visit? The events just described are taken from my 2011 diary. I remember returning and fishing on quite a few occasions in the same area hoping to put my hooks into that impressive fish. For the rest of 2011, my diary has no record of any further big pike from Kens Fishery. On into 2012. Personally, I find that the mid-January to mid-February generally provide the best chances of catching the season's best. This year was no exception. From Kens water I eventually caught pike of 21lb and 22lb on dead bait and on lure, respectively. The River Wye also fished well that year with quite a few doubles and two 20lb fish up to 26lb.

Sadly, for the angling community, my diary notes that on the 2nd of March I received confirmation from Ken that he had sold his land to the Yorkshire Wildlife Trust. The season end will be the final chance to fish Kens superb waters. It was a very enjoyable season finishing on a reasonably high note and I thank Big Dave, Dean and Ken for giving me the opportunity. I would also like to thank Kevin Clifford for sharing his knowledge about the River Hulls Pike History.

Red Letter Day Ten
A SUB-ZERO TWENTY POUNDER

'December is good, January is better, but February is best.' This is a very valuable pike fishing adage which of course refers to the condition of the pike and how they improve towards the back end of the coarse fishing season. It is the very reason pike anglers of long experience are on high alert during this exciting part of the year.

For this very reason, I invited my friend Barrie up to Yorkshire in February to share some premium pike fishing time on a part of a northern river that I knew contained a good head of 'Barrie worthy' big pike. As luck had it Barrie was working on the Friday at Lancaster University so he found a small hotel to stay in just a couple of miles from our chosen venue. I set off from Harrogate at 6.00am to meet Barrie at our arranged time of 7.00am. It took me several minutes to de frost my windscreen so I was running late for my appointment with the doctor but fortunately I knew the road well so I soon made up the lost time on the straight flats along the road!

When I arrived at our rendezvous Barrie had just arrived and he was sat on the sill of his hatchback getting his fishing gear together, not just fishing tackle, but also cooking equipment, and heaters already for a good breakfast. One of Barrie's favourite treats whilst fishing was to cook a good fried breakfast including his favourite delicacy, well cooked bacon. Quite often he would share a few rashes with me, it tasted delicious. Oh yes, Barrie certainly knew how to live life to the full! The worse the weather, the better Barrie's culinary treats tasted, he was such a great bloke to be with.

On this particular day, the temperature was minus five degrees centigrade. I directed my visitor to the best cold weather pike spot that I knew on the river. It was on a wide bend and about two thirds of the way across near the outside bend there was a twenty-foot-deep banana shaped trough about forty feet long and fifteen feet wide. This trough itself was over twenty feet deep and was surrounded on all sides by water averaging only ten feet deep. The fringes of the river were covered in quite thick cat ice which extended about ten feet out into the river but this was no problem. I immediately bombarded the hotspot with lots of sardine chunks just upstream of the feature so they would flow nicely into Barrie's deeper water below. I set up my rods fifty yards upstream and fished a float ledgered trout bait in mid river. Not the best position, but that had been reserved for my special guest. We had only been set up for two hours or so when on the far bank a big group of match anglers arrived and settled in right opposite us. Barrie was quite happy to stay put; the river was fifty yards wide so they were not crowding us but I didn't like it and decided to move upstream a mile. I tried to get Barrie to come, but he was quite happy in his deep-water hotspot. We arranged to rendezvous mid-afternoon to exchange notes.

On the additional one-mile march north to the new venue I certainly burnt off the calories I had consumed eating Barrie's bacon sandwich, I really needed them for the extra push and I was quite tired when I finally arrived at the new venue. Once I regained my breath the change to my new venue just 'felt so good,' I had the whole river to myself. Out went some pre bait into a deep area similar to my fishing partner one mile downstream, only this one was on a straight north south run of the river. One of my sardine baits was positioned hard against the willow bushes on the opposite bank the other mid river in comparably shallow water of ten feet. I was sat on the right riverbank looking east and the sun was climbing slowly in the sky but the air temperature was still sub-zero. The sun was actually coming from behind the thick bank of willow bushes on the far bank casting a shadow which ran right along the eastern riverbank. A big pike lying in this shadow would be just about invisible and yet could see everything. I just knew I was in for some fun.

Sure enough, after only about forty minutes the right-hand float fishing in the shadows began to 'nod' ever so slightly. I immediately lifted the rod from the rest and wound down hard onto a very heavy resistance in over twenty feet of water. I felt that oh so familiar low frequency powerful head shake which can only mean one thing, 'Big Pike on'. She was on too and made a deep nerve-wracking sweep of the riverbed to find a log to snag up on. Slowly, very slowly she succumbed to the upward pressure of the rod. Now though, I had to hold the pike rod with one hand and smash a large hole in the cat ice to get my prize within reach of the net. I soon achieved this using the handle of the landing net. Now at last I was ready to net this beauty. Netting was not so difficult though as when the pike approached a lot of the ice was broken up in the turbulence of the water. As soon as I lifted her out of the water I felt a very solid weight, at that point I knew she was a twenty. Wow, wait until I tell Barrie, I hope he has had one too!

Sub Zero pike weighing in at 21.5 lb. This fish had a fork length of 46 inches, its continental full length over 121.9 cm or four feet! This is one of the longest Northern River Pike I have ever caught.

As I unhooked this wonderful pike, I could see she was scale perfect, a real beauty measuring forty-six inches long. In Sweden it would be forty-eight inches long (extreme length) a full four feet in length. Wow! Although perfectly healthy she was a slim girl but still weighing twenty-one and a half pounds. I was ecstatic and as I quickly measured her dimensions, I noticed the frost was freezing my net solid, so I returned her back to the relative warm river to stay safe. In very cold temperatures the pikes gill filaments can be damaged by the frost so I took no chances.

That was it, I had achieved my target for the day so I quickly packed up and headed south to meet back up with Barrie. The only thing which worried me was that Barrie might have blanked after coming all the way up from Cambridge. Also, up to that point Barrie had never taken a Yorkshire River twenty, as a born and bred Yorkshireman I knew that was important to him and if he had blanked, I would feel really guilty. As it was Barrie had blanked but I immediately invited him back up to help rectify the situation. This we did and Barry came up two weeks later with his fishing partner Tim Cole. They came up together in one car to share driving and save petrol expenses too. Tim and Barrie came up on the Saturday which I could not make owing to family commitments but the good news is they did catch a twenty-two pounder in the same place I had fished. I am fairly sure it was my pike which had put on half a pound during the intervening fortnight. The only trouble was the twenty-two pounder fell to Tim's rod, at least they scored though and avoided a blank. To the best of my knowledge Barrie never did get his Northern River Twenty, it just seemed it wasn't meant to happen. If not, he certainly made up for it on his home Fenlands waters where he succeeded like no other on the Fenlands. Overall, he caught about four times more twenties than me, plus a record six fenland thirties which was quite amazing. Somehow it never materialised for him on the northern rivers though which is more evidence to suggest that methods which work well on the Fens or Norfolk Broads do not necessarily translate to our Northern Rivers (see the chapter dealing with hook rigs).

If I could only turn the clock back, I would give Barrie one of my home-made river rigs. I had never tried to hide the rig from him and I did not push it onto him (as I had with my friend Nigel). If I had pushed it might have looked somehow disrespectful and I didn't want that. I really should have though because I did promise him a Northern River Twenty and therefore should have done whatever it took to make that happen. Over the years I have noticed there is often a lot of cruel irony in Pike fishing. Like Fred Buller lending his spinner to the bloke who straight away caught the record pike on that same 'lucky' spinner! Or the number of times you take a complete novice pike fishing for the first time and they catch the biggest pike of a lifetime. There are hundreds of other cruel ironies, but that would fill an entire book.

Such is Pike Fishing and it's all part and parcel of what makes it so uniquely intriguing.

Red Letter Day Eleven

HOW TO CREATE THE 'GOOD OLD DAYS' ON THE RIVER AIRE
By Guest Writer Mr Mark Green

After a long summer break from pike fishing there is no better feeling than welcoming the cold frosty mornings and preparing a winter campaign targeting pike. Over the years I have fallen into the trap of thinking about fishing too many far-off pike venues dotted about all over the country. Long range trips involve staying at expensive hotels and with the increasing costs of petrol and day tickets it can work out very costly, and over the years I was amazed at how much my pike fishing trips had actually set me back financially.

If you have a couple of Stillwater's and a river or two within a short distance from home and they both contain numbers of pike the best cost-effective plan is to stick with them. I have spoken to pike anglers in the past who have also travelled all over the country in search of big pike and beating their own personal bests only to find that the best pike fishing venues are actually on their doorstep.

River pike fishing is without a doubt my favourite form of pike fishing. The pike fight a lot harder due to the current and I can travel light, keep mobile and cover a lot of water in a day's fishing. Due to the amount of rain, we experience nowadays during the winter months having a good back up still water is essential for when the rivers become unfishable due to floods.

In November 2021 I started to think a lot about pike, I had set up the rods, sorted all the tackle out and filled the bait freezer to the brim but for some reason I just could not quite find the motivation to go out fishing. I had walked the banks of my local river and the conditions were ideal. My usual spots where I had caught pike from before were heaving with baitfish and the pike were in attendance and crashing about having a good feed.

During a telephone conversation with a good mate and fellow pike angler, he asked if I had been out fishing and he was very surprised to hear I was no longer motivated to get out onto the riverbanks after the pike. I had in fact been in this position for a while due to heavy work and family commitments. Furthermore, the passing of my main fishing buddy and father caused me to somehow lose my motivation to fish. Looking back, I now realise I was in mourning which naturally just took the edge off life in general for a time.

When I finally did get motivated and got out fishing it certainly improved my state of mind and mental health, just being out fishing in the fresh air really made me feel so much better. During the telephone conversation my friend reminded me of how going fishing has always helped rejuvenate both body and spirit, it's just too good to miss. Now I was really fired up and ready to go and by good fortune my companion had a day off the following Tuesday, a catch up combined with a good day's fishing would do us both a power of good.

During our conversation I mentioned I had seen numbers of good pike moving about on our local river so that provided a good place to start and hopefully put a few pike on the bank. For the next few days, I kept a lookout on the river phone app and even after a couple of days rain the rivers looked spot on and perfect for pike fishing.

Over the years the river phone app has saved me a lot of wasted time travelling to rivers which were just unsuitable for fishing due to snow broth or flooded fields making it impossible to even reach the river, and I would recommend this technology to river anglers in particular.

This Photo captures the mood of the River Aire on a misty autumnal dawn. After a struggle with pollution lasting over seventy years the beautiful River Aire has now been transformed into a good quality mixed fishery. Photo courtesy of Mark Green.

Tuesday finally arrived and whilst loading the car I was full of anticipation and really looking forward to having a good catch up with my friend too. Fishing is fine whilst alone but is often so much better when you meet up with friends. On this day we arranged to fish next to each other near an old bridge in a swim which had produced well for us in the past. The bridge, as well as been an excellent feature in itself for pike is also an area where the river depth shelves up from seventeen feet up to eleven feet. Both the bait fish and pike hang about together on the bottom of the slope.

I had purchased the *'Castable Deeper'* a couple of years ago. This device, when attached to your mobile phone via Bluetooth relays valuable information back to you phone. Not only does it tell you the depth of the water but it also gives details of any fish present onto your mobile screen in real time. The water column of the river shows up well on the mobile screen. The bottom and shape of the riverbed shows up clearly as a distinct line. Above the riverbed weeds show up well as structures, sometimes they only grow a few inches tall, in other areas they may grow almost to the surface. All this is valuable information for the angler to be aware of in selecting what rigs to use on the day. Most exciting of all individual fish show up on the screen indicating where they are in the water column, all very interesting and useful in helping to choose where to fish.

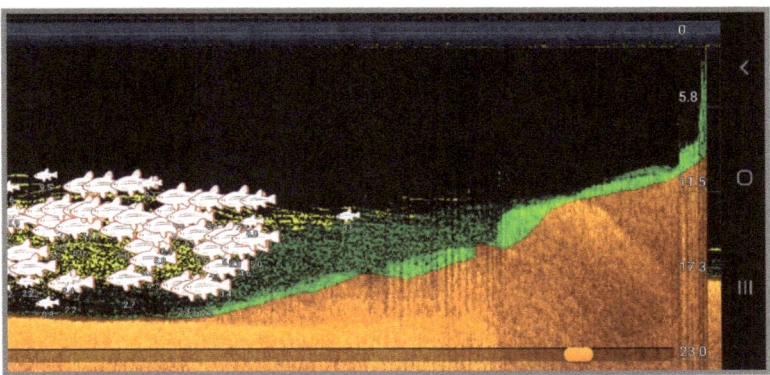

This is the Deeper image showing up on the I phone showing where and how many fish are within the survey area. Not only does the Deeper give the location of the fish but it also provides details of the depth and shape of the underwater contours. A special phone holder is available which can be clipped onto the rod providing in effect an underwater windscreen for the angler!

On this day we located a good feature containing fish so we set up together to fish this promising part of the river. We had done our 'homework' using the latest technology so now we began to fish. Using one rod each we fished together so we could have a good catch up and fish at the same time, who could ask for more? I decided to use a running ledger rig with my favourite bait, a full lamprey with just an inch cut off the tail end. Lampreys are full of blood and the pike home in on the blood leakage, they are we believe attracted in this way from hundreds of yards downstream. In this river pike are accustomed to lamprey as they form an important part of the River Aire food chain, that's another reason we really believe in their effectiveness. I have lost count of the number of times I have been unhooking river pike when a Lamprey has been protruding from its stomach. Yes, there is no doubt at all that these are one of the best baits of all for pike fishing on rivers. Due to the constantly flowing river water the blood tends to get washed out of the bait after a couple of hours or so, that's why it pays to replace the bait with a fresh one after about two hours or so.

My fishing partner set up a paternoster rig with a sardine set to fish mid water with the plan of altering the depth the bait was fished every hour or so. After stowing away my expensive river app and phone in a very safe place I cast my bait towards mid-river where the *Deeper* had identified some fish providing an excellent starting point. Sure, enough it was not long before the bite alarm was singing. I wound down firmly to set the hooks and knew instantly it was a good fish. It swam off downstream using the flow of the river to lever its way from danger. It took some time and a hard battle to finally get this wonderful fish under the net. Oh yes, what a fantastic feeling, we weighed her in at fifteen pounds, what a beauty, my mood went from just over zero up to ten out of ten after seeing that superb fish. It was caught thanks to a mixture of using old fashioned river craft with the latest high-tech gear, so rewarding!

A few years ago, I purchased a device called the *Water Wolf underwater camera*. This device is attached to the float ledger rig and monitors what is going on under water near the bait. The recordings are then downloaded onto the computer when you get home. I was fascinated to learn how long pike can just look at the bait before taking it, or sometimes just swimming off with no interest. It also showed that pike mouth the bait then drop it without even moving the float! This behaviour is discussed in the earlier chapter on hooks and rigs. On one occasion using the *Water Wolf camera* I could see a pike circling the suspended bait several times before taking it.

Back to the river though, the runs kept on coming to the ledgered lamprey baits but not on my mates. I offered to share runs to make it fair, in any case I had already banked a big pike so I wanted to share out the sport a bit. Thankfully, several more pike came fighting to the net so we both had plenty of fun. During all the action I began to realise how much fun I had been missing being in good company and catching these superb Northern River Pike.

The action from the pike slowed down a bit in the late morning session which was a good thing really. It gave us time to reflect on the wonderful fish we had just taken and gave us time to settle back a bit and enjoy a brew with some delicious biscuits providing much needed fuel to keep us going. The weather was very mild and the pike were still crashing into the roach shoals. I was Kicking myself for not bringing my spinning rod with me! Whilst waiting for action on the static dead baits I normally cast around the floats and over the years I have found this a very effective way of catching extra pike. Not just by catching them on the lure rod, but more often by stimulating big pike to move around a bit to find our baits.

I can remember one occasion whilst fishing a very large water the first three hours were very slow with no action at all. I then started to fish artificial lures around the dead baits which were positioned near the side. After only about six casts I had a follow in from a good double figure pike which had a mark on its nose. Just five minutes later the dead bait float shot off at last, an immediate strike was met with a very heavy force out in the deeper water, it turned out to be a very welcome eighteen pounder, a truly great fish. Although the lures did not produce that day, they certainly helped to get the pike moving and making it all worthwhile. This has happened so many times that I rarely go out without my lure rod and a few spinners, it really is a valuable part of the river pikers tool kit.

In those nice quiet spells between runs I was already planning my next pike trip. I thought I must make the most of it whilst the river was still good and before it was spoilt by the freezing rain causing the annual temperature shock which spoils the river for weeks on end. In the past I had suffered many poor days when the river was high with cold water and snow broth. Part of the problem is there are very few slacks where the pike can get out of the main current. Big, bladed spinnerbaits have produced the odd pike rather than using dead baits and I know a lot of anglers who have experienced the same with flooded rivers and therefore focus on using spinners with good results.

Our day had passed by too quickly, but there was still a couple of hours left so we were not finished yet. I was already fully satisfied and would be perfectly happy even if we caught no further fish as the day had already been a great success. Just to make things a little more interesting, and using my knowledge gleaned from my *Water Wolf* footage shown on the computer screen in previous sessions, I decided to twitch the lamprey bait intermittently back to just inject some extra interest into the bait. A few minutes after a recast, near where I had seen fish scatter, I noticed that line was beginning to peel off my reel spool! Very interesting, I could feel my heart beating harder in my chest with anticipation, without any hesitation I closed the bail arm and pulled into what I thought was a small jack pike as it came straight up to the surface. It was only then that I saw it and realized it was no jack at all, in fact it was at least a double, but it was difficult to tell at first. Then it woke up and wrenched line off the spool in a series of deep powerful runs. This was a big fish and like the earlier fifteen pounder it was using the force of the river current to gain advantage. Following some heart stopping runs the fish eventually came over the net. At this point my friend shouted excitedly "If it isn't a twenty its very close." I could see the pike was long, but it was only when I could see it on the unhooking mat, I realised just how very big it was! At first, I said, "Oh it's about nineteen pounds I think." I did not want fate to think I was getting above myself by being greedy. That after all would be bad Karma!

In fact, the scales settled at twenty-two pounds and nine ounces. Wow, that is a truly amazing pike and without a shadow of doubt the very best river pike I have ever seen. It was in pristine condition, not a mark or line burn on its flanks or anywhere else. Judging by the pike's immaculate jaws it probably had never been caught before. I really was in awe of this pike as it swam off back to the safety of the river depths from which it came.

It was the first trip out of the pike season and we had scored a twenty-two-pounder backed up by a string of big doubles too! I heartily thanked my mate for a really good day out and for giving me the nudge I needed to get back out fishing.

As the title suggests a Red-Letter Day for me is not just about catching fish, but also about sharing good times with friends, catching up on life and catching pike, they don't even have to be big pike as it's the quality of the experience which really counts. Whatever the future holds my good mate and I can look back on this day with joy forever and reflect on how things were better back in the good old days!

Mark displays his stunning River Aire twenty-two-pound and nine-ounce pike! What an immaculate looking fish, scale perfect and such beautiful markings. To think not long-ago great parts of the lower River Aire, including where this fish was caught from, was a dead river. It has taken millions of pounds of anglers funding to clean the rivers up. A process started by the late John Eastwood featured in the first part of this book. Mark deserves extra congratulations for tracking down this fish using the latest technology. Photo courtesy of Mark Green.

Bill Winship

Red Letter Day Twelve

BIG DURHAM PIKE ON THE RIVER WEAR.
By Guest writer Jonathan Chandler

The River Wear in county Durham is in my opinion one of the finest rivers in England. As a born and bred Geordie I would say that wouldn't I? Yes, the River Wear is a lot smaller than say the Tyne to the north, in fact only half the size actually, but what it lacks in size is made up for in its growing big fish potential and easy accessibility.

Fly fishing is my favourite fishing method and I use it to catch trout, salmon and coarse fish along the full length of the river. In the upper reaches many of the waters are fly only and the main target fish are brown trout, sea trout and salmon. Lower down though, below Wolsingham game fish give way to coarse fish like chub, dace, grayling, perch and pike. This area, just a few miles above Durham city lie some of my favourite beats. There are slow deep areas interspersed with faster shallow runs where a lure can be striped through the shallows causing big chub to erupt into action, some of them grow to over six pounds in weight. They are truly wonderful fish to catch.

Not long-ago fishing clubs along the river encouraged all coarse fish to be removed with the intention of providing better conditions for the trout and salmon. Thankfully, these older authorities have been gradually replaced by a more enlightened management. Old dogma has been replaced by modern science and in this process the new Environment Agency and the Angling Trust have truly worked wonders. Decade after decade of persecution never quite removed the indigenous coarse fish, they still managed to survive somehow, but now they are really thriving and the whole river is benefiting from what we now call natural biodiversity.

Flyfishing for salmon is one of my many passions on the River Wear and to catch a big twenty-pound salmon requires some serious fishing tackle like a purpose-built salmon fly rod, a strong reel and a fifteen-pound leader. I like to buy my game fishing tackle from Hardy's of Alnwick, their shop is less than an hour north on the A1 and they have such great tackle. Their tackle is not cheap, but the quality of it means it will last so long it is not so expensive overall. In any case, nothing is too good for fishing the River Wear and as keen salmon angler Jack Charlton once said, "Nothing is too good for a true Geordie." Jack was of course once a coal miner from Ashington and became a football celebrity and highly respected angling author.

On the subject of quality fishing, I have noticed that the quality of pike fishing on the river has improved considerably over the past decade or so. Going back forty years I can always remember catching pike on the salmon fly from time to time, but they were normally just small jack pike under around three pounds. Now, largely thanks to the work of the environment agency pike fishing has improved so much I have had to start using a fourteen-inch wire trace on my salmon leaders!

About ten years ago my attitude to the pike was changed forever. I had booked a week off work and decided to treat myself to a three-day session of salmon fishing on my favourite mid-section of the River Wear near Durham. In this section there are plenty of deep runs and swims to just die for. For some reason, the salmon were not responding and on the third day at lunch time my score was still zero. I repeatedly told myself. "There is more to fishing than just catching fish." By two thirty in the afternoon even this 'diffuser' was wearing thin. Finally, at about 2.45pm I finally had a fish on, it was only a small grayling though but at least it was something. I gently brought my fish towards the net when an invisible force took hold of my only catch. The unseen force powered off into deep water. I felt the rod shudder as something happened out in mid river. I then saw a huge pike come to the surface and erupted skywards shaking its head and flinging the grayling across the water surface, somehow the double hooks on the fly re connected in the pikes open mouth providing a strong hold in the pike's jaw. Without a wire trace I feared it would only be a short fight as the pike would quickly snap the unprotected mono trace. By a freak of good luck, the line was held out of the pike's deadly teeth so all was well, though I had no idea of this for the first ten minutes or so. It was a very heavy fish and put a lot of strain on the rod. As the fight progressed, I began to realise the hook was outside the pike's mouth. Still, the fight was far from over and I kept a very strong hold to prevent the line crossing over into the pike's jaws. With a fifteen-pound leader I was able to exert considerable pressure and leverage with my purpose-built salmon rod, but I had never had to play a fish this big before. As I drew the fish closer to within about twenty feet of the net it appeared impossible to make further headway, it just seemed as if there was a barrier preventing it from getting closer. The water was gin clear so it could obviously see me which made matters worse. At this stage I was really desperate to get my fish to the net. If I lost it, I would be gutted, really gutted, but still the struggle continued and my arms were aching like never before. After a further five minutes of absolute torture, she did finally come to the net. Hallelujah! Finally, she was mine. I just collapsed on the bank and carefully held the net above the water level whilst I regained my senses. "How big is it?" Unbeknown to me two fellows on the far bank had been carefully watching my every move for the last fifteen minutes. "Oh, it's about fifteen or twenty pounds I think." They had no idea it was a pike so I just kept quiet and regained my breath. I uncoupled the landing net handle and got out the little Sampson weighing scales. Without taking the fish out of the net I weighed this beauty. The scales only read up to 25lb and they bounced down heavily to the extreme limit leaving a good weight of the fish unrecorded. I then lifted the full weight of the fish and estimated roughly that there was a further five or six pounds which went beyond the limits of the scale! I was neurotically aware I was being watched all the time, but at least my actions were shielded by a bank tall waterside reeds which protected me from the onlookers. "Oh, it's just over twenty pounds" I shouted to the bystanders who still probably thought it was a salmon. No one asked anyway so I returned the pike to the water within the net still feeling stunned and shocked by the sheer size of it. The pike was just over forty-eight inches long, streamlined with a steely evil looking face!

As a salmon angler brought up in a salmon fishing mindset, I had always removed pike as that was the unthinking culture of my upbringing. This pike went back though, and so has every single pike ever since. From now on I also resolved to only fish with a wire trace. I had been very lucky to land this specimen, but luck like that was obviously a 'one off' event nothing short of a miracle in fact, but from this point forward it was wire traces every time. An angler can only push one's luck so far.

I will never know the true weight of this fish; I don't really care. What I do know is that this fish turned a near blank three-day fishing trip into one of the most memorable days of my life. I have since heard on the grapevine that well witnessed pike up to twenty-nine and a half pounds have been caught on the Durham River Wear. There are also rumours of fish over the thirty pounds mark, both pike and salmon. This is a fantastic prospect and the pleasure of fishing the beautiful River Wear is a great privilege and so deeply enjoyable. Who could possibly ask for more?

The River Wear is second to none for its charm and beauty. Here the river scene is further enhanced by Durham Cathedral which overlooks the river in the heart of Durham City. Thanks to a more enlightened approach to the value of coarse fish the River Wear has a fast-growing reputation for producing very large pike which can now rival any of the Northern Rivers.

APPENDIX

The Pike Condition or 'Fatness' Scale

The Northern Rivers of England are quite special in that throughout their course the waters have a wide range of variable conditions ranging from being fast and shallow in the upper regions to markedly slower and deeper towards the lowland valleys. As we have already seen big pike can adapt and thrive in all these conditions but to do so their physical morphology changes in order to cope with each separate environment.

I did not fully realise this until I acquired transport providing the opportunity to fish a wide variety of rivers and noticed from an early stage that pike caught from upland faster rivers tended to be more streamlined than those which were fifty miles or more downstream along the river course. Both sections produced pike to over twenty pound or more, but interestingly, they just looked quite different in the separate river sections. I noticed that the pike seemed generally fatter further downstream to measure these changes I devised a scientific device called the Pike condition scale which is shown on the diagram. On this scale very slim pike are shown at the top with the fattest at the bottom. The condition or fatness of the pike can be measured scientifically by simply dividing girth measurement by length. For example, a pike with a length of thirty inches and a girth of only six inches would be very thin and give an elongation ratio of just 0.2 on the scale. By measuring the differences, we can record what is going on in a very interesting way. Yes, it was obvious that pike generally became better conditioned further downstream, also, that pike living in the same river section were mostly identical as they lived within the same feeding conditions. Pike in the lower sections of our rivers are generally a lot better conditioned owing to all year-round availability of roach and bream stocks which are not present in the upper reaches. It is not all bad news for the pike in the upper reaches though as they get the winter benefit of vast shoals of grayling moving into the upper deeps during winter. Therefore, even in the upper limits you can still get pike approaching the thirty pounds mark, so we can still enjoy promising pike fishing in most sections.

We do realise that for many pike anglers this kind of scientific analysis is very boring and we fully respect that opinion. However, if you apply it to your own fisheries, the ones you know and love we are sure you will immediately realise how fascinating and useful it is to study your pike at this more advanced level. Once you start to collect your measurements, log them down in your fishing diary as you have a bank of knowledge which becomes so valuable and even more so as time goes on. Just one example, in 2005 the northern rivers became seriously affected by the cormorant onslaught. Suddenly, our rivers were attacked by tens of thousands of cormorants which effectively wiped-out whole sections of fodder fish from rivers like the Wear, Tyne, Ouse, Ure, Ribble and many others. At first it did not seem to affect our pike because they were too big for the cormorants to swallow! After a year or so though we found our pike were becoming unusually easy to catch and when caught they were much thinner and even emaciated in some instances. Thanks to our measurements we could see our pike stocks were becoming thinner from their normal condition of 0.6 on the scale down to 0.3 over a period of about three years. Worse still, our catch rates were falling badly. Pre 2005 we could expect to catch three or four twenty pounders each year, now it is down to one every year showing the scale of the devastation. This evidence makes depressing reading, but we still enjoy fishing the same venues, only with lower expectations and somehow, we still catch some big pike up to over twenty-five pounds, but just not so often.

On a more positive note, one thing we have become aware of is that pike tend to feed up to whatever food availability there is. For example, in a water rich in fodder fish all year-round pike will naturally feed heavily and put on weight very quickly. In these waters pike in the twenty-to-thirty-pound class can still be caught. In less well stocked waters in the faster upland areas pike still grow big, but it takes them much longer and the weight ceiling tends to be about a third lower. Yes, their maximum length will be the same at perhaps forty-two to forty-six inches long and if a fast river pike they will fight harder and longer than their heavyweight cousins further downstream, yet their weight will be nowhere near its full potential for its length. In effect a forty-six-inch inch long fast river pike, though perfectly healthy, has only reached possibly less than a third of its upper weight potential under ideal food supply conditions.

As we saw earlier in the chapter on Northern Rivers, the Swale is the fastest river in England, and as one would expect the pike are often very thin. Yet even in the River Swale there are small sections of water which provide better shelter and food supplies where even the River

Swale pike feed better and are a few points fatter on the scale. Overall though the Swale is a thin pike water whilst at the other end of the scale the lower River Ouse is a relatively fat pike water. Thankfully though, both rivers produce our much loved twenty plus pounders but much more often on the Ouse.

In over fifty years of river pike fishing, we have caught several fish over forty-four inches long, and a few up to forty-six inched long (fork length) weighing only twenty-four pounds. This is because they only measured 0.4 on the attached condition scale. In effect, big as they were, they were only at approximately one third of their full weight potential. On the scientific condition scale, just imagine the weight of a forty-six-inch pike with a condition scale reading of 1.0! Such a pike would need a massive food supply to expand to this size. The kind of food supply once available every year with salmon runs which as our living link and witness Norris described as "made the river go black" with their annual runs upriver, not only in the Ure, but in all our northern rivers. The few pike which measured forty-six inches fork length were in fact forty-eight inches long if measuring their extreme length as they do in Sweden.

When Norris caught his 56lb river pike the River Ure enjoyed massive runs of salmon, mostly between three to ten pounds in weight. These salmon often shoaled up below river weirs for weeks on end until a flood made it possible for them to continue their journey upstream. These were ideal feeding conditions for any large pike, but a pike with a length of forty-six inches could become progressively fatter and deeper in its girth. This part of the river was at that time also blessed with a sheltered ox bow lake where all fish could retreat during periods of high water. In short, this part of the River Ure literally had it all in terms of ideal growing conditions for a super obese pike!

Norris told me his big pike was well over four feet long so let us just assume it was only 48 inches long, if it measured say 0.9 on the condition scale it could have easily been sixty pounds in weight, it was over 56lb as it counter weighed a 56lb weight on the scales. If only they had measured its length, we could get a better estimate. No matter, Norris and his father Tom went to a lot of trouble getting the fish weighed at the Bruce Arms stables and they confirmed its weight as over 56lb. For many years I did not believe this claim as it was so much larger than my own best efforts. Now though, having studied the wider circumstances,

I now actually believe every ounce of it. Of course, it would not satisfy the British Records Fish Committee of course, but neither was Tommy Morgan's Loch Lomond 47lb 11oz accepted. Now there is an interesting link between Morgan's Pike and the Sturdy pike in that they were both salmon fed giants caught when the salmon runs were in full flow. We would guess though that within the confines of a river weir, the Sturdy pike would have richer feeding conditions providing better growth. As mentioned earlier over the last fifty years I have caught several very large pike up to a fork length of forty-six inches. From this evidence we know under current feeding conditions forty-six inches is about the length limit we can expect. Crucially though, in the past when feeding conditions were infinitely better perhaps a greater length could be expected too in addition to the obvious weight? We will only know this when the big runs of salmon and sea trout finally return to put the theory to the test. What I do know for certain from the condition scale is that even a forty-six-inch pike has the potential to grow to be a fifty pounder under the correct feeding conditions. The pike I have caught at that length have varied in weight from twenty-two pounds up to twenty-six pounds and have only measured a third of the way up the condition or fatness scale at around 0.3 to 0.4 on the scale. In short, they have had the capacity to double or even treble their weight if they had the chance to graze on a regular crop of five-pound salmon which were once available to them twice a year, each and every year. These regular salmon runs ceased around the 1930s due to chronic pollution in the Humber estuary preventing migratory runs for many years.

River Pike in Northern England

CONDITION SCALE	ELONGATION RATION
	0.2
	0.4
	0.6
	0.8
	1.0

This is one of the authors largest Northern River Pike caught or seen in over fifty years of fishing these northern rivers. Its fork length was forty-six inches giving an extreme length of forty-eight inches and yet it was only a mid-twenty pounder. It only reached a third of the way up the condition scale. Just look at the size of those jaws! This fish would have no problem feeding on quality five-pound salmon and with its huge but empty frame it could easily reach its full growth potential of fifty or even sixty pounds.

As already mentioned in the biography of Norris Sturdy I was fully aware of Norris's big pike story and how he caught his 56lb pike. For forty years, I discounted his story as just another 'Tall Story', especially when my best lifetimes dedicated efforts only produced pike half his weight! However, in researching the past for this book I have discovered that the Northern Rivers in Edwardian England were completely different to what they are today. There really were salmon caught by the hundredweight and individual fish occasionally caught up to over fifty pounds! The pike too were much bigger, understandably so when they could gorge on an almost limitless supply of migratory salmon. Norris died thirty-four years ago but I now feel guilty I ever doubted his word and the very detailed circumstances he gave me about his big pike capture.

More recently in 2020 we have had a fully authenticated big pike found dead within a mile or so of Norris's great pike weighing well over fifty pounds. Yes, it was grown under artificial circumstances in an enclosed pond stocked artificially with sizable pellet fed rainbow trout. The point here is that under good growth conditions with almost unlimited food pike really can grow to their full-size potential which is well over fifty pounds. This is not just another tall story but an absolute proven fact.

Nurseries for River Pike

Pike are generally known to spawn between February and June but the actual time can vary according to local conditions. So, the earlier the water temperatures reach the trigger point of around forty degrees Fahrenheit, the earlier they will spawn. Our northern rivers tend to warm up later than the rivers of southern England and hence spawning may be over a month behind thanks to the colder high-altitude feeder becks and gills of the Pennines. This means that whilst pike on the River Thames may spawn in February or March, the northern rivers may be as late as April, May or June depending on mother nature and the ficklety of spring weather conditions.

Although forty degrees is the temperature at which spawning can begin to take place the hatching process is much more efficient if the hen pike can find temperatures of forty-five to fifty degrees. Fertilised eggs hatch out twice as fast in warmer waters. Pike eggs are sticky and evolved to become attached to weed stalks. If these tiny eggs can hatch out in say seven days as opposed to twenty-five days their survival rates will be infinitely better. Pike instinctively know this and migrate from their normal haunts to find shallow warmer pockets of water which benefit from direct sunlight.

In our northern rivers there are many local conditions which give rise to these pockets of warm water. The three main ones we have witnessed are as follows. Firstly, the weedy sheltered channels which are created below lock gates. In these protected conditions the standing water can build up its temperature above the main river and hold it for long periods of time. The sheltered nature of these places provides a microclimate separate and more viable than those found in the main river. Secondly, in fast rivers like the Swale or the Ribble pike often migrate up into quieter feeder streams or even shallow ditches where the water may only be eighteen inches deep but several degrees warmer than the main river. Such waters are often choked with weeds. It is well known that male pike enter the spawning shallows a few weeks before the female hen pike enter. Once the females appear on the spawning grounds the male fish, which often outnumber the larger females two or three to one begin to swim in exact unison together. As the females move around the water the males move in accord, almost looking as though they are attached by an invisible bond. At the same time, the male pike gently massage the hen pike to encourage the release of eggs and simultaneously liberate clouds of their own milt in order to fertilize her eggs. Depending on the size of the female, they can hold between 25,000 and 225,000 eggs in a mating process which can take up to two weeks. If weather conditions suddenly turn very cold the whole process is stopped but will continue once the temperatures return to the required level. We have often witnessed the whole process at close hand from the vantage point of our boat. Only last week on the third of April we were fly fishing for trout from our boat in the weedy shallows and a very large pike of at least twenty pounds came right alongside our boat and just stayed there. This memorable pike turned its head upwards to look at us as if to say, "Good day". It was only eighteen inches from the row locks, so I took a photo of its impressive size. Despite all our movements in the boat it was completely indifferent to our presence. Normally fish of this size are very wary and keep a very safe distance and are super cautious, but not during the spawning process. This leads us to believe that the hormonal changes needed to complete reproduction must override their sense of danger. Certainly, they are temporarily off-guard during spawning and very vulnerable to predators like mink, otters, or cormorants. At least after a successful spawning period they eventually return to the safety of their normal haunts which may be three or four miles away or more and you never see them again unless of course, they succumb to your bait late at the back end of the season. The third type of spawning site which can replenish the river with future generations of pike can be found in connected lakes. For example, in upper Wensleydale there is a natural lake called Semerwater with numerous feeder streams including one which drains Cragdale Moor at a height of over two thousand feet only three miles to the south. This natural large lake, which lies over eight hundred feet above sea level, has a weedy shallow spawning ground right next to the outflow stream which empties into the River Ure three miles to the north. During periods of flood a lot of tiny pike fry get washed out of the lake into the outflow stream and thus seeds the River Ure with future generations of pike. This example shows that not all river pike or even trout are born in the rivers they grow up in. It is a great survival advantage though in terms of the natural restocking of rivers which so often become seriously polluted in the lower river course.

Another similar situation can be found on a tributary of the River Swale. In this instance the tributary was used to create a duck decoy by the late Earl of Holderness in the eighteenth century. In this case an artificial lake was built by creating a dam to hold back the stream creating an ideal duck decoy and fishpond of about three acres in size. Pike and perch were stocked to form a wonderful scenic lake within the deer park designed by the famous landscape gardener Capability Brown. The weedy shallow nature of the lake became a prodigious breeding ground for pike and perch. We took the fishing rights of this water over twenty-six years ago and it became a wonderful pike and trout fishing haven. It is still essentially the original stream, but just temporarily widened and improved for sporting purposes. When we first took over the fishing rights the largest pike in the lake was about eight pounds. By artificially stocking the water with a few rainbow trout we created a water capable of holding twenty-pound pike. These new twenty-pound pike grew from the original stock in just four years to reach their full potential. Yes, it was artificial, but we continued with it because it has been so very interesting fishing for both trout, perch and pike. In summer, the outflow stream becomes well stocked with newly hatched four-to-six-inch pike which again, as with the upper Wensleydale example were washed out of the lake into the outflow stream during the floods. How did we find this out? Well before spawning in the lake there were no pikelets to be seen in the outflow stream, but about six weeks after spawning the small pikelets were there in good numbers to see in the stream, the evidence was there to see. Interestingly, we found none of the bigger sized pike in the outflow stream as they seem to know how lucky they were to have such a safe environment. We did however get rainbow trout escapees from time to time, but they were easy to re catch and return to the safety of the lake. Apart from the trout, it was just the small pike which found their way out through the overflow channel during progressive floods, eventually finding their way into the River Swale which lies fifteen miles downstream. This is of course just another clever mechanism of nature to distribute the species throughout the whole river network.

Moving south to the majestic River Aire there are several large weirs along the lower river course which were built to deepen the river to allow access to navigation of the large barges which carried coal up and down the river. Just below these weirs there are several shallow weedy pools near the northern banks which provide ideal spawning conditions for a variety of coarse fish including pike. After spawning the big females move downstream into their deeper haunts, but jack pike seem to hang about these areas all year round.

The River Nidd is a much smaller river but has very good weed growth especially where it meets the mighty River Ouse. There are fast runs which alternate with some very slow and shallow pools which provide extensive weed beds, tailor made for spawning. It is so good that even big pike from the River Ouse move up into the Nidd shallows to spawn.

On the fast rivers the Ure, Swale and Nidd we have seen pike spawning in the river itself, but mainly where various features create sheltered shallow areas of warm water. In one section there is a major geological fault which acts like an underwater dam holding back the water creating a length of shallow but slow water. This natural feature is south facing and full of natural water weeds. It is full of small bait fish like dace minnow gudgeon and grayling and has been a pike spawning ground and nursery for pike for the fifty years I have known of it. This feature is the result of the solid geology of the area and has probably been a good spawning site for coarse fish for thousands of years. It is interesting to note that half a mile upstream and then half a mile downstream of this spawning site there are other smaller spawning areas for coarse fish, so the future of pike fishing looks good on this part of the river.

Looking at the map of pike rivers in northern England it is noticeable that some of the west flowing rivers are very poor pike waters. This could be because of a lack of good spawning sites, after all if they are unable to spawn there will be no pike. Certainly, the River Eden is a very fast river so may simply lack the exacting conditions needed to make successful pike nurseries. Perhaps with global warming the whole situation could change finally making the River Eden a good pike river. It certainly has a food chain strong enough to support a good head of big pike, it will be interesting to see.

A good spawning site on the Northern Rivers. Every year pike can be seen spawning in these shallow weeds which are full of dace and minnows. They usually spawn about April, slightly later than southern rivers in England.

Modern Threats to Angling

Within the pages of this book, we have discussed how many of our northern rivers have been rescued from the scourge of industrial pollution thanks to the conservation work funded to a great extent by the angling community. It is ironic therefore that just as our waters are recovering towards their natural pure state, our newly recovering fish stocks are being compromised by a range of new invasive predators, in particular the cormorants and mink.

Back in the 1990s I can remember Dr Barrie Rickards writing an article where he warned us all about the devastating effects that cormorants were having in the Fenlands of England. At that time we associated cormorants as harmless seabirds like puffins and shags which inhabit our rocky shorelines, I do not remember even seeing any on our northern rivers. Then later in the 2005 we first began to see them show up on the River Ouse in increasing numbers. They started building nests next to our fisheries, it was then we fully realised they had expanded north just as Barrie had predicted about a decade or so earlier. At first, they were a fully protected species and so their numbers built up quickly. At the same time silver fish and trout from many of our lakes and rivers were simply wiped out. Thankfully, cormorants are not capable of eating pike over a weight of about five pounds, so it did not affect pike fishing right away. However, in time it did as our pike were left with nothing to eat. Now after about fifteen to twenty years of cormorant activity pike fishing on the rivers is still tolerable, but roughly, only about a third as prolific as it previously was. Thankfully, by some miracle of nature there are still reasonable numbers of twenty-pound pike. I suspect such big pike can in fact extend their dietary intake to small ducklings or any small living creature on the water's surface. We have witnessed a cormorant being taken by a big pike on the river Ouse. My fishing partner Nigel was alerted to an area just below where he was fishing by a desperate calling sound of a distressed bird. When Nigel arrived, he saw a commotion on the water surface. An adult cormorant was being towed backwards along the surface of the water. He saw the caudal fin of a big pike before it decided to take its meal underwater. This was an amazing event we have only witnessed once, but it shows beyond doubt that pike have very Catholic eating habits! This unlucky cormorant supplied good nourishment to the pike, though it would not be able to digest the feathers so there is no doubt it would have been passing black feathers for some time after its substantial meal! Thankfully, it is now possible to obtain a permit from Natural England to shoot cormorants on waters where they are a nuisance. Therefore at least their numbers can be controlled to some extent. Also, now they have virtually emptied a lot of our waters their numbers should reduce owing to food shortages. As always, nature has the final say.

Another fierce predator every bit as destructive as the cormorant is the mink. Again, these invasive animals feed on fish and breed very fast. Over recent years they have multiplied along the banks of our northern rivers and not only kill fish but also ducks, coots, swans and moorhens. Also, farm animals like hens, geese, pheasants, and other domestic birds. Last October I was fishing on the river Ouse near a farm which was set up on a bank about two hundred yards from the river. I heard a squawking sound about fifty yards down the bank from where I was fishing. When I looked across, I could see a large domestic hen being dragged kicking right into the river where it was dragged underwater.

A freshly killed pike, a casualty of the otter. Even big pike are no match for otters and mink who often kill big fish of all species just for fun. It is ironic that just as our rivers are recovering from a century of pollution the fish are now falling prey to invasive predators like the mink and cormorants. Photo courtesy of David Harrison.

Again, this was the work of the mink, a cute looking animal but very ferocious. Thankfully, the mink is classed as vermin, so we can control them. Thanks to their greedy nature they are also very easy to capture in small humane cage traps. Their numbers really must be controlled though as they devastate small living creatures in our rivers and along the bankside. Only about twenty years ago the coots and moorhens were a regular sight and sound on our waterways. Now, thanks to the mink they are fast becoming nothing more than a distant memory.

A Moorhens nest hidden along the water's edge. Just fifteen years ago this was a regular sight every spring but not anymore, the mink and otters have simply decimated their numbers in many areas.

Henry Williamson was born in London in 1895. He became a very successful writer and author of many books to do with the countryside. He was so successful that in 1928 he was awarded the Hawthornden Prize for outstanding literature. His successful book was called Tarka the Otter. Over the following years this book became recognised as a British Classic and has been enjoyed by generations of both adults and school children for over ninety years.

Before 1928 Farmers and Fishermen hunted the otter to extinction because, like the mink it was known to devastates freshwater fisheries. It also kills waterside birdlife by eating both eggs and the offspring of waterside fowl. During the Victorian and Edwardian period country folk depended on fish and fowl for their livelihoods. Otters were therefore a real threat to their existence. If otters had just killed for what they needed to eat there would have been no problem. However, they kill for fun, leaving dozens of dead fish to just perish. That is why they were so ruthlessly pursued. In his lovely book Tarka the Otter, Williamson humanises a family of otters and fantasises a story about their life and adventures. As a result of his successful book otters have been romanticised and are regarded in modern society as almost human and because of this have been reintroduced and protected on our rivers. Be warned, anyone found killing an otter in modern times will face a six-month prison sentence so although they are ruthless fish killers, they are something with which we must live. Again, like the mink, once they have destroyed our fish stocks, they may well wither naturally so nature will at some stage intervene to redress the balance. There are some plans afoot to reintroduce beaver into our rivers, and they kill both mink and otters, not for food, but to protect their young from competing predators. That may be a natural solution to help equalise the predator prey balance.

As our rivers continue to recover from past pollution, and as the fish stocks increase as they surely will, let us hope there will be so many fish through natural regeneration that the otter problems will be minimised as fish stocks expand naturally. They did once find a balance when natural fish stocks were more prolific. If you are interested in seeing our rivers thrive as they did before the industrial revolution it would be wise to sign up to become members of the Angling Trust who are our best hope to both maintain and develop or river systems in the future.

In 2004 the 'Yorkshire Dales Rivers Trust' was established as a registered charity and they too are working hard to improve our northern rivers. They are involved with all kinds of conservation projects like flood management. Only recently they have been awarded a £ 267,000 grant from the Environment Agency to plant 28,000 trees in the upper dales to help slow down potential flood waters and also improve biodiversity. These and many other project are wonderful steps in the right direction and further support in new and separate ways what anglers have been working on hard for over a century, which is the conservation of the rivers in this country for everyone to enjoy.

River Pike Slide Shows
FUNDRAISING FOR THE A.C.A

In 1984 my old school friend and fishing partner Kevin Russell and I decided to join the Pike Anglers Club of Great Britain which had been formed seven years earlier to campaign for pike conservation. Within about three months of joining Graham Stead, a prominent P.A.C. official in Bradford, invited us to form our own Ripon branch as there were very few representatives in our home county of North Yorkshire. At first, we were a little taken aback, we were not political animals and felt it was not really our scene. Then, after further prompting and thought we considered what it would involve. All we had to do was hold regular meetings in our local area, report back to the central committee on any local anti-pike issues, and of course recruit new members. We put an advert in the 'Angling Times' and in the P.A.C. magazine 'Pikelines' to test the waters and invited anyone interested to join us at our local meetings in Ripon. In this way we attracted a dozen or so people. Our first meeting was very low key, we basically just met up and had a good talk about our shared interest in fishing. We discovered right away that we all had special interests within the subject of pike fishing. For example, Tim had his own fishing tackle shop in Leeds and was very keen on all the latest pike fishing tackles. Kevin was a keen lure angler had an in-depth knowledge baits from America. My own special interest was supporting the 'Anglers Cooperative Association' to fight water pollution in our rivers. All in all, it was very enjoyable, and we agreed that in future meetings we could all give a half hour talk on our own favourite pike related subjects. In this way everyone was felt to play an important part and respected for their specialist knowledge. From the very start this worked well, and we reported back into the quarterly magazine 'Pikelines' on our activities in a section of the magazine called 'Regional Reports'. This aroused interest from other regional clubs, and we were duly invited to do talks and slide shows in the more established clubs in Northern England and even Scotland! At each slide show we always had a collection to raise funds for the A.C.A. who we supported with a great deal of passion. At that time there was still a battle raging to just keep several of our Yorkshire rivers clean enough to support fish life!

Happy memories. Delegates at the Ripon P.A.C. branch meeting held this time at the Bull Inn on the river Ure at West Tanfield. Fully fuelled by a mutual interest in pike and of course the beneficial effects of the local beer!

The problem was that in the early stages we had no slide projector and we needed one fast. Being at that time newly married with a huge mortgage money was tight to put it mildly. By chance I called in at an antique shop in Castleford to look for classical vintage fishing reels and there in the window was a large Aldis slide projector just like the one our Geography teacher used back in our school days. It was at least twenty years old, but it still worked and had a very powerful lamp. Best of all it was on offer to clear at just £ 2.99! Now, almost forty years on it still works well and has been used for everyone's entertainment all over the U.K. The Aldis projector has earned me the reputation of been "Financially cautious" I am comfortable with that tag and even wear it as a badge of honour, indeed, as the amazing Tom Jones once said, "If you have still got it, and it works, then use it!". A great piece of worldly advice if ever I heard one!

One of our first ever slide shows was at the Lincoln branch of the P.A.C. We were invited over for the night by Lincoln Regional Organiser Brian Mundy. I must say I was very apprehensive about addressing a room full of strangers, even Brian was new to me, I had only spoken to him over the phone, so it was a very strange experience. Once at the venue, a large Pub in the centre of Lincoln, I set out my trusty Aldis projector and checked the slides were in order. Brian kindly bought me a pint of Ale and off we went. After brief introductions I invited members of the audience to stop at any point to ask questions. This meant the presentation was more of a two-way process which kept the audience involved and created a friendly interactive atmosphere. Most of the bigger pike displayed were the thirty-pound Stillwater trout fed pike. Other slides shown were of smaller mid-twenties from the northern rivers. During the question/answer parts of the show I noticed all the questions were focused on the river pike section. I thought the audience would be more interested in the massive artificial trout water thirties presented, but no, their main appetite was to learn about the wild river pike. The colour slides of twenty-pound spate river pike on the northern rivers with sand and gravel runs and northern hill backdrops was more of a novelty. By the end of the talk many fishermen in the audience were already seriously planning to make the journey north, which from Lincoln was manageable, especially if organised on an overnight weekend basis.

Around the same time, we were invited to do a slide show for the Nottingham branch of the P.A.C. by the then Regional Organiser Peter Haywood. Again, I was very apprehensive, I did not know Peter except for talks on the phone so once again I was faced with a room full of complete strangers. Thankfully, they turned out to be great hosts and a very nice and friendly team of budding pike anglers. Learning from the Lincoln talk we crafted the slide show more towards river piking. This meant greater depth was given to the techniques associated with northern river pike. At this stage I only had about twenty years of experience and I was fully aware some of the audiences were a lot older than me with more years of experience under their belts. I was not phased though as they were very friendly positive people, I was more than ready to debate on any subject. It was not after all a competition, however, with the Nottingham club the questions were very detailed, I sensed these fellows were extremely keen on pike and wanted to wring out of me every piece of knowledge and compare it with their own experiences. One thing I discovered was that they were using a much wider range of dead baits than me. At that point I was only using sardines, trout, mackerel, and eel section, they were using double that number of bait options. I suspect they needed a wider range because their waters received a lot of pike fishing attention. In contrast, on the northern spate rivers I had no competition from other pike anglers at all so had no need for a wider range of baits. It was a very interesting discussion and good to consider the wider options. As a specialist piker on the northern rivers, I included a section on fishing in coloured flood water conditions and fishing both a rising river and a falling river, both with very peat-stained water. Now this audience were no strangers to river pike as the mighty river Trent flows right through Nottinghamshire. I was therefore quite astonished when they asked me to just confirm my findings about coloured flood waters being beneficial to sport. Indeed, their experiences fishing the river Trent were the exact opposite. They much preferred clear water in trim. To our Nottingham friends the idea of fishing in flooded highwater was a no-go area. Now, as I write this some twenty-eight years later my tally of river pike over the twenty-pound mark is over fifty and over half of these have been taken in high water conditions. All I can say is that high water works for me on the northern rivers and that is why the subject is frequently referred to in this book. The fact that the Trent in Nottinghamshire was not so good just illustrates how different rivers vary across the country. This is exactly the kind of thing which can get thrown up in group discussions and why we enjoy presenting pike slide shows/discussions in good company with like-minded people. All facilitated in a marvellous way by the Pike Anglers Club and of course, the froth of a few freshly pulled pints of beer!

Test run at home. The writer prepares for another slide show on Northern River Pike. Note the 1950s vintages Aldis slide projector, still working well after over sixty years!

Another memorable slide show we did was presented in Glasgow. Now this involved a lot of planning and an overnight stay in Glasgow as the 260-mile trip there made it too far to cover in one day. Fortunately, I was able to stay over with my half-brother in law and friend Malcolm who lived in Glasgow and was interested in attending the event. The Legendary Ralston Mc Phearson invited Malcolm and I to the event but again it was a daunting prospect, over five hundred miles round trip to a foreign country to meet a room full of potentially hostile Scott's! Before we went to the venue Malcolm invited me to his house for tea so at least we went on a full stomach. I was so glad that Glaswegian Malcolm was with me to guide me straight to the venue. It was right in the centre of Glasgow and needed very special local knowledge just to find a parking place! As soon as we entered the venue Ralston gave us a hero's welcome. Free food, free drinks and a room full of wonderful people. I can honestly say that I have never been made to feel so welcome anywhere, not ever! How wrong I was to feel concerned about the evening. Before the slide show we had time to mix with members of Ralston's Glasgow branch of the P.A.C. This was a great ice breaker and enabled us to get to know each other a little before the main event. Some of Ralston's members had brought with them photos of the great pike they had caught on the Scottish Lochs within traveling distance from Glasgow. There were no river pike, but the Loch pike were most impressive indeed. They were even kind enough to offer to take us on a tour of these wild fastnesses, it really was just mind blowing. I often stop and consider what a great sport angling is that brings strangers together like this in a sense of kinsmanship second to none. That is the true magic of angling, it is not at all just about fish, but equally about the human relationships it forges. The one thing I regret is that I never took our Glaswegian friends up on their offer to fish on their secret pike hotspots, but we do keep in touch, indeed Ralston did take me up on my invite to the northern rivers. We had a good day and Ralston caught some good honest Yorkshire pike. I was very pleased to return some of the friendship he had shown us on that memorable evening. It really was one of the best nights out I have had, way up there in Glasgow of all places.

The Wakefield branch of the P.A.C. was run by Peter Green who also invited us along to present our slide show on Northern River Pike. Peter and his group were of course centred close to the northern rivers and were very close to many of the best fisheries in the north. Peter had retired from full time work and became very involved in with the P.A.C. at Committee level, in fact it was Peter who invited me to become part of the National Committee. He invited me to his home in Wakefield where we discussed various matters in his office. The whole room was in fact dedicated to his work in angling administration, not just the P.A.C. but he also organised numerous other fund-raising activities like fishing days on various exclusive waters. The money raised was given to local charities and reported in the local press. Peter was indeed a real force for good and cultivated a very good public image for angling. Peter also secured the pike anglers access to the Fairburn Ings wildlife preserve. This was no mean feat as it was a wildlife reserve but Peters negotiating skills won through providing us all with some truly fantastic pike fishing opportunities.

Peter and Bill enjoy time together at the P.A.C. National Convention in Harrogate. Peter had a razer sharp whit and a tremendous dry sense of humour. Few if any have contributed more to Angling in Northern England than Peter.

Another notable invitation was received from the Radcliffe/Manchester region which was run by Howard Buffett and Steve Ormrod. Our meeting was in a classical Victorian style Pub. This was only about ninety minutes' drive from my home, and I arrived a little early so I had the car park to myself. Within just a few minutes there was a tap on my car window and there was Steve and Howard, so we went in to meet the Landlady who made us feel at home. This was of course 'Coronation Street' country and the local Lancashire accents made us feel we were sat in the 'Rovers Return' from the UKs number one top family programme. Howard and Steve's members were all very experienced pike anglers and open to discuss our fishing venues and favourite big pike waters. Howard did in fact join our local club on what was and still is one of Yorkshires top pike waters. Also, Steve was to become the editor of Pikelines magazine, the quarterly magazine for the Pike Anglers Club of

Great Britain. The quality and size of Pikelines improved substantially during Steve's tenure as editor of the club magazine.

Alan Palmer the Regional Organiser for the Southport branch of the P.A.C. also invited us to do a slide show. This was a 200-mile round trip shared with fellow speaker Dave Tipping the popular angling author and broadcaster from Harrogate. Southport is the home of many famous pike anglers like Gordon Burton, Malcolm Bannister and of course our host Alan Palmer himself who made Dave and I very welcome. After an interesting talk and discussion Alan introduced me to angling author Malcolm Bannister. After the show Malcolm invited me back to his home where he kindly shared his very extensive angling library including some out-of-print works from the Victorian Era. One book from the 1920s was of particular interest called 'Pike Fishing' and written by Tom Seccombe Gray first published in 1923. Malcolm lent me this book to read later in my own time. It was in fact half past midnight and I still had a long drive home. I was particularly interested in Tom Gray's book because it was written during the early 1920s, the same golden era that my friend Norris and Tom Sturdy fished in. There are some very good accounts of big pike in Tom Greys book, but nowhere near as big as the pike which Norris recalled on the Yorkshire rivers, which at that time enjoyed massive runs of sea trout and salmon.

Eric Edwards from St Helens also invited us to speak. Eric was of course the Regional Organiser for the St Helens branch of the pike club and was famous for his lure angling exploits all over the U.K. and Ireland. Eric also presented a very professional slide show and he kindly offered to come back to Yorkshire to return our favour. Eric presented his marvellous show at the 'Bruce Arms' public house in West Tanfield. The same hostelry where Francis Walbran was a regular speaker and guest over one hundred years earlier. The stable is still there where Norris weighed his fifty-six-pound pike and the front room where poor Max was laid out after his final fishing trip remains. Yes, this place was Max Walbrans favourite haunt for over thirty years and for well-informed anglers is heady with our rich angling culture, but so few realise it, even in Yorkshire. The Bruce Arms still offers great hospitality and excellent food, the one thing which has changed since Walbrans days is that grayling no longer feature on the menu!

Well, these are just six examples of slide shows and meetings we have held since 1984, all presented on the 1950s Aldis projector of course. Five out of over sixty presentations which are listed below.

A LIST OF SLIDE-SHOW INVITATIONS/HOSTS AND VISITS.

Region	Host	Number of Shows.
Glasgow	Ralston MacPherson	1
Southport	Alan Palmer	2
St Helens	Eric Edwards	2
Teesside	Chas White	2
S.E. Northumberland.	Mark Haughton.	1
Newcastle upon Tyne	Martin Langman	2
Amber Valley	David Holmes	2
Nottingham	Pete Haywood	2
Holbeach	Fenland Tigers	1
East Yorkshire.	Adrian Brayshaw.	2
Manchester.	Tony Bolger.	2
Blackpool	Paul Dickinson	1
Hull	Clive Melhuish	1
Lincoln	Brian Mundy and Chino	3
Selby	Chris Betts/Mark Green	2
Wakefield	Peter Green	2
Ripon	Kevin Russell/ Y.T.	31
Manchester/Radcliffe	Howard Buffey/Steve Ormrod	2
Wetherby	John Smith	1
Leeds	David Harrison	1
Loughborough (National Conf.)	Martin Gay.	1

Please note all the above slide shows were presented using the now famous Aldis slide projector, all that is except for the show done at the P.A.C. conference at Loughborough University. In this presentation a large format projector was used owing to the huge size of the auditorium. Phil King kindly set up my slides in correct order but, unknown to me added a wobbler slide as a joke. It was in fact two wobblers showing a naked lady! This was a total surprize to me in front of about five hundred delegates. My comments were. "This is another example of a well-conditioned lady!" It was all great fun. Even Liz my wife was amused, it was a memorable day indeed!

We cannot finish off this section without giving special mention to some of the speakers who have travelled from far and wide to tread the boards at our home Ripon branch of the P.A.C. One of our most famous speakers was Barrie Rickards who honoured us with at least ten talks and slide shows. Thanks to this he was very well known to our members who so appreciated getting to know him. Barrie was such a very sociable person and would generously give his time to all, regardless of who they were. His talks were always riveting too. I can remember him telling us about his fishing trip to the Amazon Basin in Brazil. He caught lots of colourful fish and showed us photos of the giant anaconda, a nonvenomous snake which lives on both land and water. He also showed us some wonderful photos of the giant Nile perch he caught on lake Nasser in southern Egypt. Barrie went with his friend Martin Gay. They caught Nile perch to over one hundred pounds weight in temperatures approaching forty-five degrees centigrade! When they became too hot, they just dived into the water to cool down. This too was a bit risky as the local crocodiles were often over twenty feet long and very partial to unsuspecting anglers! It became so hot they completely ran out of water so were forced to drink directly from lake Nasser to stave off heat exhaustion. It was not so long after that one of Barrie's friends died from internal organ failure. His premature death may not be related to this, but I often wonder. The local Nubian Tribesmen have lived in this part of Africa for thousands of years so are well adapted. In contrast our immune systems are completely vulnerable in this alien environment. Barrie's talks were always so interesting, and his pike talks were second to none, looking back we all feel very privileged to have known him so well.

We also owe a lot to Harrogate angling author and broadcaster Dave Tipping who has provided us with lots of great angling shows on subjects ranging from giant skate to roach and very large pike too. On one of Dave's enthralling slide shows he explained how he tracked down a twenty-pound pike in a stream so small you could jump over it. The depth of water was only about six inches, but the pike was taken in a deep pool with just eighteen inches depth. This massive pike came from one of the river Derwent tributaries in the upper network of feeders and proved beyond all doubt that big pike can be found in the most unlikely places.

Gordon Burton delighted us with his 'Pike Spinning' talk and presentation at the Leeds Anglers Club venue in central Leeds. Gordon has fished for pike all over the world and in addition to having caught lots of giant pike he also has a giant personality Gordon, more commonly known as 'Lord Gord' has great charisma and when he talks about pike spinning his enthusiasm is highly contagious! When he addressed the P.A.C. Conference at Loughborough University he really was in top gear with his talk entitled 'Where Eagles Dare'. This was of course the title to his talk on his beloved Loch Lomond. A place where real Eagles are seen from time to time hovering along the slopes of Ben Lomond. Above all Gordon is a natural extrovert and we were all enthralled by his Pike Spinning show. Gordon is good at talking the talk, but he is also good at walking the walk. His amazing catches using mainly plugs and spinners is testament to his real skill as a catcher of big truly wild pike. It is interesting to note though that all though Gordon had taken lots of big pike from all corners of the earth I do not recall him showing a single pike from the Northern rivers.

Famous pike fishing Guru Neville Fickling also did us the honours with his interesting slide show. Neville attracted a very large audience, and we were all keen to hear about his secrets to his success. Neville, who lives in Gainsborough very kindly wavered his fee and only accepted petrol money for his long journey and slide show. This was one of our best shows and we all learned a lot from Neville's interesting approach to his favourite sport. Neville also developed his famous tackle shop in Gainsborough, probably the best all round shop for pike fishermen in the whole world, not only supplying all the tackle needed, but also a wide range of baits too. Best of all, Neville's product knowledge is based on first-hand experience and as such is fully trustworthy and based on his pike catches second to none.

Finally, I would just like to say that these 'Great Angling Nights Out' gave us all the opportunity to meet our angling heroes in real life, I have only mentioned a few here, but would like to thank all the many speakers we have had over the years. Many of our guest speakers were Authors of Fishing books so there were often book signings after the shows fuelling a great sense of camaraderie. These events also provided a great opportunity to sign up new members to join the P.A.C. and the A.C.A. (Now the Angling Trust). As a result of this activity, we have not only struck a blow for the P.A.C. but also helped fight for clean rivers by supporting the A.C.A. On the 13$^{th\ of}$ April 1995 we were rewarded handsomely with honorary life membership to the A.C.A. from (Ms) N Jones and the late Allen Edwards the Director of the A.C.A.

Writing this chapter has been a very nostalgic journey, bringing to life some of the great events and people who made it all possible. Sadly, many have now passed away, but the memory of their kindness and good deeds lives on, this chapter is therefore dedicated to them, and all anglers who fight for pike conservation and the right to fish clean rivers.

P.A.C. Senior Club Official Graham Slater awards Peter Green his well-earned trophy. Which is thus engraved. "For commitment and dedication to the Pike Anglers Club of Great Britain" Sadly, Peter passed away in December 2013 but his good conservation work lives on. It is particularly fitting that Peters son Mark is featured in the Red-Letter Days section with his incredible 22lb River Aire Pike, from a river which was polluted for over seventy years of has now been saved thanks to dedicated voluntary conservationists like Peter.

The Trout in Spring

From the 14th of March each year all coarse fishing must stop on the northern rivers to allow our fish time to spawn without interruption. Fishing is then resumed on the glorious 16th June by which time they have usually recovered from their domestic duties.

The beginning of the trout fly fishing season falls perfectly into this gap in the pike anglers calendar providing a wonderful diversion to our sport. If you have never fished for trout before then you are in for a real treat and we purposefully include this chapter as it is a delightful diversion away from pike fishing at a time the pike are best left alone. A three- month fence period of abstinence is an important part of pike conservation and for us is completely indispensable, so much so that for the last twenty-five years we have leased our own trout fishery which we stock heavily with rainbow, blue and brown trout. We stock on the first Saturday in March every year when water temperatures are often just hovering above freezing. Our membership is limited to twenty, in line with Max Walbrans model to prevent overfishing.

The sight of the trout rising on a spring morning creates a sense of anticipation beyond all measure. Fly fishing for trout really is an indispensable sport during the early part of the year. This photo captures the sheer beauty of the northern trout water we are privileged to fish. Photo courtesy of Phil Fowler Jones.

One of the wonderful things about fly fishing is that everything is so light, just a small shoulder bag to carry one's flies, a light rod and net and off you go. Our small private water is owned by Tom who is a great enthusiast and supporter of rural sports. He is very down to earth too. When we first had the possibility of taking over the lease, I asked Tom if we needed some sort of written contract. Tom just said, "Billy, if you get fed up with me just tell me, and if I get fed up with you, I will tell you!" That was over twenty years ago and our little club still runs seamlessly based on a strong foundation of mutual respect. Most of our members are over seventy years of age, mainly retired professionals with expensive cars. For this reason, we keep the three-hundred-yard woodland track to the water in good repair, and the six boats too, which takes quite a lot of time to maintain, but it is a pure joy trying to keep everything ship shape. Above all though, in the coolness of the spring morning the sight of those rising trout, some up to ten pounds in weight, creates a sense of anticipation which is beyond measure. Indeed, after seeing dozens of trout rising right across the inky black water with pine trees reflecting over the dark green surface, you really do know life is good and with spring in the air it is a great way to start the sporting year. On our first trip out this year my fishing partner Nigel and I gently rowed the boat out next to some pine trees and then anchored our position by quietly lowering the mooring weight and set up the fly rod. Before starting to fish though we first pour out a hot coffee accompanied by a few pieces of dark chocolate made in Switzerland by Lindt. This chocolate is known as the millionaire's chocolate, simply the best money can buy. This five-minute pause before fishing allows time for the trout to acclimatize to our presence and of course a little time to assess the mood of the water. On this occasion and with consideration for the insect activity, a mayfly was cast out twenty yards and just allowed to settle proudly on the water surface. For the first few minutes nothing happened. Then we see a hump of water close to the fly, then another, something is swimming round the bait without taking it. Then the water around the fly becomes even more turbulent as more than one trout circles round the fly, then the surface of the water is broken as one of the trout takes the bait. "Fish on," the light fly rod bends into a satisfying curve, "Yes, we are in"! That first fish of the season is always the best, no matter what size. In this case it is a four-pound blue rainbow which on the light Hardy eight-foot fly rod gave a good account of itself on the four-pound breaking strain line. After using heavy pike fishing tackle all year everything is so sensitive and light, a wonderful contrast to our normal routine, yet on light four-pound leaders every bit as sporting!

Following three hours of great sport we returned towards the landing stage, just before we reached the moorings, we saw a huge pike right next to our boat, it was obviously spawning in the shallows and had no fear of us whatsoever. It was so close we could have almost reached out to stroke it. Instead, we took photos, we saw its back was about five inches wide and it was certainly over twenty pounds, a real bruiser, but out of season so we moved away. Once onto the bank we could still see her in the water looking very vulnerable in her hostile world. Only a week previously we found a Fifteen-pound pike dead on the bank killed by a mink which only ate part of the poor things head.

A 5lb brown trout taken during the May hatch. It only comes once a year, just too good to miss!

The rest was left for the foxes to scavenge. There had been fifteen prime trout killed the same week, again all dragged up onto the bank and decapitated by mink.

On a more cheerful note and on another occasion, this time in August we had been fly fishing in shallow water no more than four feet deep, the trout were in good fettle and we had caught several fish on a dull overcast day. Then, at about eleven thirty in the morning the sun burst out and instantly illuminated the whole water scape beneath us. It was just as though someone had turned on some underwater lights making it visible for the first time. We could see every minnow and weed stalk in good definition. Then, gradually to the left we became aware of two very large pike laying peacefully and parallel to each other only fifteen feet from the boat. They must have been there all the time, possibly attracted to us by the constant stream of trout coming to our net. Just for our amusement we flicked some small pieces of bread just over their heads to see if they were hungry. They were not it seemed, but a few trout intercepted the bread which vanished in a flash. We then threw a couple of handfuls of broken crust above the pike's head. These slowly fell downwards and in between our two big pike. To our amazement the trout frantically swam between the pike with no regard to their own safety. Some of the bread had rolled over the pikes back and directly underneath them. We were even more amazed to see the trout butting the pike upwards so they could swim under the pike through the narrow gap to get at the bread, between and underneath the pike! This was so interesting to watch, both Nigel and I were amazed at the sight of those pike appearing completely at ease with the situation as were the trout. The pike were not it in feeding mode and somehow the trout knew this!

The great thing about trout fishing from the boat in spring is that if you are quiet and fish for a long period of time the fish seem to accept you as part of their environment. In this way, and when conditions are good you can see fish chasing your baits in pairs, and it is clear the competitive element makes the trout grab the lure in their rush to be first. They are not always so obliging though, on several visits just a few weeks after stocking the fish just seem to vanish. The reason is usually extremely cold weather. Cold sub-zero conditions in April or May cause the fish to just 'Shut down' and lie low in deep water. One of our members who owned a fish finder reported to me. "There are no fish in the water at all" this poor bloke had taken time off work to fish just a couple of weeks after stocking. He had completely blanked, even though I knew there were over five hundred freshly stocked trout present. In this case I suspect the trout must have been simply comatose on the bottom and that is why they did not show up on his screen. Thankfully, about two weeks later and after a steady warm southwest wind the trout were back into action. I phoned my friend and he returned on a weekend visit, this time he caught fifteen trout and was really made up. He rang me to apologise for his mistake. I told him there was no need to apologise, it was perfectly understandable why he had reacted so badly. I thanked him for his honesty as we had both learned two good lessons. Firstly, never rely on electronic gadgets in shallow water environments. Secondly, in very cold conditions our trout really can completely switch off their feeding habits.

All this is good experience and feeds back into our understanding of both pike and trout. Together they form the best of what the northern rivers can offer us. It therefore makes a lot of sense to fish seriously for both species especially as it gives us the opportunity to fish almost the full year-round!

Although pike fishing on the rivers starts again on the 16$^{th\ of}$ June, we continue trout fishing later and later as each year passes. The main reason is that fly fishing is such a delight in the warm weather. Also, it gives the pike more time to recover from spawning and gives them time to thrive during the warmer months when they are quite vulnerable in warm water conditions. Once September arrives, they are well rested and ready to provide good sport again. With pike fishing, we believe that 'Less is more' when it comes to fishing for them, they do indeed thrive on neglect. For some angler's tench or bream provide that summer diversion, but for us its most definitely the trout which have lived in balance with the pike since time immemorial.

No Pressure! Bill, grandson Harry and Bogul the dog are all ready for trout fishing action.

No, she is not ready yet! A 5lb rainbow trout makes its bid for freedom. On a 4lb leader this is great sport, for us it is completely indispensable.

A Glossary of Pike Fishing Terms

Over the years the sport of pike fishing has developed its own specialist language. Some of these terms have a specific meaning known only to pike fishermen themselves. For the benefit of newcomers and overseas readers we have defined a few of these terms so readers can enjoy their full meaning in this book.

TERM: 'BIG PIKE' for the purpose of this book we define a big pike as one above the weight of ten pounds. This was the benchmark used by Dr Barrie Rickards in his classic book called 'Fishing for Big Pike.' By A&C Black.

TERM: 'A DOUBLE' This term refers to any pike above ten pounds in weight.

TERM: 'A TWENTY' There is something very special about catching a pike weighing over twenty pounds. Many waters simply don't have the conditions to produce them. A pike angler knows he has arrived when he has caught his first twenty pounder and can die a happy man!

TERM: 'WILD RIVER PIKE' The Northern Rivers are massive waters which are very lightly stocked by artificial means. The volume of fish artificially introduced are wiped out several times over by cormorant and mink predation. This means the indigenous pike survive on wild natural food sources like minnows, dace, wild brown trout, grayling, salmon, other coarse fish and waterfowl. Only the fittest pike survive which alone gives them a primeval quality second to none.

TERM: 'MAMMOTH PIKE' In Fred Buller's book on Mammoth Pike the benchmark used for entry into his book was 35lb. Therefore, giving birth to this term. Fred never qualified for an entry into his own book even though he was a very capable and successful all-round pike angler.

TERM: 'JACK PIKE' A reference to a pike below three pounds in weight. As defined by Norman Marston in his classic tome 'Encyclopaedia of Angling.' By Paul Hamlyn.

TERM: 'WIRE TRACE' Pike's teeth will cut through mono or braid main lines very quickly. When pike fishing the hooks must be attached to a wire trace to prevent this happening.

TERM: 'UP TRACE' An additional length of wire to be attached above the main wire trace. This gives added protection to the main line when a pike strikes upwards towards the reel line. The uptrace should be about five inches longer than the lower trace. An illustrated example of the authors favourite design is featured in the chapter on wire traces.

TERM: 'BITE OFF' When the uptrace is not used there is a danger of pike cutting through the main line causing a bite off. Also, when game anglers are playing trout pike can attack the fish causing a bite off when the pikes teeth make short work of severing the main line.

TERM: 'FISHING GAZETTE PIKE FLOAT' An egg-shaped slotted float with peg to adjust fixed depth. A popular float with Victorian origins. (Illustrated in float section).

TERM: 'PILOT FLOAT' A round float with hole in centre. Its original purpose was to sit above the fishing gazette float and helped to keep old fashioned silk line afloat. Still highly effective as a simple slider float. (Illustrated in float section).

TERM: 'STOP KNOT' A short length of line or other material tightly tied to the main line. It can slide up or down the main line to set the float at any chosen depth. If the depth of river is more than the length of rod the knot needs to be cast through rod rings. Wide rod rings greatly help free passage of stop knots.

TERM: 'SLIDING FLOAT' When fishing deep water, a sliding float can be used to help prevent the line from snagging up on sunken obstacles. The float is attached to the line by either a loop on the float or through a central hole in the float itself. The float can be set to fish any depth by setting the stop knot on the line at the chosen depth. (Illustrated in float section).

TERM: 'DUMBELL FLOAT' Two pilot floats attached by four-inch peg. Pike master Dennis Pye invented this float for live baiting on the shallow Norfolk Broads. It Is equally effective on shallow weedy parts of the river course.

TERM: 'WEEDLESS FLOAT' A special streamlined float for fishing weedy shallows. (See section on floats). Described by Barrie Rickards as "Admirable" in his book on 'Success with Pike'.

TERM: 'PENCIL FLOAT' Very popular streamlined pike floats. Can be used for fixed float fishing or slider application.

TERM: 'SUNKEN FLOAT' A float fixed to line by stop knot set below water surface. It is anchored in position by a ledger weight. Often used to suspend baits off the riverbed.

TERM: 'SNAG FRIENDLY FLOAT' A pike float which can be retrieved when tackle becomes snagged. (Read the section on floats on how to make one). This float is the writer's invention and favourite design. It is purpose built for fishing snag ridden northern rivers.

TERM: 'DEEPER RIVER APP' A very useful app to survey the riverbed and water column. We recommend its use on Northern Rivers. Its value is demonstrated by Mark Green in his Red-Letter Day Chapter.

TERM: 'ESOX LUCIUS' Latin term for pike meaning 'water wolf.'

TERM: 'NATURAL BAITS' Natural baits include any sea or freshwater fish used as bait or even worms.

TERM: 'FRESH BAITS' Fish wholesalers and retailers sometimes can provide fresh fish. These are fish which are fresh from the sea and have not been deep frozen. Not always available and are more expensive but worth it as they are particularly productive for catching river pike when you can get them. They really are superior to deep frozen baits in our experience.

TERM: 'ARTIFICIAL BAITS' These are wooden or plastic baits better known as spoons, spinners and plugs. All are designed to imitate natural fish, crustacea or small mammals.

TERM: 'LEDGER' To fish at ground, or in our context on riverbed using ledger weight as anchor.

TERM: 'A PATERNOSTER RIG' A three-way rig arrangement. Mainline at top, wire trace below, then thirdly a two or three-foot leger link to hold rig in flowing water. Very good river rig. The rig is illustrated in chapter on floats.

TERM: 'SUSPENDED DEADBAIT' When fishing deep water, say fifteen feet deep, the bait can be suspended one foot off the riverbed by fixing the stop knot at a depth of fourteen feet. Also, highly effective method in shallow water too.

TERM: 'TROTTING THE SWIM' When you cast a suspended dead bait into flowing water it can 'trot' its way downstream in a very enticing manner. This is one of our well proven methods of catching big river pike.

TERM: 'SPATE RIVER' A river which has its source on very high land and is prone to sudden floods. Most of the rivers in this book are spate rivers with sudden floods caused by heavy downpours on high ground across the vast uplands. The regular floods create well washed gravel beds in the upper reaches which often attract salmon for spawning purposes.

TERM: 'RIVER IN TRIM' When any river is said to be in trim it means it is in a settled state, neither in flood nor in drought but flowing steadily within its normal average levels.

TERM: 'RIVER IN FLOOD' When the river is high and coloured, though not necessarily bursting its banks the river can be said to be in flood.

TERM: 'RIVER FLOODING OVER' This is when a river bursts its banks flooding the surrounding fields. This is a regular event on the River Ouse, Derwent, Hull and Ribble.

TERM: 'PIKE ROYALTY' This is a term reserved for P.A.C. Committee members who donate three years or more unpaid service to the club. An act of genuine altruism deserving huge respect.

TERM: 'RED LETTER DAY' An old country term often used to describe an exceptional day's sport, usually fishing but equally applied to shooting too.

TERM: 'TO BLANK' This is of course when an angler fishes all day without catching anything. Not good of course, but in this book just part of the journey to success!

TERM: 'SNOW BROTH' During settled winter periods good fishing conditions can be disrupted by sudden snow and sleet storms on the high Pennines. Following these winter storms, the rivers are flooded by icy freezing waters containing a mixture of ice and water or snow broth. These conditions can often be associated with blank days!

TERM: 'WATERWOLF UNDERWATER CAMERA' This is a special underwater camera which enables one to see pike approach the bait. Valuable film footage is recorded and can be analysed at home by downloading results onto the home computer. (See Mark Greens success in his Red-Letter chapter).

TERM: 'LEVEE' An earth embankment running along the side of the lower rivers to help contain high waters and prevent the river flooding adjacent fields. Most of the productive lower valley sections have these features running all along both banks.

TERM: 'MAXIMUM WATER TEMPERATURE' For safe pike fishing is defined as sixty-two degrees Fahrenheit or sixteen point six degrees Centigrade. Above this temperature pike are at risk of succumbing to heat exhaustion. Very warm water contains less oxygen. It is best to avoid pike fishing in these conditions as it will almost certainly result in pike fatalities which results in more blanks in winter. In all conditions we recommend no pike should be kept out of water for over two minutes. There is no need to worry about fishing in very cold water as pike are fine in even the lowest possible water temperatures. Sub-zero air temperatures are dangerous though as they can freeze the delicate gill filaments. In these conditions pike should be returned as soon as possible to the relatively 'warm' water at zero degrees centigrade.

Bill Winship

The Road to Success

NEVER FEAR THE INEVITABLE BLANK SESSIONS

The Pike angler who claims he never blanks is very probably a liar! All our rivers are dynamic systems which change from day to day and no matter how well you know your local water it will often deliver surprises, some good and some bad. I will never forget when Barrie Rickards once joined me on a thirty-six-hour pike fishing weekend on the river Ure. It was October, the river was in trim, we had pre baited some good swims so all was set to enjoy some pike fishing action. At the end of that session neither Barrie nor myself had caught anything. The one thing which really impressed me was that Barrie was completely unphased, he openly said that up to the last minute he was fishing with high expectations. As everyone in pike fishing circles knows, Barrie was to Pike Fishing what Sir Patrick Moore was to astronomy, he was and still is a true star. In fact he was a Northern Star, and like the celestial version had a guiding influence on thousands of anglers. Barrie was born in Leeds; I like to think of him as one of our own and that is why this book includes a healthy amount of Barrie Biography! Following that experience I never again felt bad about blanking . As the great man himself said, "Blanking is just an inevitable part of the road to success." When viewed in this positive way those blank sessions are suddenly not so bad after all and certainly nothing to feel disappointed about.

One of the good things about not catching is that it makes you more circumspect and question more carefully exactly what happened and that critical process can lead to some positive outcomes on future trips. Here are some of the learnings we have discovered on our own blank studded road to catching big pike.

(1) High Summer droughts. In these rare conditions the water temperatures can become very high, up to over seventy degrees Fahrenheit, and oxygen levels become very low. Under these circumstances pike are vulnerable and are best left alone.

(2) The Autumn temperature shock. The very nature of rivers mean the whole river system can change virtually overnight. At some time before wintering our rivers can experience a

sudden temperature shock when waters cool down to winter levels. We have noticed it can take a couple of weeks or more for fish to acclimatise before they start to feed again and bring our blanking days to an end.

(3) Moving house in spring. During an early spring, the pike can suddenly disappear from their normal haunts to visit their regular annual spawning sites. This can result in blanks caused by fishing for pike which are not there. The chapter on 'Pike Nurseries' in this book explains in detail where the pike can move to. These pre spawning temporary hotspots can be very productive as before they spawn the pike often feed heavily. Once they decide to commit to the actual spawning process they usually stop feeding and are best left alone. At this stage we recommend it is time to store the pike rods away and dust down the fly rods in readiness for the spring trout fishing bonanza. A short chapter and guide on trout fishing is provided in the appendix. This allows the pike time to spawn and then recover after their taxing domestic duties. For many weeks after spawning the pike are in very poor condition. They are often thin and have red sore marks across their flanks showing clearly what a poor state they are in. Year after year we have found dead pike in the month of May whilst fly fishing. Some of these dead pike are often spawn bound, one we found dead was over thirty pounds! This pike was fully bloated with eggs which she had failed to deliver.

(4) Our angling diaries show that settled relatively warm periods of winter (temperatures hovering around the 36-degree Fahrenheit) can be quite 'reliable' conditions for catching pike. However, a sudden very cold storm high up in the Pennines can flood the rivers with snow broth causing a second temperature shock again causing poor conditions which result in the blank days.

These are just a few examples of river conditions which can lead to poor results, but there are many more of course. On most visits though we catch something, even a three-pound Jack Pike is at least something and after a series of blanks can be very welcome!

The more familiar one becomes with local rivers the less time one will spend blanking. After a few years and after many good and bad days one can build up a natural 'feel' for the water. There have been many days when I have been at work knowing the rivers are just perfect for pike fishing but having to wait for the weekend to take advantage. In most cases the anticipation proved very worthwhile as favourable conditions normally last a week or more, but it is all part of the gamble which is pike fishing at its best. It is great to shorten the odds by being knowledgeable about your local rivers, paradoxically though some of the best fun can also be had exploring new unknown waters where the unlocked mystery itself becomes an exciting challenge.

On an unfamiliar river all one's previous experience is almost turned back to zero. Of course one still has the basic transferable skills but on a new water the blanks can soon start to mount in the time it can take to get to grips with the new swims. Unknown waters with unknown snags can be very expensive with lost tackle too, and yet when you do eventually score it is one of the most satisfying feelings ever, and one soon forgets the blanks endured on the way. For this reason I always like to have a few new waters up my sleeve to prospect, it takes the pressure off the old favourite waters which have produced many big pike over the years. These new prospect waters are possibly just a section of my local river Ure or Nidd never fished before or it may be a completely new river. They are both equally exciting. As mentioned in the introductory section on main northern rivers, there are hundreds of miles of rivers to fish and most of them just waiting to be discovered.

Part of the fun lies in researching waters using the Ordnance Survey maps, the detail on these maps is truly amazing, bends in the rivers are shown, weirs, lock cuttings and in general all the features typical of a good pike venue. Google Maps are also fun to view too. On these you can even see the shallows and rapids, but they do not highlight pubs and car parks or public rights of way as well as the maps. Best to employ both method's in researching new pike fishing opportunities, this gives us the best of both worlds. A lot of this initial prospecting can be done from the comfort of your armchair on those cold winter nights. Using the computer one can research further by looking at the big city club waters too. For example, look up York fishing clubs and there are numerous alternative venues available with maps and very helpful notes on the waters available. There are even photos of the rivers themselves and photo galleries showing big fish catches. Most of the photos show barbel, trout, roach and carp, but there are the odd photos of big pike too with the exact locations appropriately masked.

Never let the fear of blanking get between you and those undiscovered pike hotspots. Blank days are just the price we pay for getting to know those untapped venues which are out there to be fished. The alternative is to just go on flogging the same old venues and where pike can develop line marks and slotted jaws from repeat captures. On many modern waters the pike are so well known they have names! They also have fins missing and red cancerous sores. We avoid such places like the plague, just look at the photos of the pike in this book, they are all pristine scale perfect pike, wild as the hills which produce them and provide both you and your pike with ample living space. Yes, the northern rivers are hard places to fish, but the rewards of catching big wild river pike by far make up for the testing challenge. The results of winning through are so worth it!

Bill holds a lovely twenty-two-pound pike taken on a section of the river never fished before.

About the Author

Bill Winship was born in West Tanfield in 1954 the son of a dairy farmer and was raised in a rural idyll. At the age of eighteen he went to college and university where he secured a degree in Geography and met his wife Elizabeth. He now lives in Harrogate and has two children and five grandchildren. He has been a keen angler for over fifty years fishing mainly for pike and trout. He is best known locally as the founder of Sunwood Lake Trout Club near Ripon. On a national scale Bill is best known for his catches of big river pike and is an Ex-President of the Pike Anglers Club of Great Britain. Bill is also a regular contributor to the 'Pikelines' quarterly P.A.C. magazine and has been for thirty-seven years. Bill is also an Honorary life member of the Anglers Cooperative Association. (Now Angling Trust) and was awarded this for his fund-raising work undertaken to combat water pollution. Bills first book 'Pike Waters' was published in 1989 by Boydell and Brewer. At the age of sixty-six Bill has just retired from his job as a National Account Executive for the Swiss Chocolate Manufacturer Lindt where he worked for twenty-six years. Now, newly retired, he is finally released to spend more time with his family and concentrate on his lifelong ambition to write this book to record at last some of the cultural history of the northern rivers passed on to him from his late and great angling friends who take pride of place in the opening chapters of this book. Bill also reveals for the first time the secret methods and tackles he has employed and invented to catch literally hundreds of double figure Northern River Pike and over fifty above the twenty-pound mark. He has caught much bigger pike to over thirty pounds in weight from artificial trout waters but he rates the smaller but natural wild river pike as the more 'worthy' quarry. Fishing for artificial trout water pike and trout make a very close second place.

www.ingramcontent.com/pod-product-compliance
Lightning Source LLC
Chambersburg PA
CBHW042046280426
43661CB00114B/1460/J